Contents

Introduction to the course

Syllabus overview

In the Level 2 *Bookkeeping Transactions* accounting unit, students were introduced to the books of prime entry, double entry bookkeeping and an initial trial balance.

In the Level 2 *Bookkeeping Controls* accounting unit, students learnt to perform a bank reconciliation, reconcile the control accounts with the memorandum ledgers and re-draft a trial balance following the correction of errors.

Advanced Bookkeeping builds on this knowledge by introducing more challenging topics such as accounting for non-current assets. Period end adjustments are studied, including accruals, prepayments, inventory, and accounting for irrecoverable and doubtful debts.

This takes the student to the position of being able to draw up a trial balance using adjusted figures, and extend it to identify the profit or loss for the period.

To support this learning, the policies an organisation may adopt to ensure strong internal controls and the ethical principles which guide the day-to-day work of accountants are also studied.

Test specification for this unit assessment

Assessment method	Marking type	Duration of assessment
Computer based assessment	Computer marked	2 hours

Learning outcomes	Weighting
1 Apply the principles of advanced double-entry bookkeeping	24%
2 Implement procedures for the acquisition and disposal of non-current assets	20%
3 Prepare and record depreciation calculations	13%
4 Record period end adjustments	20%
5 Produce and extend the trial balance	23%
Total	**100%**

AAT

Advanced Bookkeeping

Level 3

Advanced Diploma in Accounting

Course Book

For assessments from September 2017

Third edition 2017

ISBN 9781 5097 1202 1
ISBN (for internal use only) 9781 5097 1221 2

British Library Cataloguing-in-Publication Data
A catalogue record for this book is available from the
British Library

Published by

BPP Learning Media Ltd
BPP House, Aldine Place
142-144 Uxbridge Road
London W12 8AA

www.bpp.com/learningmedia

Printed in the United Kingdom

Your learning materials, published by BPP Learning Media
Ltd, are printed on paper obtained from traceable
sustainable sources.

Assessment structure

2 hours duration

Competency is 70%

*Note that this is only a guideline as to what might come up. The format and content of each task may vary from what is listed below.

Your assessment will consist of 5 tasks.

Task	Expected content	Max marks	Chapter ref	Study complete
Task 1	**Non-current assets** Update a non-current asset register to show: • Acquisition of non-current assets • Disposals of non-current assets • Depreciation	21	Purchase of non-current assets Depreciation of non-current assets Disposal of non-current assets	
Task 2	**Ledger accounting for non-current assets** Record non-current asset information in the ledger accounts. This may include: • Acquisitions • Disposals • Depreciation	17	Purchase of non-current assets Depreciation of non-current assets Disposal of non-current assets	
Task 3	**Ledger accounting, including accruals and prepayments, and applying ethical principles** You will be required to calculate and record accruals/prepayments. This may include determining whether balances in a trial balance will appear as a debit or credit. Ethical principles, organisational procedures or the accounting equation may also be tested.	19	Accounting principles Accruals and prepayments	

Task	Expected content	Max marks	Chapter ref	Study complete
Task 4	**Accounting adjustments** Calculate adjustments and enter them in a trial balance extract or record journal entries to correct errors and clear the suspense account Record period end adjustments and respond appropriately to period end pressures	23	Accounting principles Accruals and prepayments Inventories Irrecoverable and doubtful debts The trial balance, errors and the suspense account	
Task 5	**Period end routines, using accounting records and the extended trial balance** Identify the adjustments required in a bank or control account reconciliation Show knowledge of accounting for payroll or organisational procedures Complete an extended trial balance	20	Accounting principles Bank reconciliations Control account reconciliations The trial balance, errors and the suspense account The extended trial balance	

Skills bank

Our experience of preparing students for this type of assessment suggests that to obtain competency, you will need to develop a number of key skills.

What do I need to know to do well in the assessment?

To be successful in the assessment you need to:

- Be confident in the topics previously studied in the Level 2 accounting papers

- Know how to update a non-current asset register to reflect the acquisition, disposal and depreciation charges for non-current assets

- Understand the ledger accounting treatment of non-current assets

- Be able to adjust income and expense items to reflect accruals and prepayments

- Process accounting adjustments and enter these items in a trial balance extract

- Perform period end routines, including correction of errors, reconciliations and preparing and extended trial balance

Assumed knowledge

The following topics were studied at Level 2 and are still relevant in *Advanced Bookkeeping*:

- **Double entry bookkeeping** – *Advanced Bookkeeping* is largely a test of your double entry skills albeit set in the context of more complex accounting transactions. It is imperative that you revise these skills.

- **Irrecoverable debts** – This area is revisited and extended to include doubtful debts.

- **Bank and control account reconciliations** – Bank and control account reconciliations can be a difficult topics so you need to revise your knowledge.

- **The correction of errors and suspense accounts** – This is another area which you may need to revisit.

You can see from the list above how important it is to consolidate your understanding of double entry bookkeeping.

Assessment style

In the assessment you will complete tasks by:

1   Entering narrative by selecting from drop down menus of narrative options known as **picklists**

2   Using **drag and drop** menus to enter narrative

3   Typing in numbers, known as **gapfill** entry

4   Entering **ticks**

You must familiarise yourself with the style of the online questions and the AAT software before taking the assessment. As part of your revision, login to the **AAT website** and attempt their **online practice assessments**.

Introduction to the assessment

The question practice you do will prepare you for the format of tasks you will see in the *Advanced Bookkeeping* assessment. It is also useful to familiarise yourself with the introductory information you **may** be given at the start of the assessment.

You have 2 hours to complete this assessment.

This assessment contains 5 tasks and you should attempt to complete every task.

Each task is independent. You will not need to refer to your answers to previous tasks.

Read every task carefully to make sure you understand what is required.

The standard rate of VAT is 20%.

Where the date is relevant, it is given in the task data.

Both minus signs and brackets can be used to indicate negative numbers unless task instructions state otherwise.

You must use a full stop to indicate a decimal point. For example, write 100.57 NOT 100,57 OR 100 57

You may use a comma to indicate a number in the thousands, but you don't have to. For example, 10000 and 10,000 are both acceptable.

Assessment preparation

1   As you revise, use the **BPP Passcards** to consolidate your knowledge. They are a pocket-sized revision tool, perfect for packing in that last-minute revision.

2   Attempt as many tasks as possible in the **Question Bank**. There are plenty of assessment-style tasks which are excellent preparation for the real assessment.

3   Always **check** through your own answers as you will in the real assessment, before looking at the solutions in the back of the Question Bank.

Key to icons

  Key term

Key term

A key definition which is important to be aware of for the assessment

 Formula to learn

A formula you will need to learn as it will not be provided in the assessment

 Formula provided

A formula which is provided within the assessment and generally available as a pop-up on screen

 Activity

An example which allows you to apply your knowledge to the technique covered in the Course Book. The solution is provided at the end of the chapter

 Illustration

A worked example which can be used to review and see how an assessment question could be answered

 Assessment focus point

A high priority point for the assessment

 Open book reference

Where use of an open book will be allowed for the assessment

Real life examples

A practical real life scenario

AAT qualifications

The material in this book may support the following AAT qualifications:

AAT Advanced Diploma in Accounting Level 3, AAT Advanced Diploma in Accounting at SCQF Level 6 and Further Education and Training Certificate: Accounting Technician (Level 4 AATSA).

Supplements

From time to time we may need to publish supplementary materials to one of our titles. This can be for a variety of reasons, from a small change in the AAT unit guidance to new legislation coming into effect between editions.

You should check our supplements page regularly for anything that may affect your learning materials. All supplements are available free of charge on our supplements page on our website at:

www.bpp.com/learning-media/about/students

Improving material and removing errors

There is a constant need to update and enhance our study materials in line with both regulatory changes and new insights into the assessments.

From our team of authors BPP appoints a subject expert to update and improve these materials for each new edition.

Their updated draft is subsequently technically checked by another author and from time to time non-technically checked by a proof reader.

We are very keen to remove as many numerical errors and narrative typos as we can but given the volume of detailed information being changed in a short space of time we know that a few errors will sometimes get through our net.

We apologise in advance for any inconvenience that an error might cause. We continue to look for new ways to improve these study materials and would welcome your suggestions. Please feel free to contact our AAT Head of Programme at nisarahmed@bpp.com if you have any suggestions for us.

Bookkeeping transactions

1

Learning outcomes

1.2	Classify assets, liabilities and equity in an accounting context
	• Classify general ledger accounts as income (revenue), expense (cost), asset, liability or equity (capital)
1.3	**Demonstrate the purpose and use of books of prime entry and ledger accounting**
	• The different books and records that make up the accounting system: books of prime entry: sales and purchases daybooks (sales, sales returns, purchase and purchase returns), cash book, journal (including narratives), general ledger accounts, control accounts, value added tax (VAT, may be known by another name in other countries)
	• What information should be recorded in each record
	• How these records relate to each other, including dealing with VAT
	• Write up general ledger accounts correctly and accurately
	• Close off accounts to the statement of profit or loss, where appropriate
	• Carry down balances, where appropriate
1.5	**Carry out financial period end routines**
	• That income or expense accounts will carry a balance prior to closing off to the statement of profit or loss at the end of the financial period
	• Which account balances to carry forward and which to close off to the statement of profit or loss at the end of the financial period

Assessment context

This chapter is an introductory chapter and serves to remind you of your Level 2 AAT bookkeeping studies. Key topics are revised including the books of prime entry, double entry bookkeeping and balancing off ledger accounts.

Qualification context

As mentioned above, the knowledge covered in this chapter is largely a reminder of the key skills learnt in the Level 2 bookkeeping units. The topics studied in this chapter are also important in the next Level 3 accounting unit, *Final Accounts Preparation*.

Business context

Maintaining proper accounting records is essential for all businesses. Accounting records which are complete, accurate and valid will provide both internal and external users with good information. This may then assist a business in assessing its performance, raising finance and meeting its statutory requirements.

Chapter overview

The books of prime entry include:

- Sales day book
- Sales returns day book
- Purchases day book
- Purchases returns day book
- Cash book
- Discounts allowed day book
- Discounts received day book
- Journal

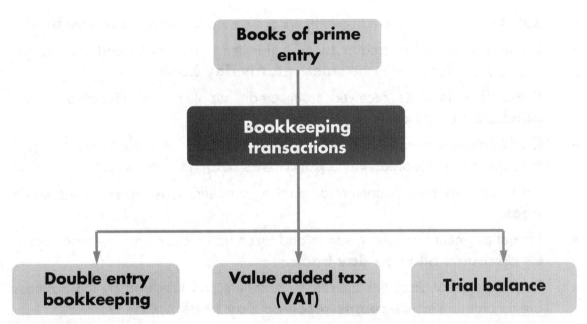

Books of prime entry

Bookkeeping transactions

Double entry bookkeeping	**Value added tax (VAT)**	**Trial balance**
• Business transactions are posted from the day books to the ledgers • The ledgers are balanced off • SOFP balances are carried forward to the next period • SPL balances are transferred to the profit or loss account	• VAT on sales increases the amount owed to HMRC • VAT on purchases decreases the amount owed to HMRC	• At the period end, the closing balances on the general ledger accounts are listed in the trial balance • The trial balance has separate columns for debit and credit balances • Once all adjustments have been made, the column totals will agree

Introduction

The Level 2 units *Bookkeeping Transactions* and *Bookkeeping Controls* explained how to:

- Record business transactions in the books of prime entry
- Post information from the books of prime entry to the ledger accounts
- Use the ledger accounts to draft a trial balance

These principles are important in *Advanced Bookkeeping* and will be revised in this chapter.

1 Books of prime entry

In earlier studies we have seen that business transactions are recorded in the **books of prime entry**. In particular:

- **Sales** invoices sent to credit customers are recorded in the **sales day book**.

- Credit notes issued to credit customers (for items returned by customers to the business) are recorded in the **sales returns day book**.

- **Purchases** invoices received from credit suppliers are recorded in the **purchases day book**.

- Credit notes received from credit suppliers (for items returned by the business to suppliers) are recorded in the **purchases returns day book**.

- Cash received from customers or paid to suppliers is recorded in the **cash book**.

- Prompt payment discounts given to and taken up by customers are recorded in the **discounts allowed day book**.

- Prompt payment discounts offered by suppliers and taken up by the business are recorded in the **discounts received day book**.

- The **journal** book is used to record transactions that do not appear in any of the other books of prime entry, so they can then be posted to the ledgers.

Note that the cash book is one book; however, in the study material it is useful to split it into the 'cash book – debit side' and the 'cash book – credit side'.

> ## Illustration 1: The accounting system for credit sales
>
> We will see how to prepare the sales day book, the sales returns day book, the cash book – debit side and the discounts allowed day book.
>
> G Mason has two credit customers, H and I. On 1 July 20X1, customer H owes £200 on one outstanding invoice and customer I owes £150 (therefore £350 in total).
>
> In July the following transactions occur and are recorded in the day books.
>
> The sales day book is used to record all invoices sent to customers buying on credit.

Sales day book (extract)

Date 20X1	Details	Invoice number	Total £	VAT £	Net £
4 July	H	0015	192	32	160
10 July	I	0016	96	16	80
15 July	H	0017	120	20	100
29 July	I	0019	144	24	120
	Totals		552	92	460

If items are returned by customers, credit notes are recorded in the sales returns day book.

Sales returns day book (extract)

Date 20X1	Details	Credit note number	Total £	VAT £	Net £
18 July	I	CN041	96	16	80
25 July	H	CN042	120	20	100
	Totals		216	36	180

Money received from credit customers is entered into the debit side of the cash book. Customer H takes advantage of a 6% prompt payment discount and pays £188 to settle the £200 owing on 1 July. Customer I pays the full amount of £150 owing on 1 July.

Cash book – debit side (extract)

Date 20X1	Details	Bank £	Trade receivables £
15 July	H	188	188
20 July	I	150	150
	Totals	338	338

Where the customer decides to take a prompt payment discount, the business issues a credit note which is recorded in the discounts allowed day book. The £12 entry for the prompt payment discount was calculated on H's outstanding invoice of £200 as (6% × £200). This is shown below:

Discounts allowed day book (extract)

Date 20X1	Details	Credit note number	Total £	VAT £	Net £
15 July	H	CN035	12	2	10
	Totals		12	2	10

Illustration 2: The accounting system for credit purchases

We will see how to prepare the purchases day book, the purchases returns day book, the cash book – credit side and the discounts received day book.

G Mason purchases goods on credit from suppliers J and K. On 1 July 20X1, G Mason owes supplier J £120 on one outstanding invoice and owes supplier K £70 (therefore £190 in total).

In July the following transactions occur and are recorded in the day books.

The purchases day book is used to record all invoices received from suppliers when purchasing on credit.

Purchases day book (extract)

Date 20X1	Details	Invoice number	Total £	VAT £	Net £
6 July	J	JC24	168	28	140
11 July	J	JC25	72	12	60
20 July	K	K93	108	18	90
29 July	K	K104	60	10	50
	Totals		408	68	340

If items are returned to suppliers, credit notes are recorded in the purchases returns day book.

Purchases returns day book (extract)

Date 20X1	Details	Credit note number	Total £	VAT £	Net £
17 July	J	CN045	72	12	60
31 July	K	CN159	60	10	50
	Totals		132	22	110

Money paid to credit suppliers is entered into the credit side of the cash book. G Mason takes advantage of a 5% prompt payment discount from supplier J and pays £114 as full settlement of the £120 owing at 1 July. G Mason pays the full £70 due to supplier K on 1 July.

Cash book – credit side (extract)

Date 20X1	Details	Bank £	Trade payables £
11 July	J	114	114
16 July	K	70	70
	Totals	184	184

Where the business decides to take a prompt payment discount, the supplier issues a credit note which is recorded in the discounts received day book. The entry for the prompt payment discount of £6 (5% × £120) on supplier J's invoice is shown below.

Discounts received day book (extract)

Date 20X1	Details	Credit note number	Total £	VAT £	Net £
11 July	J	CN243	6	1	5
	Totals		6	1	5

Having recorded this information in the relevant day books, it can then be posted to the ledgers. In Chapter 10 *Control account reconciliations*, the business transactions for G Mason are posted to the ledgers.

However, before we post the transactions in the books of prime entry to the **ledger accounts**, it is important to revise the principles of double entry.

BPP LEARNING MEDIA

2 General ledger accounts (T-accounts)

Ledger accounts in the **general ledger** can be structured as **T-accounts**. This is an example of a bank ledger T-account:

Bank

Debit (Dr)	£	Credit (Cr)	£
Increases the money held in the bank		Decreases the money held in the bank	

The left hand side is known as the debit side (abbreviated to Dr) and the right hand side is known as the credit side (abbreviated to Cr).

A **debit entry** is an entry into the ledger on the **left hand side**. So money paid into the bank would require debit entry in the bank T-account.

A **credit entry** is an entry into the ledger on the **right hand side**. So money paid out of the bank would require a credit entry in the bank T-account.

Every transaction has a **dual effect** and therefore should be recorded in two places. This means that every debit in the ledger accounts must have an equal credit in another ledger account. Therefore, at all times:

> **TOTAL DEBITS = TOTAL CREDITS**

2.1 Principles of double entry bookkeeping – general rules

There are some general rules for **double entry bookkeeping** which can help you to decide where debit and credit entries should be made in the ledger accounts:

(a) A **debit** entry represents:

    (i)   An increase in an asset
    (ii) An item of expense
    (iii) An increase in drawings
    (iv) A decrease in liabilities, income or capital

(b) A **credit** entry represents:

    (i)   An increase in a liability
    (ii) An item of income
    (iii) An increase in capital
    (iv) A decrease in assets, expenses or drawings

A helpful way to remember this is to use the mnemonic DEAD CLIC:

Debit	Credit
(increase)	(increase)
Expenses	**L**iabilities
Assets	**I**ncome
Drawings	**C**apital

2.2 Elements of the financial statements

Assets, liabilities, capital, income and expenses are known as the elements of the financial statements.

- **Assets** are items that the business owns, such as cash and machinery, and amounts owed to the business by credit customers.

- **Liabilities** are amounts that are owed to other parties, such as loans, overdrafts and amounts owed to credit suppliers.

- **Capital** is the amount of cash injected by the owner, plus the profit the business has made, less any drawings the owner has taken. **Drawings** are the money and goods that the owner takes out of the business.

- The main sources of **income** for a business will be from sales of goods and services, but may also include sundry income, such as interest paid to the business by its bank, rent received from tenants and commission received from acting as an agent.

- The main **expenses** of the business will be the goods that it purchases for resale as well as the other ongoing costs of running the business such as wages to employees (**not** the owner), rent paid for its premises, utilities and stationery.

Activity 1: Double entry bookkeeping

The following transactions took place during the first week of trading for Williams & Sons.

(1)   Started business by depositing £30,000 into the bank account
(2)   Bought goods for resale and paid £800 by cheque
(3)   Paid rent of £500 by cheque
(4)   Sold goods for £400, customer paid directly into the bank account
(5)   Paid rates of £150 by cheque
(6)   Sold goods on credit to a customer, M Brown, for £1,150
(7)   Bought goods for resale on credit from Y Hillier for £450

Required

Record the transactions above in the general ledger accounts. Ignore VAT.

GENERAL LEDGER

Bank

	£		£

Capital

	£		£

Purchases

	£		£

Rent

	£		£

Sales

	£		£

Rates

	£		£

Sales ledger control account

	£		£

Purchases ledger control account

	£		£

3 Balancing off the ledger accounts

We have seen how business transactions are recorded in the books of prime entry and how that information is then transferred from the books of prime entry and summarised in the general ledger.

At the end of the financial period end and in preparation for drafting the accounts, the accountant must:

- Balance off the income and expense accounts, and transfer the remaining balance to the statement of profit or loss

- Balance off the statement of financial position accounts, and identify the amounts to be carried forward to the next financial period

The steps to balance off a ledger account are:

Step 1 Add up the debit side and the credit side separately.

Step 2 Put the larger of the two totals as the column total for both the debit and credit columns.

Step 3 Calculate the balancing figure on the side with the lower total and describe this as the balance carried down (balance c/d).

Step 4 Show this balancing figure on the opposite side, below the totals line, and describe this figure as the balance brought down (balance b/d).

Illustration 3: Balancing off a statement of financial position (SOFP) ledger account

We will illustrate the balancing off process by considering Robin & Sons' bank account in the general ledger.

The following transactions have been posted to the bank T-account.

Balance off the bank account. Show the balance c/d and balance b/d at the end of the period.

Bank (SOFP)

	£		£
Capital	15,000	Purchases	4,000
Sales	1,500	Rent	600
Sales ledger control account	2,500	Purchases ledger control account	1,400

Before adjustment, the debit and credit columns are not equal.

Step 1 Total both the debit and the credit columns, making a note of the totals for each.

Debit column total: £19,000
Credit column total: £6,000

Step 2 Put the larger of the two totals as the column total for both the debit and credit columns, leaving at least one empty line at the bottom of each column.

Step 3 Calculate the balancing figure on the side with the lower total. In this case, in the credit column, put in £(19,000 – 6,000) = £13,000. Describe this as the balance carried down (balance c/d).

Step 4 Show this balancing figure on the opposite side, below the totals line, and describe this figure as the balance brought down (balance b/d).

Bank (SOFP)

	£		£
Capital	15,000	Purchases	4,000
Sales	1,500	Rent	600
Sales ledger control account	2,500	Purchases ledger control account	1,400
		Balance c/d	13,000
	19,000		19,000
Balance b/d	13,000		

The closing balance shows that Robin & Sons has an asset (a debit balance) of £13,000 in the bank account. In the next period, the bank account will be opened with a balance b/d of £13,000.

When balancing off a statement of profit or loss (SPL) account, the process is similar. However, when closing off an SPL account, the period-end balance is transferred to the profit or loss account.

Activity 2: Balancing off ledger accounts

The general ledger accounts prepared in Activity 1 are reproduced below.

Required

Balance off the ledger accounts.

For the statement of financial position (SOFP) ledger accounts, show the balance c/d and the balance b/d.

For the statement of profit or loss accounts (SPL), show the balance transferred to the profit or loss account.

GENERAL LEDGER

Bank (SOFP)

	£		£
Capital (1)	30,000	Purchases (2)	800
Sales (4)	400	Rent (3)	500
		Rates (5)	150

Capital (SOFP)

	£		£
		Bank (1)	30,000

Purchases (SPL)

	£		£
Bank (2)	800		
Purchases ledger control account (7)	450		

Rent (SPL)

	£		£
Bank (3)	500		

Sales (SPL)

	£		£
		Bank (4)	400
		Sales ledger control account (6)	1,150

Rates (SPL)

	£		£
Bank (5)	150		

Sales ledger control account (SOFP)

	£		£
Sales (6)	1,150		

Purchases ledger control account (SOFP)

	£		£
		Purchases (7)	450

4 Value added tax (VAT)

Value added tax (VAT) is a consumer tax imposed by the government in the UK on the sale of certain goods and services. In other countries, VAT may be known by another name.

VAT rules are quite complex but for the purposes of *Advanced Bookkeeping*, the following are the main points to remember.

The tax-collecting authority in the UK is Her Majesty's Revenue & Customs (HMRC). VAT is a tax on consumers that is collected on behalf of HMRC by VAT-registered businesses.

Not all businesses are registered for VAT. Non VAT registered businesses cannot charge VAT on their sales or reclaim it on their purchases.

Output VAT is charged on sales and **input VAT** is incurred on purchases.

Many business transactions involve VAT, and most invoices show any VAT charged separately.

If output VAT (on sales) exceeds input VAT (on purchases) the difference is paid over to HMRC. If output VAT is less than input VAT in a period, HMRC will refund the difference to the business. In other words, if a business pays out more in VAT than it receives from customers it will be paid back the difference.

4.1 Accounting for VAT

The tax paid to or recovered from the tax authorities in each accounting period is the balance on the VAT control account.

Listed below are the items that are typically debited and credited to the VAT control account.

A debit in the VAT control account

Item	Explanation
Balance b/d	Occasionally a **debit** balance when the business is owed amounts by HMRC (where output VAT < input VAT) and the **VAT control account** represents an **asset**.
Purchases (cash and credit)	When a business makes a purchase, it can reclaim the VAT paid on that purchase from HMRC. Therefore, it represents a **decrease in liability**.
Sales returns	The product has been returned by the customer so the business no longer owes the VAT to HMRC – this represents a **decrease in liability**.
Discounts allowed	If a credit customer takes advantage of a prompt payment discount, they owe less money to the business than is shown on the original sales invoice. Therefore, the VAT due to HMRC decreases so discounts allowed represent a **decrease in liability**.
Bank	If the business owes VAT to HMRC (where output VAT > input VAT), there is a credit balance on the VAT control account. When the business pays the VAT to HMRC, this represents a **decrease in liability**.

A credit in the VAT control account

Item	Explanation
Balance b/d	Usually a **credit** balance (where output VAT > input VAT) representing amounts owed by the business to HMRC and the VAT control account represents a **liability**.
Sales (cash and credit)	When a business makes a sale, the business collects VAT on behalf of HMRC and therefore must pay this VAT to HMRC, representing an **increase in liability**.
Purchase returns	The amount of VAT reclaimable has gone down as the business is returning the goods. Therefore, the VAT cannot be reclaimed from HMRC and the **original debit** recorded at the time of purchase must be **reversed with a credit**.

Item	Explanation
Discounts received	If a business takes advantage of a prompt payment discount from a supplier, they will pay less money to the supplier than shown on the original purchase invoice. Therefore, the **VAT reclaimable from HMRC decreases**, resulting in an increase in the amount that the business owes HMRC.
Bank	If VAT is recoverable by the business from HMRC (because output VAT < input VAT), HMRC refunds the business. The VAT control account asset balance (a debit) will therefore be reduced (with a credit) as the **business has recovered the VAT** from HMRC.

Illustration 4: Preparing the VAT control account

In Illustration 1, the day books show the following VAT amounts:

- Sales day book: £92
- Sales returns day book: £36
- Discounts allowed day book: £2

In Illustration 2, the day books show the following VAT amounts:

- Purchases day book: £68
- Purchases returns day book: £22
- Discounts received day book: £1

In this illustration, assume that the balance b/d at the start of the period is £80 credit. The amount paid to HMRC during the period is £78.

Record this information in the VAT control account. Show the balance c/d and balance b/d at the end of the period.

VAT control account

	£		£
VAT on purchases	68	Balance b/d	80
VAT on sales returns	36	VAT on sales	92
VAT on discounts allowed	2	VAT on purchases returns	22
Bank	78	VAT on discounts received	1
Balance c/d	11		
	195		195
		Balance b/d	11

In this illustration, there is a liability to HMRC of £11 at the end of the period.

5 Trial balance

Once the general ledger accounts have been totalled, a **trial balance** is drawn up by taking the closing balance on each of the general ledger accounts and placing them in a list.

The list is divided into two columns with one column for all the items with debit balances and another column for all the items with credit balances. This is known as an initial trial balance.

The trial balance forms a check on the accuracy of the entries in the ledger accounts. The total of the debit balances should equal the total of the credit balances. If the debits in the trial balance do not equal the credits then this indicates that there has been an error in the double entry.

Illustration 5: Trial balance

Review the closing balances calculated in Activity 2. List them in the trial balance.

Trial balance as at 31 December 20X1

Account name	Debit £	Credit £
Bank	28,950	
Capital		30,000
Purchases	1,250	
Rent	500	
Sales		1,550
Rates	150	
Sales ledger control account	1,150	
Purchases ledger control account		450
Totals	32,000	32,000

The trial balance balances which suggests that the transactions have been recorded correctly in the general ledger accounts.

6 Knowledge test preparation

The *Advanced Bookkeeping* assessment may include short-form, objective-style requirements on any area of the syllabus. If the requirements are based on bookkeeping transactions, they could be structured as follows.

Activity 3: Advanced bookkeeping – knowledge

This task is to test your knowledge.

(a) **Which ONE of the following would you expect to find in the general ledger?**

	✓
Statement of profit or loss	
Purchases day book	
Trial balance	
Purchases ledger control account	

(b) **Which ONE of the following best describes liabilities?**

	✓
The amount of cash injected by the owner of the business	
The ongoing expenses of the business	
Amounts due from other parties	
Amounts owed to other parties	

Assessment focus point

The topics studied in this chapter form the basis of the more challenging accounting issues and adjustments that will be studied in *Advanced Bookkeeping*.

Chapter summary

- A business's transactions are first entered into the books of prime entry. The books of prime entry are then totalled and two entries will be made in the general ledger accounts with the total – this is called double entry bookkeeping.

- Each transaction is recorded in ledger accounts with a debit entry in one account and a credit entry in another account.

- A debit entry is an entry into the ledger on the left hand side. A debit entry represents:

  - An increase in an asset
  - An item of expense
  - An increase in drawings
  - A decrease in liabilities, income or capital

- A credit entry is an entry into the ledger on the right hand side. A credit entry represents:

  - An increase in a liability
  - An item of income
  - An increase in capital
  - A decrease in assets, expenses or drawings

- A helpful way to remember this is to use the mnemonic DEAD CLIC.

- Balancing the ledger accounts enables the business to know the closing amount on each account.

- Output VAT is charged on sales and is recorded in the VAT control account with a credit entry. Input VAT is incurred on purchases and is recorded in the VAT control account with a debit entry. At the period end, the VAT control account is balanced off to show the amount owing to or owed from HMRC.

- A trial balance is prepared by listing all the debit balances brought down and credit balances brought down and checking the totals of these balances to ensure that they agree.

Keywords

- **Books of prime entry:** The records in which transactions are initially recorded

- **Cash book:** The book of prime entry used to record money received and paid out by the business

- **Credit:** The credit side of a ledger account is the right hand side

- **Debit:** The debit side of a ledger account is the left hand side

- **Discounts allowed day book:** This day book lists credit notes issued by the business for prompt payment discounts taken up by customers

- **Discounts received day book:** This day book lists credit notes issued by suppliers for prompt payment discounts taken up by the business

- **Double entry bookkeeping:** A system of accounting where the two effects of each transaction are recorded

- **Drawings:** The money or goods that the owner takes out of the business

- **Dual effect:** Every transaction a business undertakes has two effects on the business (a debit and a credit)

- **General ledger:** A collection of ledger accounts, where the double entry takes place for all the transactions of the business

- **Input VAT:** VAT on purchases reclaimable by VAT-registered businesses from HMRC

- **Journal:** The book of prime entry for non-standard transactions

- **Ledger accounts (or T-accounts):** The accounts in which each transaction is recorded

- **Output VAT:** VAT on sales collected by VAT-registered businesses from the consumer on behalf of HMRC

- **Purchases:** Purchases either of materials that are to be made into goods for resale or purchases of goods that are to be resold to customers

- **Purchases day book:** This day book lists the invoices received from credit suppliers

- **Purchases returns day book:** This day book lists the credit notes received from suppliers for items returned by the business to suppliers

- **Sales:** Sales of goods or services to customers either for cash or on credit

- **Sales day book:** This day book lists the sales invoices sent out by the business to credit customers

- **Sales returns day book:** This day book lists credit notes issued to customers for items returned by customers to the business

- **Trial balance:** A list of the closing balances on each of the general ledger accounts with one column for all the items with debit balances and another column for all the items with credit balances; total debits should equal total credits

- **Value added tax (VAT):** A consumer tax imposed by the government on the sale of certain goods and services which is collected by the business on behalf of HMRC

- **VAT control account:** Summarised totals of all VAT transactions are posted to this account; on a regular basis, it is balanced off to give the amount due to or recoverable from the tax authorities.

Test your learning

1 **Show the journal entries required to record the following transactions in the general ledger. The business is VAT registered. VAT is charged at 20%.**

   (a)   Receipt of capital into the business bank account of £40,000.

Account name		Debit £	Credit £
	▼		
	▼		

   (b)   Purchase of goods for resale on credit of £12,000 inclusive of VAT.

Account name		Debit £	Credit £
	▼		
	▼		
	▼		

   (c)   Payment for goods purchased on credit for £8,000 to a credit supplier.

Account name		Debit £	Credit £
	▼		
	▼		

Picklist:

Bank
Capital
Purchases
Purchases ledger control account
VAT control account

2 **Show the journal entries required to record the following transactions in the general ledger.**

(a) **Payment of electricity from the bank account of £5,500.**

Account name		Debit £	Credit £
	▼		
	▼		

(b) **Sale of goods to a credit customer for £15,000. Ignore VAT.**

Account name		Debit £	Credit £
	▼		
	▼		

(c) **Receipt from a credit customer for goods sold on credit for £12,000.**

Account name		Debit £	Credit £
	▼		
	▼		

Picklist:

Bank
Electricity
Sales
Sales ledger control account

3 **Identify the general ledger accounts that are debited and credited for each of the following transactions.**

	Debit		Credit	
Money withdrawn from the bank account by the owner		▼		▼
Cash purchase (ignore VAT)		▼		▼
Cash sale (ignore VAT)		▼		▼

Picklist:

Bank
Capital
Drawings
Purchases
Purchases ledger control account
Sales
Sales ledger control account

4 **Balance off the bank ledger account. Show the balance c/d and the balance b/d.**

Bank

	£		£
Balance b/d	15,000	Purchases ledger control account	10,000
Sales ledger control account	18,000	Rent	1,000
▼		Electricity	600
▼		▼	
▼		▼	

Picklist:

Balance b/d
Balance c/d
Profit or loss account

5 **Balance off the sales account and show the balance transferred to the profit or loss account.**

Sales

	£		£
Sales returns	2,000	Sales ledger control account	42,000
▼		▼	

Picklist:

Balance b/d
Balance c/d
Profit or loss account

6 **Select the correct day book from the picklist to match each description.**

Description	Day book	
Where sales invoices issued to credit customers are recorded		▼
Where non-standard transactions are recorded		▼
Where cash payments and cash receipts are recorded		▼
Where prompt payment discounts taken up by customers are recorded		▼
Where credit notes issued to customers for items returned are recorded		▼
Where credit notes issued by suppliers for items returned are recorded		▼
Where prompt payment discounts offered by suppliers and taken up by the business are recorded		▼
Where invoices received from suppliers for credit purchases are recorded		▼

Picklist:

Cash book
Discounts allowed day book
Discounts received day book
Journal
Purchases day book
Purchases returns day book
Sales day book
Sales returns day book

7 On 1 December 20X5, a business has a credit balance b/d on its VAT control account of £6,000.

During December 20X5, the following information regarding VAT is recorded:

Description	Amount £
VAT on credit sales	10,000
VAT on sales returns	1,000
VAT on cash sales	600
VAT on purchases	8,000
VAT on purchases returns	1,200
VAT on discounts allowed	400
VAT on discounts received	200
Bank payment to HMRC	2,800

Prepare the VAT control account for December 20X5. Show the balance c/d at the end of the month and the balance b/d at the start of the next month.

VAT control account

	£		£
▼		▼	
▼		▼	
▼		▼	
▼		▼	
▼		▼	
▼		▼	

Picklist

Balance b/d
Balance c/d
Bank
Cash sales
Credit sales
Discounts allowed
Discounts received
Purchases
Purchases returns
Sales returns

Accounting principles

2

Learning outcomes

1.1	**Demonstrate the accounting equation**
	• The importance of the accounting equation for keeping accounting records
	• The effect of accounting transactions on elements of the accounting equation
1.2	**Classify assets, liabilities and equity in an accounting context**
	• Definitions and examples of assets: non-current (tangible, intangible) and current; liabilities: current and non-current; equity and capital; income (revenue); expenses (costs)
	• Classify general ledger accounts as income (revenue), expense (cost), asset, liability or equity (capital)
1.3	**Demonstrate the purpose and use of books of prime entry and ledger accounting**
	• The importance of following organisational policies and procedures
	• The importance of the integrity and accuracy of records
	• Why the records need to be kept secure, and how
1.4	**Apply ethical principles when recording transactions**
	• The meaning of objectivity and its importance in accounting
	• The importance of transparency and fairness
	• That only valid transactions for the period must be included, and that all relevant transactions must be included
	• Apply the ethical principle of confidentiality
	• Identify whether entries are made with integrity, professional competence and due care
	• Identify whether transactions are genuine and valid for inclusion in the organisation's records
	• Identify professional behaviour, including dealing with the pressures of familiarity and authority

Assessment context

The accounting equation, organisational policies and procedures and ethical principles may well be tested in short-form objective test questions.

Qualification context

The Level 2 *Bookkeeping Transactions* unit introduced the accounting equation. This topic is recapped in this chapter. The classification of assets, liabilities, capital, income and expenses is tested in all the accounting units.

Organisational policies and procedures, and ethics, are important in the Level 3 and 4 synoptic assessments. Ethics is also the focus of the Level 3 unit, *Ethics for Accountants*.

Business context

Strong organisational policies and procedures are vital to all organisations. They must be implemented by those at the top of the organisation and then applied by all employees. Sound ethical principles provide a framework for the decisions made by accountants in their day-to-day work.

Chapter overview

The accounting equation can be stated as:

- Assets – Liabilities = Capital
- Assets = Liabilities + Capital
- Assets – Capital = Liabilities

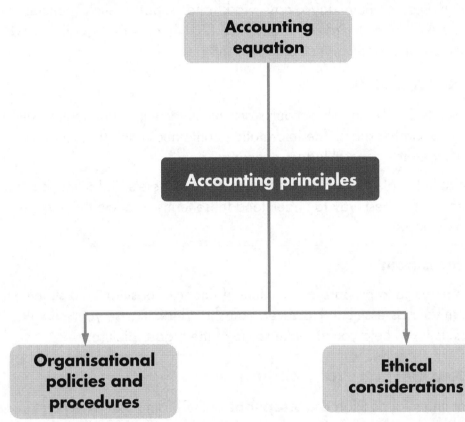

Accounting equation

Accounting principles

Organisational policies and procedures

Ethical considerations

- Financial information is used by many stakeholders
- Information must be complete and accurate
- Policies and procedures must be in place to ensure the data is reliable

The ethical principles are:

- Integrity
- Objectivity
- Professional competence and due care
- Confidentiality
- Professional behaviour

The threats to the ethical principles are:

- Self-interest
- Self-review
- Advocacy
- Familiarity
- Intimidation

Introduction

Having recapped the principles of double entry bookkeeping in the previous chapter, we now take this a stage further by looking at the definitions of assets, liabilities, income, expenses and capital, and viewing them in the context of the accounting equation.

When recording items in the accounting records, organisational policies and procedures must be in place and observed to ensure all transactions are recorded completely and accurately.

To assist accountants in their day-to-day work and support such policies and procedures, the AAT *Code of Professional Ethics* (2014) provides guidance which must be observed by all members, including students.

1 Business accounts

Two key components of a business's accounts are the statement of financial position and the statement of profit or loss. The information contained in the financial statements comes from the general ledger accounts.

You need to be able to categorise general ledger items as assets, liabilities, capital, income or expenses. The best way to understand these terms is to see them in the context of business accounts.

Assessment focus point

You will **not** be required to prepare a statement of financial position or a statement of profit or loss in your assessment. However, you should familiarise yourself with these statements as it will help you to make sense of the bigger picture.

1.1 Statement of financial position

The statement of financial position is a **snapshot** of the business at **one** point in time.

It shows what a business owns (**assets**) and what it owes (**liabilities**).

Illustration 1: Statement of financial position

Fred Designs
Statement of financial position as at 31 December 20X5

	£
ASSETS	
Non-current assets	
Property, plant and equipment	160,000
Intangible assets	20,000
	180,000
Current assets	
Inventories	35,000
Trade and other receivables	20,000
Cash and cash equivalents	15,000
	70,000
LIABILITIES	
Current liabilities	
Bank overdraft	16,000
Trade and other payables	34,000
	50,000
Net current assets	20,000
Net assets	200,000
CAPITAL	
Capital	180,000
Add profit for the year	45,000
Less drawings	(25,000)
Closing capital	200,000

The **assets** section of the statement of financial position contains '**non-current assets**', which are assets that the business will hold for more than one year and '**current assets**', which are assets the business will hold for less than one year.

Here, the **liabilities** section is made up of **current liabilities**, which are amounts the business owes that must be paid within one year. It is also possible to have **non-current liabilities**, which are amounts the business owes that are due to be paid in more than one year, eg bank loans.

The **capital** section is made up of the **cash injected** by the owner, plus the **profit** the business has made, less any **drawings** the owner has taken.

1.1.1 Points to note

Term	Consideration
Accounting equation	The statement of financial position falls naturally into two parts which are the two sides of the accounting equation – 'assets minus liabilities' and 'capital'.
Non-current assets	These relate to assets held and used in the business over the long term (ie more than one year). There are two main types of non-current assets: • **Tangible assets:** assets which have a physical substance, for example property, plant and equipment • **Intangible assets:** assets which do not have a physical substance, for example licences and brands
Current assets	These relate to assets used by the business on a day-to-day basis and include inventories, trade receivables, and bank and cash balances.
Current liabilities	These relate to liabilities owed by the business due to its day-to-day activities and include trade payables, accruals and bank overdrafts. Note that where a business is registered for value added tax (VAT), it acts as a collecting agent for the government. The balance on the VAT control account is often a current liability because businesses tend to sell items for more than they cost, and so the VAT owed on sales will be higher than the VAT due back on purchases.
Non-current liabilities	These relate to the long-term debts of the business and include items such as long-term bank loans.
Net assets	In terms of the accounting equation, total assets minus total liabilities is the business's **net assets**.
Capital	The capital or proprietor's interest section of the statement of financial position shows what the business owes back to its owner. This includes the capital contributed to date, plus the profits for the year, less any drawings taken. It is also referred to as the **equity** interest.

You can see from the statement of financial position that:

Assets	–	Liabilities	=	Capital
£250,000	–	£50,000	=	£200,000

This is known as the accounting equation.

1.2 Statement of profit or loss

The statement of profit or loss gives a summary of trading activities over a period of time (usually 12 months).

It shows amounts that the business has earned (**income**) and costs that a business has incurred (**expenses**). Income less expenses gives the **profit** the business has generated.

The following are examples of income:

(a) Revenue (or sales) – this is all the income generated from selling the business's **products**

(b) Interest received – eg interest received from bank savings accounts

(c) Rental income

The following are examples of expenses:

(a) Cost of goods sold – this is the cost associated with selling the business's **products**

(b) Interest paid – eg interest paid on bank loans

(c) Gas, electricity, stationery, rent and rates costs

Illustration 2: Statement of profit or loss

Fred Designs
Statement of profit or loss for the year ended 31 December 20X5

	£
Revenue	200,000
Less cost of goods sold	
Opening inventory	40,000
Purchases	130,000
Closing inventory	(50,000)
	(120,000)
Gross profit	80,000
Sundry income	5,000
Discounts received	3,000
	88,000
Expenses	
Rent and rates	21,000
Telephone	3,000
Electricity	4,000
Wages and salaries	9,000
Motor expenses	5,000
Discounts allowed	1,000
	(43,000)
Profit	45,000

Cost of goods sold is calculated as the **opening inventory** (all the goods the business purchased in the last period but didn't sell) plus **purchases** (all the goods for resale that the business has bought in this period) less **closing inventory** (all the goods the business has bought in this period but not yet sold).

Gross profit is the profit from the business's **trading activity**.

Discounts received are prompt payment discounts the business has received from suppliers.

The expenses listed here in this section are the business's **overheads**.

Discounts allowed are prompt payment discounts the business grants to its credit customers.

The **profit** is then transferred to the capital section of the statement of financial position.

Activity 1: Classifying items

Show whether the following items are an asset, liability, capital, income or expense.

Then indicate whether they are included in the statement of financial position (SOFP) or statement of profit or loss (SPL).

	Asset, liability, capital, income or expense	SOFP or SPL
Trade receivables (sales ledger control account)	▼	▼
Capital	▼	▼
Sales	▼	▼
Bank overdraft	▼	▼
Wages expense	▼	▼
Intangible assets	▼	▼
Cost of sales	▼	▼

Picklist:

Asset
Capital
Expense
Income
Liability
SOFP
SPL

2 Accounting equation

The **accounting equation** can be stated as:

Assets – Liabilities = Capital

The equation can also be rearranged. For example:

Assets   = Liabilities + Capital

Liabilities = Assets   – Capital

Double entry bookkeeping, and therefore financial accounting, is based on the accounting equation.

Assessment focus point

The accounting equation is very important. You should learn it! Your assessment may ask you to state the accounting equation or use it to find a missing figure. Alternatively, you may be asked to explain the effect of a transaction on the accounting equation – the technique here is to think about the double entry, which type of accounts are debited or credited (assets, liabilities, capital) and whether the debit or credit increases or decreases the balance on the accounts.

Activity 2: Accounting equation

(a) **Show whether the following statements are true or false.**

	True ✓	False ✓
Capital = assets plus liabilities		
Assets plus capital = liabilities		
Capital plus liabilities = assets		

(b) **Answer the following questions by entering the appropriate figures.**

Question	Answer £
If liabilities total £39,000 and capital totals £51,000, what is the amount of assets?	
If assets total £86,000 and liabilities total £44,000, what is the amount of capital?	
If capital totals £74,000 and assets total £162,000, what is the amount of liabilities?	

(c) The owner of a business withdraws some cash from the business for personal use. How will the elements of the accounting equation be affected by this transaction?

	Increase ✓	Decrease ✓	No change ✓
Assets			
Liabilities			
Capital			

3 Organisational policies and procedures

Each organisation will have its own policies and procedures in place to ensure the accounting records truly reflect the transactions and financial results of the business.

The accounts may be used by a wide range of stakeholders and therefore it is vital that the information is complete and accurate.

For example:

- A bank will examine the financial performance and position of a business when deciding whether to make or extend a loan.

- Suppliers may review the accounts when considering whether to offer credit to the business.

- A potential employee may review the accounts to assess the stability of the business.

An accounting system is effective if it meets the following objectives:

- Operates effectively: processing all transactions completely and accurately

- Reports accurately: providing financial and management information to stakeholders that is cost-effective, reliable and timely

- Complies with applicable laws and regulations

Control procedures vary depending on the nature and size of the organisation. They may include the following:

Procedure	Description
Authorisation of transactions	Transactions should be authorised by supervisors and managers to confirm that they are valid.
Processing controls	Organisations should carry out arithmetic and bookkeeping checks on whether transactions have been processed accurately and completely (eg reconciliations).

BPP
LEARNING MEDIA

Procedure	Description
Physical controls	Companies should ensure physical restrictions (including locks) are in place to limit access to the accounting records and assets such as cash and inventory.
Reviews	Organisations should review financial information; this may involve comparing the budget to the actual performance or comparing the performance and position of the business from one period to the next.
Written record of procedures	Businesses should have a user manual listing the main organisational procedures. For significant transactions, there should be a written record of whether the procedures have been followed.
Segregation of duties	Where possible, a number of people should be involved in different parts of each process to minimise the opportunity for fraud and error. For example different members of staff should (1) open the post, (2) record cheques received and (3) bank cheques received.

Activity 3: Policies and procedures

Jefferson is a medium-sized organisation with six employees in the accounts department.

On reviewing the organisation's policies and procedures, the new Finance Director has found that one member of staff processes all transactions relating to the sales ledger. This includes raising sales invoices, raising sales returns credit notes and recording money received from customers in the accounting records.

Required

(a) Which organisational procedure could be put in place to improve security over the sales ledger?

	✓
Physical controls	
Segregation of duties	
Authorisation of transactions	
Written record of procedures	

(b) As an accounting technician, why is it important to follow organisational policies and procedures? Choose ONE.

	✓
To learn about changes in accounting standards as part of your continuing professional development	
To allow you to access the records required for your day-to-day work	
To remove the possibility of any numerical errors arising	
To assist in the understanding of both individual responsibilities and team responsibilities	

4 Ethical considerations

Ethics are moral principles that guide behaviour, and ethical values are assumptions and beliefs about what constitutes 'right' and 'wrong' behaviour.

The concept of business ethics suggests that businesses are morally responsible for their actions and should be held accountable for them.

Accountants work in the public interest. This means they have a duty to society as a whole, and therefore strong moral values are essential to the profession.

The AAT's *Code of Professional Ethics* (2014) applies to all members, including students.

4.1 Fundamental principles

- **'Integrity**: to be straightforward and honest in all professional and business relationships' (AAT, 2014: p. 9)

- **'Objectivity**: to not allow bias, conflict of interest or undue influence of others to override professional or business judgements' (AAT, 2014: p. 9)

- **'Professional competence and due care**: to maintain professional knowledge and skill at the level required' (AAT, 2014: p. 9)

- **'Confidentiality**: to ... respect the confidentiality of information acquired as a result of professional and business relationships' (AAT, 2014: p. 9)

- **'Professional behaviour**: to comply with relevant laws and regulations and avoid any action that brings our profession into disrepute' (AAT, 2014: p. 9)

Assessment focus point

Ethics is studied in more detail in the unit *Ethics for Accountants.* In *Advanced Bookkeeping* it is important to understand how ethical principles provide a guiding framework for an accountant's day-to-day work.

Activity 4: Fundamental principles

Identify the fundamental principle being applied in the scenarios below. All of the scenarios take place within an accounting practice.

Each scenario should be considered separately.

Scenarios	Fundamental principle
All accounting estimates (such as depreciation charges) are reviewed independently by two members of staff, to ensure they are fair.	▼
Employees are not permitted to make negative references to competitors when trying to win new business.	▼
The new trainee accounting technician receives training from an experienced supervisor before beginning work.	▼
A client has overpaid. The managing partner contacts the client to notify him of this and issue a refund.	▼
No client details may be disclosed outside the firm without specific consent from that client.	▼

Picklist:

Confidentiality
Integrity
Objectivity
Professional behaviour
Professional competence and due care

4.2 Threats to the fundamental principles

The *Code* identifies the following categories of threats to the fundamental principles:

Self-interest	An accountant's personal or other interest may inappropriately influence their judgement or behaviour
Self-review	Where an accountant evaluates previous judgements made by themselves
Advocacy	Threat that an accountant promotes a client's position to the point that their objectivity is compromised
Familiarity	Risk that an accountant is too trusting or accepting of information provided by a client or employer because of a long or close relationship with them
Intimidation	An accountant may act inappropriately due to actual or perceived pressure on them

(AAT, 2014)

Assessment focus point

The threats to the fundamental principles are studied in more detail in the Level 3 *Ethics for Accountants* unit. However, at this stage in your studies, it is useful to be aware of them. Tasks on ethics in *Advanced Bookkeeping* are likely to be practical in nature and revolve around a scenario.

Activity 5: Ethical behaviour

You are preparing the accounts for a client for the year ended 30 June 20X2. The business despatches goods to a customer and raises an invoice on 29 June 20X2. However, the customer does not pay until 28 July 20X2.

Your junior colleague asks you why you are considering recording this sale in the accounts for the year ended 30 June 20X2 when the cash was not received until 28 July 20X2.

Which of the following can you use in your explanation to him?

You must choose ONE answer for each row.

Reason for considering the sale	Acceptable reason ✓	Unacceptable reason ✓
The proprietor needs to increase the profit for the year ended 30 June 20X2 to encourage the bank to extend the business's overdraft limit		
The transaction is an expense relevant to the year ended 30 June 20X2		
The figure is a current asset at 30 June 20X2		

Activity 6: Professional behaviour

You are working as an accounting technician on year-end accounts. The following are situations where you may have to record adjustments.

Which ONE of these would be acceptable professional behaviour if actioned by you?

	✓
A client's sales manager wishes you to record in the current accounting period credit sales made in the last month of the year. The bank statement shows that cash was not received from customers until the second month of the next year.	
A client wants you to reduce the profit figure in order to pay less tax. She asked you to put back the date of a large sales invoice into the next accounting period.	
Your firm needs to meet its deadline for preparing the accounts. Your supervisor tells you to save time by writing off the same amount for irrecoverable debts as the prior year.	
A client has a VAT-registered business. At the year end there is a credit balance on the business's VAT control account. The client asks you to record the balance as income in the statement of profit or loss.	

Chapter summary

- Each item in the financial statements can be classified as an asset, liability, capital, income or expense.

- The accounting equation is: Assets – Liabilities = Capital. The accounting equation can be rearranged: Assets = Liabilities + Capital and Assets – Capital = Liabilities.

- The financial information provided by organisations is used by a wide range of stakeholders.

- Each organisation will have its own policies and procedures in place to ensure that the accounting records are complete and accurate and that they truly reflect the transactions and financial results of the business.

- Procedures may include:
  - Authorisation of transactions
  - Processing controls
  - Physical controls
  - Reviews
  - Written record of procedures
  - Segregation of duties

- Ethics are moral principles that guide behaviour and ethical values are assumptions and beliefs about what constitutes 'right' and 'wrong' behaviour.

- The AAT's *Code of Professional Ethics* (2014) applies to all members, including students.

- The fundamental ethical principles are:

  - Integrity
  - Objectivity
  - Professional competence and due care
  - Confidentiality
  - Professional behaviour

Keywords

- **Accounting equation:** This can be defined as assets minus liabilities equals capital

- **Capital:** The capital or proprietor's interest section of the statement of financial position shows what the business owes back to its owner; this includes the capital contributed to date, plus the profits for the year, less any drawings taken

- **Confidentiality:** 'To ... respect the confidentiality of information acquired as a result of professional and business relationships' (AAT, 2014: p. 9)

- **Current assets:** These are assets used by the business on a day-to-day basis and include inventories, trade receivables, and bank and cash balances

- **Current liabilities:** These are liabilities owed by the business due to its day-to-day activities and include trade payables, accruals and bank overdrafts

- **Equity:** Ownership interest

- **Expenses:** Costs that the business has incurred

- **Income:** Amounts that the business has earned

- **Intangible assets:** Assets which do not have a physical substance, for example licences and brands

- **Integrity:** 'To be straightforward and honest in all professional and business relationships' (AAT, 2014: p. 9)

- **Non-current assets:** Assets that are to be used in the long term within the business

- **Non-current liabilities:** These relate to the long-term debts of the business and include items such as long-term bank loans

- **Objectivity:** 'To not allow bias, conflict of interest or undue influence of others to override professional or business judgements' (AAT, 2014: p. 9)

- **Professional behaviour:** 'To comply with relevant laws and regulations and avoid any action that brings our profession into disrepute' (AAT, 2014: p. 9)

- **Professional competence and due care:** 'To maintain professional knowledge and skill at the level required' (AAT, 2014: p. 9)

- **Tangible assets:** Assets which have a physical substance, for example property, plant and equipment

Test your learning

1 **Show whether the following items are an asset, liability, capital, income or expense.**

Then indicate whether they are included in the statement of financial position (SOFP) or statement of profit or loss (SPL).

	Asset, liability, capital, income or expense	SOFP or SPL
Trade payables (purchases ledger control account)	▼	▼
Sundry income	▼	▼
Purchases	▼	▼
Bank (debit column of TB)	▼	▼
Wages expense	▼	▼
Property, plant and equipment	▼	▼
Discounts allowed	▼	▼

Picklist:

Asset
Capital
Expense
Income
Liability
SOFP
SPL

2 A new business is started on 1 November with the following assets and liabilities.

Assets and liabilities	£
Motor vehicle	20,000
Loan from bank	10,000
Inventories	6,400
Bank	3,600

Required

Show the accounting equation on 1 November by inserting the appropriate figures.

Assets £	Liabilities £	Capital £

3   Hubert & Sons have recently employed a trainee bookkeeper. It is now time to prepare the year-end accounts. The chief accountant is on extended leave and the business owner is considering asking the trainee bookkeeper to prepare the accounts.

Which ONE fundamental ethical principle is most at risk?

	✓
Integrity	
Objectivity	
Professional competence and due care	
Confidentiality	
Professional behaviour	

4   Hemmingway is a small organisation with just one member of staff (David Silcox). David's duties include maintaining the accounting records and paying suppliers. The owner has been advised that strong policies and procedures should be in place to reduce fraud and error.

In particular, the owner is concerned that David could pay high-value supplier invoices without his knowledge.

What is the most appropriate organisational procedure that could be put in place to reduce the risk of the member of staff (David Silcox) paying a fictitious supplier?

	✓
Physical controls	
Written record of procedures	
Authorisation of transactions	
Reviews	

Purchase of non-current assets

3

Learning outcomes

2.1	Demonstrate the importance of prior authority for capital expenditure
	• Why authorisation is necessary
	• The appropriate person in an organisation to give authority
2.2	**Identify capital expenditure**
	• That International Financial Reporting Standards (IFRS) exist that are relevant to non-current assets
	• What can and cannot be included in the cost of non-current assets
	• The importance of organisational policy, including applying a given level of materiality
	• That revenue expenses should be excluded
	• The effect of capitalisation on the statement of profit or loss and statement of financial position
	• Treat VAT, according to the registration status of the acquiring organisation
2.3	**Differentiate between funding methods for acquisition of non-current assets**
	• The following funding methods: cash purchase (including purchase on standard commercial credit terms); borrowing, including loans, hire purchase, finance lease (no detailed knowledge of accounting treatment); part-exchange
	• The suitability of each of the above in a tightly defined business context

Assessment context

Non-current assets and depreciation are an important part of the *Advanced Bookkeeping* syllabus and will be the main topic tested in tasks 1 and 2 of the assessment.

It is likely that you will be required to enter new non-current assets into both the non-current asset register and the general ledger accounts. You will also need to distinguish between capital and revenue expenditure, and demonstrate knowledge of the different funding methods businesses use to acquire non-current assets.

Qualification context

Recording and accounting for non-current assets is developed in the Level 4 paper *Financial Statements of Limited Companies,* where you will deal with more complex issues such as revaluations, impairments and intangible non-current assets.

Business context

Non-current assets are often one of the most expensive items purchased by a business and they can have a significant impact on the accounts. It is important therefore that a business adopts and maintains a consistent approach in accounting for these items.

Chapter overview

Capital expenditure: acquisition, replacement or improvement of non-current assets

Revenue expenditure: trading expenses or the repair, maintenance and service of non-current assets

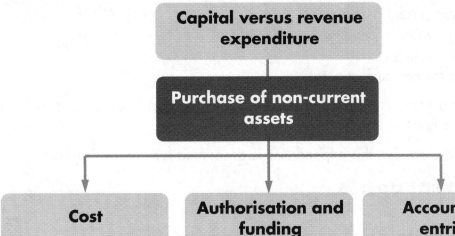

| | Cost | Authorisation and funding | Accounting entries |

Cost

The following items **are** capitalised as part of the cost of a non-current asset:

- Cost of purchase, including delivery
- Cost of construction, including own labour costs
- Cost of site preparation, including own labour costs
- Cost of installation and assembly
- Cost of testing
- Professional fees

If VAT registered, exclude VAT from the cost of the asset. If not VAT registered, include VAT in the cost of the asset

Authorisation and funding

Made prior to the purchase and by the appropriate level of personnel

Avoids items being purchased unnecessarily

Helps ensure items are bought at the best price and on the best terms

Funding methods include:

- Cash purchase
- Bank loans
- Hire purchase
- Finance lease
- Part exchange

Accounting entries

Cash purchase

DEBIT   Asset at cost
CREDIT Bank

Acquisition through loan

DEBIT   Bank
CREDIT Loan

Then:

DEBIT   Asset at cost
CREDIT Bank

Acquisition through hire purchase or finance lease

DEBIT   Asset at cost
CREDIT Liability

Introduction

This chapter considers the distinction between capital expenditure and revenue expenditure and how to account for and control the acquisition of non-current assets.

The topics covered are:

- Capital and revenue expenditure
- VAT and non-current assets
- Authorising capital expenditure
- Methods of funding
- Accounting for non-current assets

The purchase of a non-current asset is often a significant cost to a business and one which will have a notable impact on the accounts.

It is important therefore that this expenditure is accounted for appropriately.

1 Non-current assets

Activity 1: Examples of non-current assets

What examples of non-current assets can you identify?

_____

1.1 Definition

The accounting treatment of **non-current assets** is covered by IAS 16 *Property, Plant and Equipment.*

Property, plant and equipment are tangible items that:

(a) 'Are held for use in the production or supply of goods or services or for administrative purposes; and

(b) Are expected to be used during more than one period.' (IAS 16, para. 6)

1.2 Capital versus revenue expenditure

(a) **Capital expenditure:** results in the acquisition, replacement or improvement of non-current assets.

(b) **Revenue expenditure:** for the trade of the business or to repair, maintain and service non-current assets

Capital expenditure results in a non-current asset being **capitalised**. In other words, a non-current asset will be shown on the statement of financial position.

Revenue expenditure results in an expense in the statement of profit or loss.

Capital expenditure should also be recorded in a non-current asset register. This is covered in Chapter 5 *Disposal of non-current assets*.

1.3 Capitalisation policy

Businesses often purchase lots of smaller items which meet the definition of capital expenditure but are for relatively small amounts.

Many businesses will therefore set a minimum level of expenditure for items to be capitalised, say £500. This is known as the **capitalisation policy**.

If a business has a policy of capitalising expenditure over £500, then any items of capital expenditure under £500 will be recorded as an expense in the statement of profit or loss even though they meet the definition of capital expenditure.

Assessment focus point

In the assessment this will be communicated to you through the phrase **'Y has a policy of capitalising expenditure over £X'**.

Illustration 1: Capitalisation policy

Scenario (a)

LH has a policy of capitalising expenditure over £400 and subsequently purchases a printer for £200.

Question	Answer
Will this printer be capitalised as a non-current asset?	

Solution

Question	Answer
Will this printer be capitalised as a non-current asset?	No

Explanation

The printer will be expensed to the statement of profit or loss as it is below the level at which the business capitalises non-current assets.

Scenario (b)

The business then acquires a piece of furniture costing £600.

Question	Answer
Will this piece of furniture be capitalised as a non-current asset?	

Solution

Question	Answer
Will this piece of furniture be capitalised as a non-current asset?	Yes

Explanation

The item of furniture will be capitalised in the statement of financial position as its costs exceeds £400 and it therefore meets the criteria for capitalisation.

This treatment is permitted by accounting standards and is an example of the **materiality** concept.

As well as materiality, the business should also consider the lifespan of the asset. If the asset has a very short lifespan it will be written off to the statement of profit or loss reasonably quickly (say, within one or two years) and so there is not much difference in the accounts between depreciating the item and recording it as an expense.

All businesses must communicate the capitalisation policy to relevant employees.

1.4 Classes of non-current assets

A business may have several different types of non-current assets and will categorise them into separate general ledger accounts.

Most non-current assets are categorised as one of the following:

(a)   Land and buildings
(b)   Machinery
(c)   Motor vehicles
(d)   Furniture and fittings
(e)   Computers   (IAS 16, para. 37)

1.5 Cost

The cost of an item of property, plant and equipment includes:

(a) Its purchase price

(b) Any costs directly attributable to bringing the asset to the location and condition necessary for it to be capable of operating in the manner intended by management

Therefore, the following items **are** capitalised as part of the cost of a non-current asset:

- Cost of purchase, including delivery
- Cost of construction, including own labour costs
- Cost of site preparation, including own labour costs
- Cost of installation and assembly
- Cost of testing
- Professional fees   (IAS 16, para. 17)

The following items **must not** be capitalised as part of the cost of a non-current asset:

- Repair, maintenance and servicing costs
- Administrative and general overheads

Assessment focus point

You may be asked to identify items which are included in the cost of non-current assets and also the items which are excluded.

Finance costs and staff training will not be tested in the assessment.

Activity 2: Cost of the asset

On 10 December 20X7 a business bought a machine. The policy is to capitalise expenditure over £300.

The breakdown on the invoice showed:

	£
Cost of machine	20,000
Delivery costs	200
One-year maintenance contract	800
Installation costs	500
	21,500

At what amount should the machine be capitalised in the entity's records? Ignore VAT.

£ [   ]

Activity 3: Capital versus revenue expenditure

On 9 August 20X7 a business bought a building. The business has a policy of capitalising expenditure over £500 and all items listed below exceed this amount.

Required

Indicate whether the following items should be treated as capital or revenue expenditure.

	Capital expenditure ✓	Revenue expenditure ✓
Cost of the plot		
Surveyor's fees		
Legal fees for drawing up the purchase contract		
Cost of researching alternative buildings to purchase		

---

2 VAT and non-current assets

The treatment of value added tax (VAT) will depend on the registration status of the business acquiring the non-current assets.

If a business is VAT registered, then the VAT can be reclaimed from the tax authorities. Therefore, the VAT is not capitalised as part of the asset.

If a business is **not** VAT registered, then the VAT will be added to the cost of the item. In other words, the VAT will be capitalised along with the other relevant costs.

Illustration 2: Registration status of businesses and non-current assets

These principles are illustrated through the following scenarios. VAT is charged at 20%.

Scenario (a)

LV is VAT registered and acquires a machine for £20,000 plus VAT.

At what amount should the machine be capitalised?

£	

Solution

£	20,000

The VAT is reclaimable from the tax authorities and therefore does not form part of the cost of the asset.

Scenario (b)

OM is not registered for VAT and acquires a machine for £20,000 plus VAT.

At what amount should the machine be capitalised?

£	

Solution

£	24,000

The machine is capitalised at £24,000 (being £20,000 net amount plus £4,000 VAT). The VAT is not reclaimable from the tax authorities and therefore is added to the cost of the asset.

Assessment focus point

In non-current asset tasks it is important to identify the registration status of the acquiring organisation. However, some tasks will state 'you may ignore VAT in this task', in which case you do not need to worry about whether to include VAT in the cost of the asset.

3 Authorising capital expenditure

Non-current assets are often some of the most expensive items a business will purchase.

It is imperative therefore that this expenditure is appropriately authorised prior to the item being purchased.

Authorisation will help ensure:

(a) That assets are not bought unnecessarily
(b) That assets are acquired at the best prices and on the best terms

The level of authorisation required will vary according to the cost of the item. For example, organisational policy may be that the following authorisation levels apply:

- Assets costing less than £500 – supervisor
- Assets costing between £500 and £1,000 – manager
- Assets over £1,000 – business owner

It is also possible that some more-expensive items will need two levels of authorisation; for example, a business may have a policy that expenditure over £2,500 must be authorised by **both** a manager and a business owner.

Illustration 3: Authorisation levels

A business needs a new computer costing £450 for the accounts department. Organisational policy is that the authorisation levels are as follows:

- Assets costing less than £600 – supervisor
- Assets costing between £600 and £2,000 – manager
- Assets over £2,000 – business owner

Which of the following persons is most appropriate to authorise the purchase?

	✓
The accounts clerk who needs the new computer	
The accounts department supervisor	
The business owner	

Solution

	✓
The accounts department supervisor	✓

The computer should not be authorised by the employee who requests the item. However, it costs less than £600 and therefore can be authorised by the employee's supervisor.

Authorisation may be evidenced by the completion of a **capital expenditure authorisation form**. For example:

Capital Expenditure Authorisation Form	
Department	
Supplier	
Description of item	
Reason for purchase	
Cost £	
Funding method	
1st Authorisation	
2nd Authorisation (>£2,500)	

4 Methods of funding

As mentioned, non-current assets are often some of the most expensive items a business will purchase. There are different ways of funding the acquisition of non-current assets.

Method	Detail
Cash purchase	This method is used to describe both 'cash' payments for non-current assets and also purchases on standard commercial credit terms. For example, if the supplier invoice states 'Payment must be made within 60 days', this is classified as a cash purchase.
Loan	A fixed amount borrowed from a bank or other provider which is to be repaid over an agreed period of time. Interest is paid on the outstanding amount.
Hire purchase	A method of financing the purchase of a non-current asset where an initial deposit is paid to the finance company followed by a fixed number of instalments after which the asset is owned by the business.
Finance lease	A method of financing the purchase of a non-current asset which is very similar to a hire purchase agreement but where there is normally no option to purchase the asset at the end of the lease term.
Part exchange	Here an old asset is given in part exchange for a new asset. Therefore, the cash or loan payment for the new asset is reduced by the amount accepted in exchange for the old asset.

As you can see, there are many ways a business can finance the purchase of non-current assets. In deciding which funding method to use, the business will look at factors such as its own cash balances, interest rates for borrowing, and leasing conditions.

5 Accounting for non-current assets

Having acquired a non-current asset which meets the criteria for capitalisation, it must be recorded in the general ledger. The normal double entry bookkeeping principles apply; however, some new general ledger accounts are used.

When a non-current asset is purchased for cash:

(a)   It increases the cost of the non-current assets in the statement of financial position

(b)   It reduces the funds in the business's bank account

Cash purchase of a non-current asset:

Account name	Debit £	Credit £
Non-current asset at cost (SOFP)	X	
Bank (SOFP)		X

Also, and as we have seen, a business may fund a non-current asset purchase through a **loan**. First, the business takes out a loan. The effect is that:

(a)   It increases the funds in the business's bank account
(b)   It increases the loan account balance

Then the business purchases the asset and the same double entry as for a cash purchase is recorded.

Purchase of a non-current asset through a bank loan:

Account name	Debit £	Credit £
Bank (SOFP)	X	
Loan (SOFP)		X

Account name	Debit £	Credit £
Non-current asset at cost (SOFP)	X	
Bank (SOFP)		X

If the non-current asset is purchased via a **hire purchase agreement** or a **finance lease**, the effect is that:

(a) It increases the cost of the non-current assets in the statement of financial position

(b) It increases a liability account for amounts owing to the supplier of the asset

Purchase of a non-current asset through hire purchase or finance lease:

Account name	Debit £	Credit £
Non-current asset at cost (SOFP)	X	
Liability (SOFP)		X

Impact of VAT on accounting entries

If the business is VAT registered, there will be an additional debit entry to the VAT control account to record the VAT on the asset purchase recoverable from Her Majesty's Revenue & Customs (HMRC):

Account name	Debit £	Credit £
Non-current asset at cost (SOFP)	X	
VAT control account (SOFP)	X	
Bank or Liability (SOFP)		X

We will practise these journals in Activities 4 and 5.

Activity 4: Recording a machine in the general ledger

A business bought a machine costing £12,000. The machine was paid for in cash. The policy is to capitalise expenditure over £500. Ignore VAT.

Required

Record the journal entry needed in the general ledger to show the purchase of the machine.

Account name		Debit £	Credit £
	▼		
	▼		

Picklist:

Bank
Loan
Machine at cost
Repairs and maintenance

Activity 5: Recording a motor vehicle in the general ledger

A business acquired a motor vehicle costing £18,500. This was funded through a loan of £18,500 repayable in 2 years' time. The policy is to capitalise expenditure over £500. Ignore VAT.

Required

Show the journal entries needed in the general ledger to record the bank loan and then the purchase of the motor vehicle.

Journal to record the bank loan

Account name		Debit £	Credit £
	▼		
	▼		

Journal to record the purchase of the motor vehicle

Account name		Debit £	Credit £
	▼		
	▼		

Picklist:

Bank
Loan
Motor vehicle at cost
Repairs and maintenance

Activity 6: VAT and purchase of non-current assets

A VAT-registered business purchased a computer for £1,000 plus VAT. The acquisition is a cash purchase. The VAT rate is 20%. The policy is to capitalise expenditure over £300.

Required

Record the journal entry needed in the general ledger to show the purchase of the computer.

Account name		Debit £	Credit £
	▼		
	▼		
	▼		

Picklist:

Bank
Computer at cost
Loan
Purchases ledger control account
Repairs and maintenance
VAT control account

6 Double entry summary for the chapter

Cash purchase of a non-current asset:

Account name	Debit £	Credit £
Non-current asset at cost (SOFP)	X	
Bank (SOFP)		X

Purchase of a non-current asset through a bank loan:

Account name	Debit £	Credit £
Bank (SOFP)	X	
Loan (SOFP)		X

Account name	Debit £	Credit £
Non-current asset at cost (SOFP)	X	
Bank (SOFP)		X

Purchase of a non-current asset through hire purchase or finance lease:

Account name	Debit £	Credit £
Non-current asset at cost (SOFP)	X	
Liability (SOFP)		X

Impact of VAT on accounting entries

Purchase of non-current asset if VAT registered:

Account name	Debit £	Credit £
Non-current asset at cost (SOFP)	X	
VAT control account (SOFP)	X	
Bank or Liability (SOFP)		X

Assessment focus point

Non-current assets are a key part of the syllabus and feature in tasks 1 and 2 of the assessment.

Chapter summary

- Capital expenditure results in the appearance of a non-current asset in the statement of financial position.

- Revenue expenditure results in an expense in the statement of profit or loss.

- Assets which meet the criteria for capitalisation will be accounted for as non-current assets, with all relevant costs being included in the cost of the asset.

- For non VAT registered businesses, VAT will be added to the cost of the asset.

- For VAT-registered businesses, the cost of the asset is recorded net of VAT and VAT is recorded in the VAT control account as it is recoverable from HMRC.

- Non-current assets should only be acquired if the acquisition is authorised in accordance with organisational policy.

- There are various funding methods used in the acquisition of non-current assets including cash, loan, hire purchase, finance lease or part exchange.

- Non-current assets are included in the general ledger with a debit to the non-current asset account (and the VAT control account if the business is VAT registered); the credit entry will depend on the method of funding used.

Keywords

- **Capital expenditure:** Expenditure which results in the acquisition, replacement or improvement of non-current assets

- **Capitalisation policy:** The business's policy for determining when expenditure on non-current assets is capitalised

- **Capitalised:** Including the cost of a non-current asset in the statement of financial position

- **Finance lease:** A method of financing the purchase of a non-current asset which is very similar to a hire purchase agreement but where there is normally no option to purchase the asset at the end of the lease term

- **Hire purchase agreement:** A method of financing the purchase of a non-current asset where an initial deposit is paid to the finance company followed by a fixed number of instalments after which the asset is owned by the business

- **Loan:** A fixed amount borrowed from a bank or other provider which is to be repaid over an agreed period of time on which interest is paid on the outstanding amount

- **Non-current assets:** Assets acquired for long-term use within the business

- **Part exchange:** A method of disposal whereby an old asset is given in part exchange for a new asset

- **Property, plant and equipment:** Tangible items that are held for use in the production or supply of goods or services or for administrative purposes, and are expected to be used during more than one period

- **Revenue expenditure:** Any expenditure for the trade of the business or to repair, maintain and service non-current assets

1   A business bought a machine to manufacture a new product and incurred the following costs:

	£
Cost of machine	10,000
Delivery costs	150
Installation costs	600
Professional fees	300
Maintenance contract	1,000
Costs of advertising new product	500
Total cost	12,550

Ignore VAT. The policy is to capitalise expenditure over £100.

(a) At what amount will the machine be capitalised in the general ledger?

£ [   ]

(b) What is the total expense to the statement of profit or loss in relation to the acquisition of this machine?

£ [   ]

2   A business has a policy of capitalising expenditure over £500 and all items listed below exceed this amount.

Required

Indicate whether the following items should be treated as capital or revenue expenditure.

	Capital expenditure ✓	Revenue expenditure ✓
Kitchen equipment for use in the business		
Administrative costs		
Installation costs		
Professional surveyors' fees		
Repairs		

3   **Match the descriptions to the relevant funding method by selecting from the picklist.**

Description	Method
An old motor vehicle is given in part exchange for a new asset.	▼
A photocopier is financed by the business paying an initial deposit to the finance company followed by a fixed number of instalments. After all instalments have been paid, the photocopier will be owned by the business.	▼
Office furniture is acquired. The supplier invoice states 'Payment must be made within 45 days from the date of purchase'.	▼

Picklist:

Cash purchase
Finance lease
Hire purchase
Loan
Part exchange

4   A VAT-registered business acquires a machine for £16,000 plus VAT. The acquisition is a cash purchase. The VAT rate is 20%.

Required

Record the journal entry needed in the general ledger to show the purchase of the machine.

Account name	Debit £	Credit £
▼		
▼		
▼		

Picklist:

Bank
Loan
Machine at cost
Repairs and maintenance
VAT control account

5. A business which is not VAT registered acquires a machine for £14,000 plus VAT. The acquisition has been funded through a bank loan of £16,800. The VAT rate is 20%.

Required

Show the journal entries needed in the general ledger to record the bank loan and the purchase of the machine.

Journal to record the bank loan

Account name		Debit £	Credit £
	▼		
	▼		

Journal to record the purchase of the machine

Account name		Debit £	Credit £
	▼		
	▼		

Picklist:

Bank
Loan
Machine at cost
Repairs and maintenance

Depreciation of non-current assets

4

Learning outcomes

2.2	**Identify capital expenditure**
	• The definitions of cost, useful life, residual value, depreciable amount, carrying amount
	• The depreciable amount of the acquisition should be allocated over its useful life; this is an application of the accrual basis of accounting
3.1	**Calculate depreciation**
	• How charges are treated at the period end
	• Choose and use appropriate methods of depreciation, taking into account the expected pattern of usage of the asset
	• Choose and use appropriate rates of depreciation, taking into account the estimated useful life of the acquisition
	• Use the straight-line method of depreciation, using a percentage, fraction or over a period of time, including cases when a residual value is expected, for a full year or pro rata for part of a year, according to the organisational policy
	• Use the diminishing balance method of depreciation for a full year using a percentage
	• Use the units of production method of depreciation
3.2	**Record depreciation**
	• Record depreciation in the non-current assets register
	• Record depreciation in the general ledger, including the journal
	• Use the following accounts: depreciation charges, non-current asset accumulated depreciation

Assessment context

Non-current assets and depreciation are an important part of the *Advanced Bookkeeping* syllabus and will be the main topic tested in tasks 1 and 2 of the assessment. You will be required to calculate depreciation using the straight-line, diminishing balance or units of production method.

You may also need to identify the most appropriate depreciation method for a particular scenario.

Qualification context

Recording and accounting for non-current assets is developed in the Level 4 *Financial Statements of Limited Companies* unit. In particular, you will need to calculate the depreciation charges to include in the period-end financial statements.

Business context

Non-current assets are often one of the most expensive items purchased by a business and they can have a significant impact on the accounts. It is important therefore that a business adopts and maintains a consistent approach in accounting for these items.

Chapter overview

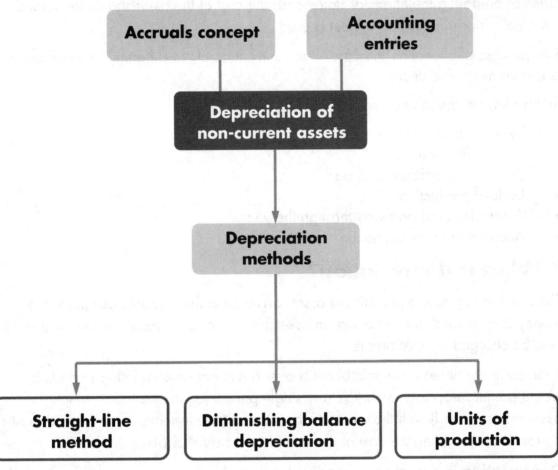

Match the cost of the asset with the consumption of the asset's economic benefits

DEBIT Depreciation charge (SPL)
CREDIT Non-current asset accumulated depreciation (SOFP)

Accruals concept

Accounting entries

Depreciation of non-current assets

Depreciation methods

Straight-line method

- Depreciation charge is the same each year
- Formula:

$$\frac{\text{Cost} - \text{Residual value}}{\text{Useful life}}$$

or

(Cost – Residual value) × %

Diminishing balance depreciation

- Depreciation charge is higher in the earlier years of the asset's life
- Formula:

Depreciation rate (%) × Carrying amount

Units of production

- Depreciation charge is based on usage of the asset
- Formula:

(Number of units produced / Life in number of units) × (Cost – Residual value)

Introduction

In the previous chapter we recorded newly acquired non-current assets in the accounting records. In this chapter we consider the accounting treatment of non-current assets **after** their initial recognition in the general ledger.

Non-current assets represent a significant cash outflow for most businesses. However, once acquired, they will often be used in the business for several years. In terms of preparing the financial statements, the cost of the asset should be spread over the periods in which the asset is used.

This process of allocating the cost of non-current assets to different financial periods is known as depreciation.

In this chapter, the topics covered are:

- What is depreciation?
- Straight-line method
- Diminishing balance method
- Units of production
- Assets acquired part way through the year
- Accounting for depreciation

1 What is depreciation?

The need to depreciate non-current assets arises from the accruals assumption. If money is expended in purchasing an asset then the amount expended must at some time be charged against profits.

If the asset consumes economic benefits over a number of accounting periods it would be inappropriate to charge any single period (eg the period in which the asset was acquired) with the whole of the expenditure. Instead, some method must be found of spreading the cost of the asset over its **useful life**.

Depreciation is a means of spreading the cost of a non-current asset over its useful life in order to match the cost of the asset with the consumption of the asset's economic benefits.

This means that instead of the cost of the asset being recorded in the accounting period when the asset is purchased, it is spread over the different accounting periods expected to benefit from the asset's use.

A formal definition of depreciation is given by the accounting standard IAS 16 *Property, Plant and Equipment* (para. 6):

Key term

> **Depreciation** is... 'is the systematic allocation of the **depreciable amount** of an asset over its useful life.'

The following terms are also useful:

Depreciable amount:	the cost of the asset less the residual value
Residual value:	the amount the asset is expected to be sold for at the end of its useful life (scrap value)
Useful life:	the period of time the business expects to make use of the asset
Carrying amount:	the value at which the asset is shown in the statement of financial position, calculated as the cost of the asset less **accumulated depreciation**

Generally all non-current assets should be depreciated as they will only last for a certain period of time.

However, land normally has an unlimited useful life and therefore is not depreciated. Buildings, though, do have a limited life and are depreciable assets.

There are three main methods for calculating depreciation:

(a) Straight-line method
(b) Diminishing balance method
(c) Units of production

2 Straight-line method

This is the most commonly used method of depreciation.

The total depreciable amount is charged in equal instalments to each accounting period over the expected useful life of the asset. In this way, the carrying amount of the non-current asset declines at a steady rate, or in a 'straight line' over time.

The **depreciation charge** is the same every year.

Formula to learn

There are two ways of calculating straight-line depreciation:

$$\text{Depreciation} = \frac{\text{Cost} - \text{Residual figure}}{\text{Useful life (years)}}$$

or

(Cost – Residual value) × %

The **straight-line method** of depreciation is **suitable for assets which are used up evenly over their useful life**.

Activity 1: Straight-line depreciation – machine

A business buys a machine for £2,500. It is expected to have a useful life of 3 years, after which time it will have a scrap value of £250.

Required

(a) Calculate the annual depreciation charge.

£ [   ]

(b) Calculate the cost, accumulated depreciation and carrying amount for each year of the asset's life.

Year	Cost £	Accumulated depreciation £	Carrying amount £
1			
2			
3			

Activity 2: Straight-line depreciation – building

A business has the following balances relating to non-current assets:

Balances as at:	30 June 20X5 £	30 June 20X6 £
Buildings at cost	100,000	100,000
Buildings accumulated depreciation	12,000	To be calculated

Depreciation is provided at 2% on a straight-line basis.

Required

(a) Calculate the depreciation charge for the year ended 30 June 20X6.

£ [   ]

(b) Calculate the updated accumulated depreciation as at 30 June 20X6.

£ [   ]

3 Diminishing balance method

This method of depreciation calculates the annual depreciation charge as a fixed percentage of the carrying amount of the asset, as at the end of the previous accounting period.

The **diminishing balance method** may be used when it is thought that the benefits obtained by the business from using the asset decline over time. An example of this could be a machine in a factory, where productivity falls as the machine gets older.

Formula to learn

Depreciation   =   Depreciation rate (%) × Carrying amount

Note. This method does not take account of any residual value, since the carrying amount under this method will never reach zero.

Activity 3: Diminishing balance depreciation – machine

A business buys a machine costing £6,000. The depreciation rate is 40% on a diminishing balance basis.

Required

Calculate the depreciation charge, accumulated depreciation and carrying amount of the asset for the first three years.

Year	Carrying amount b/d £	Depreciation rate	Depreciation charge £	Accumulated depreciation £	Carrying amount c/d £
1					
2					
3					

Activity 4: Diminishing balance depreciation – vehicle

A business has the following balances relating to non-current assets:

Balances as at:	31 January 20X8 £	31 January 20X9 £
Vehicle at cost	50,000	50,000
Vehicle accumulated depreciation	32,850	To be calculated

Depreciation is provided at 30% on a diminishing balance basis.

Required

(a) **Calculate the depreciation charge for the year ended 31 January 20X9.**

£ ☐

(b) **Calculate the updated accumulated depreciation as at 31 January 20X9.**

£ ☐

4 Units of production method

The **units of production method** of depreciation involves charging depreciation according to the actual usage of the asset.

The life of the asset is measured in terms of the number of units of output it is likely to produce (or the number of hours it is likely to be used). It is then depreciated according to that rate.

This method is useful where a business has non-current assets with varying usage.

In the units of production method, higher depreciation is charged when there is greater activity and less is charged when there is lower usage.

The following formula is used to calculate depreciation under this method:

Formula to learn

$$\text{Depreciation} = \frac{\text{Number of units produced}}{\text{Life in number of units}} \times (\text{Cost} - \text{Residual value})$$

Activity 5: Units of production depreciation – machine

A business acquired a machine costing £40,000. The machine is expected to produce 100,000 units over its useful life.

Over the last three years it has produced the number of units shown below.

Required

Calculate the depreciation charge, accumulated depreciation and carrying amount of the asset for the first three years.

Year	Number of units produced	Carrying amount b/d £	Depreciation charge £	Accumulated depreciation £	Carrying amount c/d £
1	10,000				
2	24,000				
3	30,000				

Workings:

Note that whichever depreciation method is chosen (straight-line, diminishing balance or units of production), the method should be reviewed from time to time to ensure that it is still appropriate. The useful life and residual value should be reviewed at least at every financial year end.

5 Assets acquired part way through the year

In our examples, the assets were held by the business for an entire year and so a full 12 months of depreciation has been charged.

Should an asset be acquired part way through the year then the business has a choice:

Options	Task instructions
Either to charge 12 months' worth of depreciation in the year of acquisition irrespective of when the asset was acquired	Here the exam task may state that **'a full year's depreciation is applied in the year of acquisition'**.
Or to calculate depreciation on a **pro rata** basis which means it will only charge depreciation on the asset for the **number of months it was held**.	Here the exam task is likely to say **'depreciation is calculated on an annual basis and charged in equal instalments for each full month an asset is owned in the year'**.

Assessment focus point

This will not be tested for the diminishing balance method as the syllabus learning outcome is 'use the diminishing balance method of depreciation for a full year using a percentage'.

Illustration 1: Pro rata depreciation

A business bought a machine for £10,000 on 1 October 20X9. It charges straight-line depreciation on a pro rata basis at a rate of 20% and has a year end of 31 December.

What is the depreciation charge for the year ended 31 December 20X9?

£	

Solution

£	500

Explanation

Here the business buys the asset with three months of the year remaining; it will therefore charge only three months' depreciation.

The depreciation for the year is calculated as:

£10,000 × 20% × $^{3}/_{12}$ = £500

Activity 6: Assets acquired part way through the year

A business has the following information relating to non-current assets:

- A piece of furniture described as 'FUJ838' was acquired on 1 April 20X8 for £8,000.

- Furniture is depreciated at 10% using the straight-line method.

- Depreciation is calculated on an annual basis and charged in equal instalments for each full month an asset is owned in the year.

Required

(a) **Calculate the accumulated depreciation and carrying amount for the year ended 31 December 20X8.**

Accumulated depreciation	Carrying amount
£	£

(b) **Calculate the accumulated depreciation and carrying amount for the year ended 31 December 20X9.**

Accumulated depreciation	Carrying amount
£	£

---

6 Accounting for depreciation

6.1 Dual effect

Depreciation has a **dual** effect which needs to be accounted for:

(a) It **reduces the carrying amount of the non-current asset** on the statement of financial position by increasing the accumulated depreciation on the non-current asset. The accumulated depreciation account (a credit balance) is offset against the non-current asset cost account (a debit balance) in the statement of financial position.

(b) It is an **expense** in the statement of profit or loss.

The asset remains at its original cost in the asset account.

Two additional general ledger accounts are set up to record depreciation:

Account name	Debit £	Credit £
Depreciation charges (SPL)	X	
Non-current asset accumulated depreciation (SOFP)		X

6.2 Non-current asset accumulated depreciation account

(a) Used to decrease the carrying amount of the asset

(b) Reduces original cost of the asset on the statement of financial position (the balance on the account is offset against the cost account for the corresponding asset)

(c) Separate account kept for each **class** of asset (eg motor vehicles, buildings, plant and machinery)

Activity 7 is longer than an assessment standard task and asks you to prepare an extract to the accounts. You will not have to do this in the *Advanced Bookkeeping* assessment. However, Activity 7 provides useful context for accounting for non-current assets in the general ledger and prepares you for exam-style questions.

Activity 7: Depreciation in the financial statements

Using the information in Activity 1, Straight-line depreciation – machine, and assuming the machine was a cash purchase:

(a) Show the journal entry to record depreciation at the end of the first year

Journal entry to record depreciation charge

Account name	Debit £	Credit £
▼		
▼		

(b) In the T-accounts record the:

- **Entries in the Machine at cost (SOFP) account; show the balance c/d and balance b/d**

- **Entry in the Bank (SOFP) account**

- **Entries in the Depreciation charges (SPL) account, showing the amount transferred to the profit or loss account each year**

- **Entries in the Machine accumulated depreciation (SOFP) account, showing the balance c/d and balance b/d at the end of each year of the asset's life**

Machine at cost (SOFP)

	£			£
▼			▼	
▼			▼	

Bank (SOFP)

	£			£
▼			▼	

Depreciation charges (SPL)

	£			£
▼			▼	
▼			▼	
▼			▼	

Machine accumulated depreciation (SOFP)

	£			£
▼			▼	
▼			▼	
▼			▼	
▼			▼	
▼			▼	
▼			▼	

Picklist:

Balance b/d
Balance c/d
Bank
Depreciation charges
Machine accumulated depreciation
Machine at cost
Profit or loss account

(c) **Show the relevant statement of profit or loss and statement of financial position extracts for each year**

Statement of profit or loss (extracts)

	Year 1 £	Year 2 £	Year 3 £
Expenses			
Depreciation charges			

Statement of financial position (extracts)

Machine	Cost £	Accumulated depreciation £	Carrying amount £
Year 1			
Year 2			
Year 3			

Activity 8: Ledger accounting for non-current assets

This task is about ledger accounting for non-current assets.

• You are working on the accounts of a business that is registered for VAT.

• The financial year end is 31 August 20X9.

• A new vehicle has been acquired. VAT can be reclaimed on this vehicle.

• The cost excluding VAT was £28,000; this was paid from the bank.

• The residual value is expected to be £4,000 excluding VAT. It is estimated it will be used for 4 years.

• Vehicles are depreciated on a straight-line basis. A full year's depreciation is applied in the year of acquisition.

• Depreciation has already been entered into the accounts for existing vehicles.

Required

(a) **Calculate the depreciation charge for the year on the new vehicle.**

£	

Make entries to account for:

(b)   The purchase of the new vehicle

(c)   The depreciation charge on the new vehicle

On each account, show clearly the balance carried down or transferred to the profit or loss account in the general ledger, as appropriate.

Vehicles at cost

	£		£
Balance b/d	36,000	▼	
▼		▼	

Depreciation charges

	£		£
Balance b/d	9,000	▼	
▼		▼	

Vehicles accumulated depreciation

	£		£
▼		Balance b/d	18,000
▼		▼	

Picklist:

Balance c/d
Bank
Depreciation charges
Profit or loss account
Vehicles accumulated depreciation
Vehicles at cost

7 Double entry summary for the chapter

Depreciation adjustment:

Account name	Debit £	Credit £
Depreciation charges (SPL)	X	
Non-current asset accumulated depreciation (SOFP)		X

Assessment focus point

In your assessment you will be asked to calculate depreciation. You must read the requirement carefully to ensure that you use the correct method.

Chapter summary

- The need to depreciate non-current assets arises from the accruals assumption.

- Depreciation is a means of spreading the cost of a non-current asset over its useful life in order to match the cost of the asset with the consumption of the asset's economic benefits.

- The cost of the non-current asset minus the depreciation charged to date is known as the carrying amount.

- The straight-line method of depreciation ensures that the same amount of depreciation is charged for each year of the asset's life.

- The diminishing balance method of depreciation charges a larger amount of depreciation in the early years of the asset's life and a lower amount in the later years of its life.

- The unit of production method of depreciation charges depreciation according to the usage of an asset in a particular accounting period.

- Depreciation is recorded in the general ledger by debiting the depreciation charges account and crediting the accumulated depreciation account.

- The depreciation charges account is cleared as an expense to the profit or loss account at the end of each year but the balance on the accumulated depreciation account is carried down as the opening balance for the following period.

Keywords

- **Accumulated depreciation:** The statement of financial position ledger account that records the depreciation charged to date on a non-current asset

- **Carrying amount:** The cost of the non-current asset minus the accumulated depreciation

- **Depreciable amount:** The cost of the asset less the residual value

- **Depreciation:** The charge to the statement of profit or loss to reflect the use of the non-current asset during the period

- **Depreciation charge:** The amount of depreciation charged to the statement of profit or loss each year

- **Diminishing balance method:** Method of calculating depreciation so that a larger amount is charged in the earlier years and smaller amounts in subsequent years

- **Residual value:** The anticipated resale value of the non-current asset at the end of its useful life to the business

- **Straight-line method:** A method of calculating depreciation to give the same charge each year

- **Units of production method:** A method of depreciating a non-current asset according to usage

- **Useful life:** The period over which the business estimates that the non-current asset will be used

Test your learning

You may ignore VAT in all of the following tasks.

1   The main accounting concept underlying the depreciation of non-current assets is the

    [▼] concept.

    Picklist:

    accruals
    consistency
    materiality

2   On 1 January 20X7 a business acquired a machine for £36,000. The machine is expected to produce 48,000 units over its useful life with a nil residual value. In the current year, it produced 12,000 units.

    What is the depreciation charge for the year ended 31 December 20X7?

    £ [   ]

3   A business purchased a car on 1 January 20X7 for £16,400. The car is to be depreciated at 35% each year using the diminishing balance method.

    (a) What is the depreciation charge for the year ended 31 December 20X8?

    £ [   ]

    (b) What is the carrying amount of the car at 31 December 20X8?

    £ [   ]

4   A business has machinery with a cost of £240,000 and accumulated depreciation at the start of the year of £135,000. The policy is to depreciate the machinery at the rate of 30% using the diminishing balance method.

    What is this year's depreciation charge?

    £ [   ]

5   A business purchased a delivery lorry for £24,000 on 1 June 20X1 which is to be depreciated using the straight-line method at a rate of 20% per annum, charged in equal instalments for each full month an asset is owned.

    What is the depreciation charge for the accounting year ending 31 December 20X1?

    £ [   ]

6 A business has the following balances relating to non-current assets:

Balances as at:	31 May 20X7 £	31 May 20X8 £
Office equipment at cost	20,000	26,000
Office equipment accumulated depreciation	8,000	To be calculated
Machinery at cost	60,000	85,000
Machinery accumulated depreciation	15,000	To be calculated

Office equipment is depreciated over 5 years on a straight-line basis and machinery is depreciated at 25% on a diminishing balance basis.

A full year's depreciation charge is made in the year of acquisition and none in the year of disposal.

Required

(a) **Calculate the depreciation charge for the year ended 31 May 20X8.**

Office equipment		Machinery	
£		£	

(b) **Calculate the updated accumulated depreciation as at 31 May 20X8.**

Office equipment		Machinery	
£		£	

7 **Which one of the following best describes the residual value of a non-current asset?**

	✓
The difference between the non-current asset's carrying amount and the estimated scrap proceeds	
The anticipated resale value of the non-current asset at the end of its useful life to the business	
The cost of the non-current asset minus the accumulated depreciation	
The amount paid for the non-current asset at the date of purchase	

Disposal of non-current assets

5

Learning outcomes

2.4	Record acquisitions and disposals of non-current assets
	• The purpose and content of the non-current assets register, including assisting physical verification and checking general ledger entries and balances
	• The carrying amount of an asset that has been disposed of at the end of the period
	• The meaning of the balance on the disposals account
	• How gains and losses are treated at the period end
	• Update the non-current assets register for acquisitions and disposals
	• Record acquisitions and disposals in the general ledger
	• Account for acquisitions and disposals by part-exchange
	• Treat VAT, according to the registration status of the acquiring organisation
	• Use the following accounts: non-current asset at cost (for example, motor vehicles at cost), non-current asset accumulated depreciation, bank/cash, loan, disposals

Assessment context

Having learnt how to record non-current assets in the general ledger and account for depreciation, it is equally important to be able to remove them from the general ledger. The disposal of non-current assets is an important part of the *Advanced Bookkeeping* syllabus and is likely to be tested in the exam.

In Task 1 you will also have to complete a non-current assets register. This is a significant task and one which assesses your understanding of acquisitions, depreciation and disposals of non-current assets.

Qualification context

Recording and accounting for non-current assets is developed in the Level 4 *Financial Statements of Limited Companies* unit where you will deal with more complex issues such as revaluations, impairments and intangible non-current assets.

Business context

Non-current assets are often one of the most expensive items purchased by a business and they can have a significant impact on the accounts. It is important therefore that a business adopts and maintains a consistent approach in accounting for these items.

Chapter overview

- List of all tangible non-current assets owned by a business
- Includes information such as:
  - Name of item and serial number
  - Date of acquisition
  - Cost at acquisition
  - Depreciation charges
  - Carrying amount
  - Funding method
  - Disposal date and proceeds

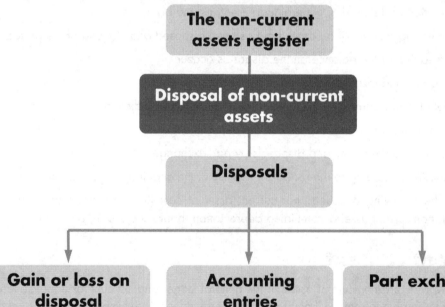

The non-current assets register

Disposal of non-current assets

Disposals

Gain or loss on disposal

- Gain or loss on disposal calculation

Proceeds	X
Less carrying amount	(X)
Gain or (loss)	X/(X)

Accounting entries

- Steps
  1. Remove the cost of the asset
  2. Remove the accumulated depreciation charged to date
  3. Account for the sale proceeds
  4. Balance off the disposals account to find the gain or loss on disposal

Part exchange

- Replace the sale proceeds in step (3) with the part exchange allowance
- Complete the entries for the purchase of the new asset

Introduction

Having considered the acquisition of non-current assets and their accounting treatment during their useful lives, the next step is to consider the process of disposing of non-current assets when they are of no more use to the business.

On disposal of a non-current asset, the business may receive cash proceeds, also known as 'scrap' proceeds. Alternatively, it may be able to part-exchange an old asset and for this to be recognised as a contribution towards the cost of a new asset. It is important to account for both types of transaction accurately.

Another key topic is the non-current assets register. This register lists all the tangible non-current assets owned by the business, and includes detailed information such as the cost, acquisition date, depreciation, carrying amount and, ultimately, the disposal details of each item.

1 Non-current assets (recap)

As has been discussed in previous chapters, the purchase of an asset such as a building, a machine or a motor vehicle will result in a non-current asset being shown in the business's statement of financial position.

Once acquired, non-current assets are generally used in businesses for several years. Depreciation is a means of spreading the cost of a non-current asset over its useful life in order to match the cost of the asset with the consumption of its economic benefits.

The actual amount shown in the statement of financial position is the carrying amount of the asset; this is the cost of the asset less the accumulated depreciation charged to date on the asset.

2 Disposal of non-current assets

Due to the fact that most assets have a finite useful life, ultimately businesses will dispose of them.

There are three main considerations:

(1)   The gain or loss that will arise on the disposal
(2)   The accounting entries to record the disposal
(3)   Offering an asset in **part exchange** against the purchase of a new asset

2.1 Gain or loss on disposal

As mentioned above, the actual amount shown in the statement of financial position is the carrying amount of the asset. When a non-current asset is disposed of, its carrying amount needs to be removed from the statement of financial position.

The sale proceeds received in exchange for the asset are unlikely to be exactly the same as the asset's carrying amount at the disposal date. Therefore, a **gain or loss on disposal** will arise.

BPP
LEARNING MEDIA

Formula to learn

Proceeds   X

Less carrying amount   (X)

Gain or (loss)   X/(X)

If:

sale proceeds > carrying amount ⇒ gain on disposal

sale proceeds < carrying amount ⇒ loss on disposal

This is not a 'true' gain or loss, but rather a 'book adjustment' to reflect the fact that the depreciation charged over the asset's life was not completely accurate.

If there is a **gain** on disposal, the asset suffered too much depreciation during its lifetime and some of this must be credited back to the statement of profit or loss.

If there is a **loss** on disposal then the asset was not depreciated enough during its lifetime and so an extra charge is needed on disposal in the statement of profit or loss.

2.2 Accounting treatment

Everything to do with the disposal is transferred to a **disposals account**.

Disposal of a non-current asset for cash (four steps):

(1)   Remove the cost of the asset:

Account name	Debit £	Credit £
Disposals (SPL)	X	
Non-current asset at cost (SOFP)		X

(2)   Remove the accumulated depreciation charged to date:

Account name	Debit £	Credit £
Non-current asset accumulated depreciation (SOFP)	X	
Disposals (SPL)		X

Note. Steps (1) and (2) have effectively transferred the carrying amount of the asset to the disposals account. Therefore, the carrying amount of an asset that has been disposed of is **zero** at the end of the period.

(3) Account for the sales proceeds:

Account name	Debit £	Credit £
Bank (SOFP)	X	
Disposals (SPL)		X

(4) Balance off the disposals account to determine the gain or loss on disposal.

A gain on disposal is shown in the statement of profit or loss as **sundry income**, a loss as an **expense**.

Activity 1: Disposal of a machine for cash

A business bought a machine for £6,000 and has held it for 2 years. The machine is sold in year 3 for £3,000. The business depreciates its machines on a diminishing balance basis at a rate of 40%. No depreciation is charged in the year of disposal.

The business has a policy of capitalising non-current asset expenditure over £500.

Required

(a) **Calculate the gain or loss on disposal of the machine. Place a tick in the relevant box to denote whether the amount is a gain or a loss.**

(b) **Show how the disposal would be accounted for in the ledger accounts.**

VAT can be ignored.

Solution

(a)

		Gain	Loss
£			

Workings:

(b) Machine at cost (SOFP)

	£		£
Balance b/d	6,000	▼	

Machine accumulated depreciation (SOFP)

	£		£
▼		Balance b/d	3,840

Disposals (SPL)

	£		£
▼		▼	
▼		▼	

Picklist:

Bank
Disposals
Machine accumulated depreciation
Machine at cost
Profit or loss account

2.3 Part exchange allowance

Instead of receiving sale proceeds in the form of cash, a **part exchange allowance** could be offered against the cost of a replacement asset. In this situation, the part exchange allowance takes the place of sale proceeds in the disposals account.

Disposal of a non-current asset in part exchange for a new asset (five steps):

(1) Remove the cost of the asset:

Account name	Debit £	Credit £
Disposals (SPL)	X	
Non-current asset at cost (SOFP)		X

(2)   Remove the accumulated depreciation charged to date:

Account name	Debit £	Credit £
Non-current asset accumulated depreciation (SOFP)	X	
Disposals (SPL)		X

(3)   Account for the part exchange allowance:

Account name	Debit £	Credit £
Non-current asset at cost **(new asset)** (SOFP)	X	
Disposals (SPL)		X

(4)   Balance off the disposals account to determine the gain or loss on disposal.

(5)   Record any additional payment made for the part-exchanged asset:

Account name	Debit £	Credit £
Non-current asset at cost **(new asset)** (SOFP)	X	
Bank (SOFP)		X

Activity 2 is a preparation question which enables you to practise these principles.

Activity 2: Disposal of a machine – part exchange

Assume in Activity 1, Disposal of a machine for cash, that instead of cash proceeds of £3,000 there is a part exchange allowance of £3,000 on a replacement machine costing £10,000.

Required

(a)   **Calculate the gain or loss on disposal of the machine. Place a tick in the relevant box to denote whether the amount is a gain or a loss.**

(b)   **Calculate the amount of cash paid for the new machine.**

(c)   **Complete the ledger accounts to show both the disposal and the acquisition. On each account, show clearly the balance to be carried down or transferred to the profit or loss account, as appropriate.**

VAT can be ignored.

Solution

(a)

	Gain	Loss
£		

(b)

£	

(c) **Old machine at cost (SOFP)**

	£		£
Balance b/d	6,000	▼	

Old machine accumulated depreciation (SOFP)

Details	Amount £	Details	Amount £
▼		Balance b/d	3,840

New machine at cost (SOFP)

	£		£
▼		▼	
▼		▼	

Disposals (SPL)

	£		£
▼		▼	
▼		▼	

Picklist:

Balance b/d
Balance c/d
Bank
Disposals
New machine at cost
Old machine accumulated depreciation
Old machine at cost
Profit or loss account

Activity 3 is representative of the type of question you may see in the assessment on the part exchange of non-current assets.

Activity 3: Vans – part exchange

During the year a business part-exchanged some vans.

- The original van was bought for £16,000.

- Four years' depreciation has been applied.

- Depreciation is provided over six years on a straight-line basis.

- The estimated residual value of the asset at the date of acquisition was £1,000.

- A part exchange allowance of £5,200 was given.

- £18,000 was paid from the bank for the new van.

- VAT can be ignored.

Required

(a) **Calculate the accumulated depreciation on the original van that was part-exchanged during the year.**

£	

Workings:

(b) **Complete the disposals account.**

Disposals (SPL)

	£			£
▼		▼		
▼		▼		
▼		▼		

Picklist:

Bank
Profit or loss account
Van accumulated depreciation
Van at cost

2.4 Assets disposed of part way through the year

In the previous chapter we saw that a business may buy assets part way through the year and that it will either charge a **'full year's depreciation in the year of acquisition and none in the year of disposal'** or will charge depreciation on a **'pro rata basis'**.

The same is true of disposals. A business may dispose of assets part way through the year and these assets may or may not need to be depreciated in the year of disposal, depending on the business's policy.

Formula to learn

If the business's policy is to charge **'a full year's depreciation charge in the year of acquisition and none in the year of disposal'** then **no depreciation** charge is made in the year of disposal. A full 12-month charge was made during the year of acquisition.

If, however, the business charges depreciation on a **'pro rata basis'** then you will need to charge depreciation on the asset for the number of months it was **held** in the year of disposal.

Illustration 1: Asset disposed of part way through the year

A business sold a van for £3,000 on 30 April 20X9. It had originally cost £12,000 and had accumulated depreciation brought forward at 1 January 20X9 of £7,200. The business charges straight-line depreciation on a pro rata basis at a rate of 20% and has a year end of 31 December.

What is the depreciation charge for the van for the year ended 31 December 20X9?

Here the business has used the asset for the first four months of the year and so should charge depreciation for four months.

The depreciation for the year is calculated as:

£12,000 × 20% × 4/12 = £800

What is the gain or loss on disposal of the asset?

Gain or loss on disposal working	£
Proceeds	3,000
Less carrying amount*	(4,000)
Loss on disposal	(1,000)
Carrying amount:	
Cost	12,000
Less accumulated depreciation (£7,200 + £800)	(8,000)
	4,000*

The next activity provides exam standard practice in recording the disposal of a non-current asset in the general ledger.

Activity 4: Part exchange of a machine

This task is about ledger accounting for non-current assets.

You are working on the accounts of a business for the year ended 31 August 20X9.

- VAT can be ignored.
- The business has a policy of capitalising expenditure over £700.
- A machine was part-exchanged on 1 January 20X9.
- The original machine was bought for £10,600 on 14 February 20X5.
- Depreciation is provided at 20% per year on a straight-line basis.
- A full year's depreciation is applied in the year of acquisition and none in the year of disposal.
- A part exchange allowance of £1,250 was given.
- £8,900 was paid from the bank to complete the purchase of the new machine.

Required

Make entries relating to the disposal:

(a) **Complete the disposals account.**
(b) **Update the bank account.**

On each account, show clearly the balance carried down or transferred to the profit or loss account, as appropriate.

Disposals

	£			£
▼		▼		
▼		▼		
▼		▼		

Bank

	£			£
Balance b/d	9,000		▼	
▼			▼	

Picklist:

Balance b/d
Balance c/d
Bank
Disposals
Machine accumulated depreciation
Machine at cost
Profit or loss account

(c) **Calculate the purchase cost of the new machine from the information above.**

£

(d) **What will be the carrying amount of the new machine as at 31 August 20Y0?**

£

Workings:

3 The non-current assets register

Nearly all large organisations will keep some form of **non-current assets register**. This register is a record of all the tangible non-current assets owned by the business. It lists detailed information on the assets, which may include:

- Item name and serial number
- Location of the asset
- Department responsible for the asset
- Asset type
- Cost
- Funding method
- Acquisition date
- Depreciation policy
- Depreciation charges to date
- Carrying amount

Ultimately, the non-current assets register will also show the disposal date and any proceeds received on disposal of the assets.

The register may take the form of a spreadsheet or a business may have a database which holds this information.

3.1 Purpose of the non-current assets register

The register is mainly for internal use and does not form part of the general ledger. Instead, it is part of the business's internal control system. The register can be used to ascertain the physical location and condition of assets and to check entries and balances in the general ledger.

A business should have policies and procedures in place to ensure that assets are accurately entered into the non-current assets register and that it is updated regularly (eg when assets are acquired or sold).

Reconciliations between the non-current assets register and the general ledger enable the business to identify discrepancies and take action, where necessary.

Likewise, on a periodic basis the physical non-current assets that a business holds should be checked against the entries in the non-current assets register. Any differences should be reported to an appropriate person in the organisation for investigation.

3.2 Structure of the non-current assets register

 Assessment focus point

In Task 1 of the assessment you will be given a partially complete non-current assets register and information regarding any acquisitions, disposals and depreciation charges for the year. You must use this information to update the non-current assets register.

3.2.1 Example non-current assets register

Description /Serial number	Acquisition date	Cost £	Depreciation charges £	Carrying amount £	Funding method	Disposal proceeds £	Disposal date
Office equipment							
Laser printer LP664	20.08.X7	6,000.00			Finance lease		
Year end 31.12.X7			1,200.00	4,800.00			
Year end 31.12.X8			1,200.00	3,600.00			
Year end 31.12.X9			1,200.00	2,400.00			
InkJet printer IP189	22.05.X8	400.00			Cash		
Year end 31.12.X8			80.00	320.00			
Year end 31.12.X9			0.00	0.00		150.00	31.12.X9
Motor vehicles							
Ford Mondeo CD06 UVS	14.02.X6	8,000			Part exchange		
Year end 31.12.X6			2,000.00	6,000.00			
Year end 31.12.X7			1,500.00	4,500.00			
Year end 31.12.X8			1,125.00	3,375.00			
Year end 31.12.X9			843.75	2,531.25			

104

3.2.2 Updating the non-current assets register

General updates to the non-current assets

- All items need to be updated for the current year depreciation charge and the subsequent change to the carrying amount.

Recording any acquisitions of non-current assets

- If an asset has been acquired in the year, as long as the capitalisation threshold has been reached, the description and serial number, the acquisition date, cost and funding method must be recorded in the non-current assets register. The cost will include the purchase price and any directly attributable costs.

- As discussed in Chapter 3 *Purchase of non-current assets*, non-current assets will be funded from cash, loans, hire purchase, finance lease or part exchange. In the assessment the funding method will be stated in the scenario. You need to select the appropriate funding method from the picklist and include it in your on-screen answer.

Depreciation

- On each row of the depreciation column the annual depreciation charge is given for each asset. For example, for the Ford Mondeo for the year ended 31.12.X6 this is £2,000.00.

- If we add up all the annual depreciation charges for each asset we can find the accumulated depreciation to date. For example, the accumulated depreciation for the Ford Mondeo by the year ended 31.12.X9 is £5,468.75 (being £2,000.00 plus £1,500.00 plus £1,125.00 plus £843.75).

- Therefore, we can establish the carrying value, which is cost less accumulated depreciation. Again, looking at the Ford Mondeo this is £8,000.00 minus £5,468.75 which equals £2,531.25.

Recording any disposals of non-current assets

- If an asset has been disposed of then it will have a nil carrying amount (£0.00) in the non-current assets register at the year end.

- The depreciation charge will depend on the depreciation policy. If there is a full year's depreciation in the year of acquisition and none in the year of disposal, the depreciation charge will be nil (£0.00). However, if the depreciation is charged on a monthly pro rata basis, you will need to work out a full year's depreciation and then pro-rate it for the number of months the asset is owned in the year.

- Enter the disposal proceeds and disposal date in your on-screen answer. It is likely that both will be entered by selecting appropriate options from the drop down menus.

Value added tax (VAT)

There are three possible scenarios in a non-current asset register task:

BPP
LEARNING MEDIA

(a) The task will say **'you may ignore VAT'** – for acquisitions and disposals, **the amounts given** in the invoices for acquisitions and disposals can be posted directly to the non-current asset register (VAT will not be shown in the invoice).

(b) The task will say that **'the business is VAT registered'** – for acquisitions and disposals, the **net amount** (excluding VAT) must be selected from the invoices to post to the non-current asset register rather than the gross amount (as the VAT on purchases is recoverable from HMRC and the VAT on disposals is payable to HMRC).

(c) The task will say that **'the business is not VAT registered'** – for acquisitions, the **gross amount** (including VAT) must be selected from the invoices to post to the non-current asset register as the VAT is not recoverable.

Activity 5 is a preparation question on the non-current assets register.

Activity 5: Non-current assets register

A business has a policy of capitalising non-current asset expenditure over £300. Ignore VAT and depreciation.

Required

(a) **Identify, by placing a tick in the relevant box, which of the items below should be recorded in the non-current assets register.**

Item	Yes ✓	No ✓
Motor van (reg. no. AT59 CBA), cost £6,000 and funded through a hire purchase agreement. Purchased on 23.09.X9.		
Optional insurance taken out on the above van for a cost of £350 paid in cash.		
A Dell laptop (serial number LT405), cost £2,000 and paid in cash. Purchased on 24.05.X9 from Dell on standard commercial credit terms.		
A second-hand scanner and printer, cost £50, purchased on 19.01.X9, paid for in cash. This item has an expected life of approximately 10 months.		
A photocopier (serial number CO132), cost £3,525 and funded through a loan. Purchased on 24.03.X9.		

(b) **Where an item should be recorded in the non-current assets register, make the relevant entry in the table below.**

Description/ Serial number	Acquisition date	Cost £	Depreciation charges £	Carrying amount £	Funding method	Disposal proceeds £	Disposal date
Motor vehicles							
▼					▼		
Computers							
▼					▼		
Office equipment							
▼					▼		

Picklist for description/serial number:

Dell laptop LT405
Insurance
Photocopier CO132
Scanner and printer
Van AT59 CBA

Picklist for funding method:

Cash
Hire purchase
Loan
Part exchange

3.3 Assessment tasks on the non-current assets register

It is important to practise the skills involved in completing a non-current assets register, as we will see in the next activity.

This will be a lengthy task in the assessment and it is advisable to have a methodical approach.

Steps

(1) Read the **requirements**.

(2) Scan the information and non-current assets register so you have an **overview** of the task. Note the **depreciation method(s)** and whether VAT is to be ignored or whether the business is VAT registered.

(3)   Read the information on the **acquisition** of a non-current asset. Make the relevant postings to the non-current assets register.

(4)   Read the information relating to the **disposal** of a non-current asset. Make the relevant postings to the non-current assets register.

(5)   Complete the **other rows** in the non-current assets register.

(6)   **Review** your answer. Does it make sense?

Activity 6: MIL Trading

This task is about recording information for non-current assets for a business known as MIL Trading. MIL Trading has a financial year end of 31 August.

The following is a purchase invoice received by MIL Trading relating to some items to be used in its office.

To: MIL Trading 18 High Road Norton NW3 9MD Item	Invoice 3920 Bordon Ltd Clapton Park BC2 9MJ	Quantity	Date: 28 May 20X7 Total £
Printer/scanner	Model BORMK95B	1	950.00
Ink and toner		2	75.00
Pre-delivery testing		1	50.00
First-year general maintenance			90.00
Total			1,165.00
Delivery date: 28/05/X7			

MIL Trading paid £1,165.00 to Borton Ltd on 30 June 20X7 with £1,165.00 borrowed interest-free from a third party. This amount is to be repaid in full on 30 May 20X9.

The following information relates to the sale of a motor vehicle no longer required by the business:

Description	1.2 litre car MN06 HNF
Date of sale	23 July 20X7
Selling price	£2,250.00

- VAT can be ignored.
- MIL Trading has a policy of capitalising expenditure over £500.
- Office equipment is depreciated at 20% per year on a straight-line basis.
- Motor vehicles are depreciated at 25% per year on a diminishing balance basis.
- A full year's depreciation is applied in the year of acquisition and none in the year of disposal.

Required

For the year ended 31 August 20X7, record the following in the extract from the non-current assets register below:

(a) Any acquisitions of non-current assets
(b) Any disposals of non-current assets
(c) Depreciation

Note. Not every cell will require an entry, and not all cells will accept entries.

Show your numerical answers to TWO decimal places. Use the DD/MM/YY format for any dates.

Picklists: (only to be used where drop down menus are provided)

Carrying amount

0.00
1,898.44
2,531.25

Depreciation charges

0.00
632.81
843.75

Description/Serial number

1.2 litre car MN06 HNF
1.6 litre van HG03 YHG
Laptop computer 081
Printer/scanner BORMK95B

Funding

Cash
Loan
Part exchange

Extract from non-current assets register

Description/ Serial number	Acquisition date	Cost £	Depreciation charges £	Carrying amount £	Funding method	Disposal proceeds £	Disposal date
Office equipment							
Laptop computer 081	30.06.X6	600.00			Cash		
Year end 31.08.X6			120.00	480.00			
Year end 31.08.X7							
▼					▼		
Year end 31.08.X7							
Motor vehicles							
1.6 litre van HG03 YHG	01.08.X5	8,940.00			Hire purchase		
Year end 31.08.X5			2,235.00	6,705.00			
Year end 31.08.X6			1,676.25	5,028.75			
Year end 31.08.X7							
1.2 litre car MN06 HNF	01.04.X5	6,000.00			Part exchange		
Year end 31.08.X5			1,500.00	4,500.00			
Year end 31.08.X6			1,125.00	3,375.00			
Year end 31.08.X7			▼	▼			

4 Knowledge test preparation

The *Advanced Bookkeeping* assessment will include questions that test your knowledge of any area of the syllabus. If the task is based on non-current assets it could be structured as follows.

Activity 7: Advanced bookkeeping – knowledge

This task is to test your knowledge.

(a) What is depreciation? Choose the ONE most suitable description.

	✓
Depreciation shows the wear and tear on an asset.	
The systematic allocation of the depreciable amount of an asset over its useful life.	
This accounting treatment helps management establish the replacement cost of the asset.	
It results in the asset being expensed to the statement of profit or loss in the period it is acquired.	

(b) Indicate whether the following statements are true or false.

	True ✓	False ✓
Directly attributable costs cannot be capitalised as part of the cost of a new non-current asset.		
The depreciable amount of an asset is its cost less residual balance.		
When a non-current asset is disposed of, if the sale proceeds exceed the carrying amount there will be a loss on disposal.		
Depreciation is an example of the accruals concept.		

5 Double entry summary for the chapter

Disposal of a non-current asset for cash (four steps):

(1) Remove the cost of the asset:

Account name	Debit £	Credit £
Disposals (SPL)	X	
Non-current asset at cost (SOFP)		X

(2) Remove the accumulated depreciation charged to date:

Account name	Debit £	Credit £
Non-current asset accumulated depreciation (SOFP)	X	
Disposals (SPL)		X

(3) Account for the sale proceeds:

Account name	Debit £	Credit £
Bank (SOFP)	X	
Disposals (SPL)		X

(4) Balance off the disposals account to determine the gain or loss on disposal.

Disposal of a non-current asset in part exchange for a new asset (five steps):

(1) Remove the cost of the asset:

Account name	Debit £	Credit £
Disposals (SPL)	X	
Non-current asset at cost (SOFP)		X

(2) Remove the accumulated depreciation charged to date:

Account name	Debit £	Credit £
Non-current asset accumulated depreciation (SOFP)	X	
Disposals (SPL)		X

(3)   Account for the part exchange allowance:

Account name	Debit £	Credit £
Non-current asset at cost **(new asset)** (SOFP)	X	
Disposals (SPL)		X

(4)   Balance off the disposals account to determine the gain or loss on disposal.

(5)   Record any additional payment made for the part exchanged asset:

Account name	Debit £	Credit £
Non-current asset at cost **(new asset)** (SOFP)	X	
Bank (SOFP)		X

- When an asset is no longer needed by a business, it will be disposed of. The carrying amount of the asset (comprising cost less accumulated depreciation) must be removed from the general ledger.

- It is likely that any proceeds received will not equal the carrying amount at the date of disposal. A gain or a loss will arise. A gain on disposal represents over-depreciation and a loss on disposal represents under-depreciation.

- In some cases a non-current asset will be disposed of by being part-exchanged in the purchase of a replacement asset – the part exchange allowance is treated as the disposal proceeds of the old asset and as part of the cost of the new asset.

- A non-current assets register lists the key details relating to an organisation's non-current assets.

- The register is mainly for internal use and does not form part of the general ledger. Instead, it is part of the business's internal control system. Reconciliations should be performed between the register and the non-current asset accounts in the general ledger.

- Likewise, on a regular basis the physical non-current assets that a business holds should be checked against the entries in the non-current assets register. Any discrepancies should be reported to an appropriate person in the organisation.

- Each accounting period, the non-current assets register must be updated to reflect:

  - Any acquisitions of non-current assets
  - Any disposals of non-current assets
  - Depreciation

Keywords

- **Disposals account:** The ledger account used to record all aspects of the disposal of the non-current asset

- **Gain or loss on disposal:** The difference between the carrying amount of the asset at the date of disposal and the disposal proceeds

- **Non-current assets register:** A register that lists all the tangible non-current assets owned by the business, and includes detailed information on the cost, acquisition date, depreciation, carrying amount and, ultimately, the disposal details of each item

- **Part exchange:** A method of disposal whereby the old asset is given in part exchange for a new asset

- **Part exchange allowance:** The value assigned to the old asset being part-exchanged by the supplier of the new asset

1 **Indicate whether the following statement is true or false.**

Statement	True ✓	False ✓
A non-current assets register is not part of the general ledger.		

2 A business purchases a computer on 1 April 20X5 for £2,200. This is then sold on 31 December 20X6 for £600. The depreciation policy is to depreciate computers on a diminishing balance basis at a rate of 40% with a full year's charge in the year of acquisition and none in the year of disposal.

The business's accounting year ends on 31 December. The business has a policy of capitalising non-current asset expenditure over £500. VAT can be ignored.

Required

Calculate the gain or loss on disposal of the machine. Place a tick in the relevant box to denote whether the amount is a gain or a loss.

	Gain	Loss
£		

Workings:

3 A business purchases a machine on 1 October 20X6 for £7,200 and this machine is then sold on 31 July 20X7 for £5,800. The machine is depreciated at a rate of 25% per annum on a straight-line basis, charged in equal instalments for each full month an asset is owned in the year.

The business's year end is 30 November. The business has a policy of capitalising non-current asset expenditure over £400. VAT can be ignored.

Required

Calculate the gain or loss on disposal of the machine. Place a tick in the relevant box to denote whether the amount is a gain or a loss.

	Gain	Loss
£		

Workings:

4 **Complete the sentences below by selecting an appropriate option.**

(a)

A loss on disposal can also be described as	▼

(b)

A gain on disposal can also be described as	▼

Picklist:

under-depreciation
over-depreciation

5 A business acquires a new motor vehicle. A part exchange allowance of £3,200 was given. £21,800 was paid from the bank for the new vehicle. VAT can be ignored.

Required

Calculate the purchase cost of the new vehicle from the information above.

£	

Accruals and prepayments

6

Learning outcomes

4.1	Record accruals and prepayments in income and expense accounts
	• That adjustments for accruals and prepayments are an application of the accrual basis of accounting
	• How opening and closing accruals and prepayments affect income and expense accounts
	• Explain the difference between the amount paid or received and the amount recognised in the accounts
	• Account for accruals and prepayments by making a double-entry in the current period and reversing it in the future period
	• Recognise the reversal of a previous period adjustment in the ledger accounts
	• Calculate adjustments pro rata
	• Enter adjustments in the general ledger, including the journal
	• Calculate the amount transferred to the statement of profit or loss
	• Use the following accounts: accruals/accrued expenses, accrued income, prepayments/prepaid expenses, prepaid income

Assessment context

Accruals and prepayments will be an important part of the *Advanced Bookkeeping* exam. There are several different styles of tasks you need to be familiar with.

You should expect to have to complete an income or expense ledger account (eg the electricity expense account) showing the reversal of the accrual or prepayment at the beginning of the year, the amount that has passed through the bank account, the accrual or prepayment at the end of the year and the income or expense that would be shown in the statement of profit or loss for the period.

You might also have to complete the accrual or prepayment statement of financial position account by showing the opening balance, reversing that opening balance then posting the closing balance.

Another task might ask you to calculate the income or expense for the year. You could also have a written task on accruals where you need to select options from a picklist to complete one or two sentences.

A separate task could ask you to produce an extract from the trial balance showing the relevant income or expense amount and also the accrual or prepayment which would be shown in the statement of financial position.

Qualification context

This area is assumed knowledge for your Level 4 paper, *Financial Statements of Limited Companies*, where you may need to take account of accruals and prepayments in calculating the final figures for income and expenses in the statement of profit or loss.

Business context

The adjustment for accruals and prepayments is an example of the accruals or matching concept. Businesses need accurate financial information in order to assess their past and current performance and make future predictions. As such, it is imperative that this information includes all income earned and expenses incurred in a particular period, even if no money has changed hands.

Chapter overview

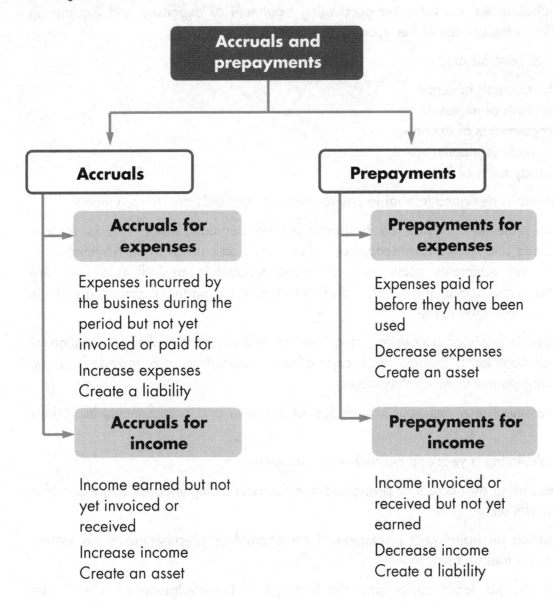

Accruals and prepayments

Accruals

Accruals for expenses

Expenses incurred by the business during the period but not yet invoiced or paid for

Increase expenses
Create a liability

Accruals for income

Income earned but not yet invoiced or received

Increase income
Create an asset

Prepayments

Prepayments for expenses

Expenses paid for before they have been used

Decrease expenses
Create an asset

Prepayments for income

Income invoiced or received but not yet earned

Decrease income
Create a liability

Introduction

In this chapter we consider the accounting treatment of expenses and income, in particular in the context of the accounting concept of accruals.

The topics covered are:

- The accruals concept
- Accruals of expenses
- Prepayments of expenses
- Accruals of income
- Prepayments of income

This chapter is designed to enable you to calculate accruals and prepayments.

Financial statements should be prepared on an accruals basis. This is so that transactions and events are recognised when they occur (even if the resulting cash receipts and payments occur in a different accounting period) and they are recorded in the accounting records and reported in the financial statements of the period to which they relate.

The accruals basis of accounting is a fundamental concept in the preparation of financial statements. Income and expenditure transactions are matched to the accounting period in which they occur.

The assessment may test your knowledge of accruals and prepayments in various ways:

(a) Calculating a year-end accrual or prepayment

(b) Recording an accrual or prepayment in the accounting records by means of a journal entry

(c) Posting an adjustment in respect of an accrual or prepayment to an extract from a trial balance

In addition, this topic could form the basis of a knowledge-based task in the assessment.

You need to understand and be able to account for:

Accrued income	Accrued expenses
Prepaid expenses	Prepaid income

1 Accrued expenses

1.1 Accruals concept

Accounts should be prepared according to the **accruals concept** which means that the income and expenses that are recognised should be those that have been **earned or incurred** in the period, not just the amounts of cash that have been received or paid.

By setting up **control accounts** for **sales and purchases on credit**, these sales and purchases are automatically recorded according to the **accruals concept** – the sale and purchase is recognised when it is made, not when the cash is received or paid.

Expenses are however treated differently – some expenses will only be **recorded** in the expense ledger account **when** they are actually **paid**.

Therefore, at the year end, the business needs to review all of its expense accounts to ensure that a **full year's expense** has been recorded and any invoices received after the year end which relate to the year which has just passed are adjusted for.

Illustration 1: Accrued expenses

Fred prepares his accounts to 31 December each year. On 1 January 20X8, he pays a telephone bill of £60 which relates to the period October–December 20X7.

Although the payment does not go through the cash book until 20X8, this expense must be included in the accounts for the year ended 31 December 20X7, as it was **incurred** during this period.

1.2 Accounting entry for accrued expenses

Key term

Accrued expenses are expenses incurred by the business during the accounting period but not yet invoiced or paid for, ie expenses in **arrears**.

Adjustments for **accruals** and **prepayments** tend to occur at the end of the year and are made by way of a **journal** entry.

Accrued expenses have a dual effect that needs to be accounted for by:

(a) **Increasing** the relevant **expense** account in the statement of profit or loss

(b) Recording a **current liability** called **'accrued expenses'** in the statement of financial position for amounts owing at the year end

Formula to learn

The journal to post accrued expenses in the general ledger is:

Account name	Debit £	Credit £
Expense account (SPL)	X	
Accrued expenses (SOFP)		X

Whenever a journal adjustment is made, a business should provide a **narrative** so that anyone reviewing the adjustment can see why the journal was made. A suitable narrative for the above journal entry is:

'Being: an adjustment to accrue the xx expense for the year ended xx.'

In the assessment some tasks will require a narrative explanation of the journal. In the exam, narrative is usually entered by selecting the correct option from a picklist.

1.3 Statement of financial position presentation

Accruals or accrued expenses are a liability of the business and are shown in the statement of financial position within the **current liabilities** section.

1.4 Approach to tasks

Read the requirement to the task carefully to identify what you are being asked to do.

Calculate the expense for the year

(1) Review all the invoices listed in the question and identify which invoices relate to the current year.

(2) If the invoice relates to the current year, include the full amount of the invoice in expenses.

(3) If an invoice has been received after the year end, check whether some or all of it relates to the current year and add any portion relating to the current year to expenses (pro-rate where necessary).

Calculate the accrued expense at the end of the year

(1) Review the task for any invoices received after the year end.

(2) Check whether some or all of that invoice relates to the current year; if so, calculate the portion of the invoice that relates to the current year – this is the accrued expense.

Record the accounting entries

(1) Record invoices paid in the year by:

DEBIT   Expenses (SPL)
CREDIT   Bank (SOFP)

(2) Record accrued expenses by:

DEBIT   Expenses (SPL)

CREDIT   Accrued expenses (SOFP)

(3) Balance off the Bank and Accrued expenses accounts by showing the balance c/d (and b/d if required) and balance off the expense account by showing the transfer to profit or loss.

Activity 1: Accrued expenses

Fiona set up a business on 1 January 20X7. Her cash payments in the year to 31 December 20X7 included:

	Date paid	Amount £	Period
Electricity			
	10.03.X7	96	Two months to 28 February 20X7
	12.06.X7	120	Quarter to 31 May 20X7
	14.09.X7	104	Quarter to 31 August 20X7
	10.12.X7	145	Quarter to 30 November 20X7

On 6 March 20X8 Fiona received an electricity bill for £168 for the quarter to 28 February 20X8.

Required

(a) Calculate the electricity expense for the year ended 31/12/X7.

£	

Workings:

(b) Calculate the accrued expense at the end of the year.

£	

(c) **Show how the above transactions would be recorded in the ledger accounts. For the electricity expense and accrued expenses accounts, show clearly the balance to be carried down or transferred to the statement of profit or loss, as appropriate.**

Electricity expense (SPL)

	£			£
▼			▼	
▼			▼	
▼			▼	
▼			▼	
▼			▼	

Bank (SOFP)

	£			£
▼			▼	
▼			▼	
▼			▼	
▼			▼	

Accrued expenses (SOFP)

	£			£
▼			▼	

Picklist:

Accrued expenses
Balance c/d
Bank
Electricity expense
Prepaid expenses
Profit or loss account
Statement of financial position

Activity 2: Accrued expenses – journal

Refer back to your solution to Activity 1.

Required

Enter the journal entry required for the year-end accrual. Include a narrative.

Account name		Debit £	Credit £
	▼		
	▼		
Being:			▼

Picklist for account name:

Accrued expenses
Electricity expense
Prepaid expenses

Picklist for narrative:

an adjustment to accrue the electricity expense for the year ended 31 December 20X7

an adjustment to record the electricity prepayment for the year ended 31 December 20X7

2 Reversal of accrued expenses

2.1 Reason for reversal of accrued expenses

At the beginning of the following period, there will be a balance b/d in the accrued expenses (SOFP) account. This will be a credit balance as the accrued expenses account is a liability account. The related invoice will be paid during this next accounting period and therefore recorded in expenses:

DEBIT   Expense

CREDIT   Bank

However, the expense relates to the prior year. Therefore, this expense needs to be removed by reversing the balance b/d on the accrued expenses (SOFP) account:

DEBIT   Accrued expenses (SOFP)

CREDIT   Expenses (SPL)

This is best explained by returning to Illustration 1:

Illustration 1: Accrued expenses

Fred prepares his accounts to 31 December each year. On 1 January 20X8, he pays a telephone bill of £60 which relates to the period October–December 20X7.

Although the payment does not go through the cash book until 20X8, this expense must be included in the accounts for the year ended 31 December 20X7, as it was **incurred** during this period. The accounting entry in 20X7 to record this expense is:

DEBIT   Telephone expenses (SPL)   £60

CREDIT   Accrued expenses (SOFP)   £60

Illustration 1: Accrued expenses continued

In the year ended 31 December 20X8, there will be a balance b/d on 1 January 20X8 in the accrued expenses (SOFP) account of £60. This is a credit balance as the accrued expenses account is a liability account. As this amount is paid on 1 January 20X8, it will be recorded in the cash book in the year ended 31 December 20X8 and therefore in the telephone expenses account for the year ended 31 December 20X8. However, it relates to the prior year (October–December 20X7) so needs to be removed from expenses by reversing the b/d accrued expenses balance:

DEBIT   Accrued expenses (SOFP)   £60

CREDIT   Telephone expenses (SPL)   £60

2.2 Accounting entry for reversal of accrued expenses

The balance b/d on the accrued expenses account is reversed at the start of the year by way of a **journal** entry.

Formula to learn

The journal to reverse the accrued expenses in the general ledger is:

Account name	Debit £	Credit £
Accrued expenses (SOFP)	X	
Expense account (SPL)		X

A suitable narrative for the above journal entry is:

'Being: an adjustment to reverse the prior period accrued expenses.'

This journal will always be dated as at the first day of the accounting period.

2.3 Approach to tasks with reversals of accrued expenses

If you are required to update the expense and accrued expenses ledger accounts:

(1) Read through the task to identify whether there is an accrued expense balance brought down from the previous year.

(2) Reverse any balance b/d on the accrued expense account:

DEBIT   Accrued expenses (SOFP)

CREDIT   Expenses (SPL)

(3) Record all invoices paid in the current year:

DEBIT   Expenses (SPL)

CREDIT   Bank (SOFP)

(4) Scan the task for any invoices received after the year end which relate to the current year – if only part of the invoice relates to the current year, pro-rate the amount to calculate the year-end accrued expense.

(5) Record the year-end accrued expense by:

DEBIT   Expenses (SPL)

CREDIT   Accrued expenses (SOFP)

(6) Balance off the expenses account by transferring the balancing figure to profit or loss and balance off the accrued expenses account by carrying the balance down.

Activity 3: Reversal of accrued expenses

Following on from Activity 1, in the year ended 31 December 20X8 Fiona paid the following electricity bills:

Date paid	Amount £	Period
12.03.X8	168	Quarter to 28 February 20X8
09.06.X8	134	Quarter to 31 May 20X8
12.09.X8	118	Quarter to 31 August 20X8
12.12.X8	158	Quarter to 30 November 20X8

During March 20X9 Fiona received an electricity bill for £189 for the quarter to 28 February 20X9.

Required

Prepare the electricity expense and accrued expenses accounts for the year ended 31 December 20X8. Show clearly:

- **The reversal of the opening accrual**

- **The cash book figures**

- **The year-end closing accrual**

- **The balance to be carried down or transferred to the statement of profit or loss, as appropriate**

Electricity expense (SPL)

	£		£
▼		▼	
▼		▼	
▼		▼	
▼		▼	
▼		▼	

Accrued expenses (SOFP)

	£		£
▼		Balance b/d	56
▼		▼	

Picklist:

Accrued expenses
Accrued expenses (reversal)
Balance c/d
Bank
Electricity expense
Prepaid expenses
Prepaid expenses (reversal)
Profit or loss account
Statement of financial position

3 Prepaid expenses

Key term

> **Prepaid expenses** arise when expenses are paid for but relate to the following accounting period, ie expenses in **advance**.

> **Illustration 2: Prepaid expenses**
>
> Fred prepares his accounts to 31 December each year. On 20 December 20X7 Fred pays £1,000 for insurance on his business premises for the 12 months commencing 1 January 20X8.
>
> Although the payment was made in 20X7, the expense should not appear in the accounts for 20X7. The accounts for 20X7 will show a prepayment for the full amount of the insurance cost (as it all relates to 20X8). The amount will also be removed from the 20X7 expenses and recorded as an expense in 20X8.

The invoice has been recorded in the current year:

DEBIT Expenses

CREDIT Bank

However, it relates to the following accounting period so must be removed from expenses.

3.1 Accounting entry for prepaid expenses

As for accrued expenses, the adjustment for prepaid expenses occurs at the end of the year and is made by way of a **journal** entry.

Prepaid expenses have a dual effect that needs to be accounted for by:

(a) **Decreasing** the relevant **expense** account in the statement of profit or loss

(b) Recording a **current asset** called **'prepaid expenses'** in the statement of financial position as effectively the next accounting period owes the prepaid amount back to the current accounting period

As for accruals, the adjustments for prepayments tend to occur at the end of the year and are made by way of a **journal** entry.

Formula to learn

The journal to post prepaid expenses in the general ledger is:

Account name	Debit £	Credit £
Prepaid expenses (SOFP)	X	
Expense account (SPL)		X

A suitable narrative for the above journal entry is:

'Being: an adjustment to record the xx prepayment for the year ended xx.'

3.2 Statement of financial position presentation

Prepayments or prepaid expenses are an asset of the business and are shown in the statement of financial position within the **current assets** section.

3.3 Approach to tasks

Read the requirement to the task carefully to identify what you are being asked to do.

Calculate the expense for the year:

(1) Add together all of the invoices paid in the year.

(2) Review each invoice paid in the year to determine if some or all of an invoice relates to the next year.

(3) If some or all of an invoice relates to the next year, remove the amount that relates to the next year from expenses.

Calculate the prepaid expense at the end of the year:

(1) Review the task for any invoices paid in the current year which relate to the next year.

(2) Calculate (where necessary) the portion of that invoice which relates to the next year – this is the prepaid expense.

Record the accounting entries:

(1) Record invoices paid in the year by:

DEBIT   Expenses (SPL)

CREDIT   Bank (SOFP)

(2) Record prepaid expenses by:

DEBIT   Prepaid expenses (SOFP)

CREDIT   Expenses (SPL)

(3) Balance off the Bank and Prepaid expenses accounts by showing the balance c/d (and b/d if required) and balance off the expense account by showing the transfer to profit or loss.

Activity 4: Prepaid expenses

Following on from Activity 1, Fiona also made the following rent payments in the year to 31 December 20X7:

	Date paid	Amount £	Period
Rent			
	01.02.X7	375	3 months to 31 March 20X7
	06.04.X7	1,584	12 months to 31 March 20X8

Required

(a) **Calculate the expense incurred by Fiona for rent for the year ended 31 December 20X7.**

£ [   ]

Workings:

(b) **Calculate the prepaid expense at the end of the year.**

£ [   ]

(c) **Show how the above transactions would be recorded in the ledger accounts. For the rent expense and prepaid expenses accounts, show clearly the balance to be carried down or transferred to profit or loss, as appropriate.**

Rent expense (SPL)

	£		£
▼		▼	
▼		▼	

Bank (SOFP)

	£		£
▼		▼	
▼		▼	

Prepaid expenses (SOFP)

	£		£
▼		▼	

Picklist:

Accrued expenses
Accrued expenses (reversal)
Balance c/d
Bank
Electricity expense
Prepaid expenses
Prepaid expenses (reversal)
Profit or loss account
Rent expense
Statement of financial position

Activity 5: Prepaid expenses – journal

Referring back to Activity 4, record the journal entry required for the year-end prepayment. Include a narrative.

Account name	Debit £	Credit £
▼		
▼		
Being:		▼

Picklist for account name:

Accrued expenses
Prepaid expenses
Rent expense

Picklist for narrative:

an adjustment to accrue the rent expense for the year ended 31 December 20X7
an adjustment to record the rent prepayment for the year ended 31 December 20X7

4 Reversal of prepaid expenses

4.1 Reason for reversal of prepaid expenses

At the beginning of the following period, there will be a balance b/d in the prepaid expenses (SOFP) account. This is a debit balance as the prepaid expenses account is an asset account. The balance b/d relates to an invoice which was paid in the prior year but relates to the current year. As the invoice was paid in the prior year, it will not appear in the cash book in the current year, nor the related expense account. Therefore, the way to show the amount in the current year's expense account is to reverse the balance b/d in the prepaid expenses (SOFP) account:

DEBIT   Expense (SPL)

CREDIT   Prepaid expenses (SOFP)

This is best explained by returning to Illustration 2:

Illustration 2: Prepaid expenses

Fred prepares his accounts to 31 December each year. On 20 December 20X7 Fred pays £1,000 for insurance on his business premises for the 12 months commencing 1 January 20X8.

Although the payment was made in 20X7, the expense should not appear in the accounts for 20X7. The accounts for 20X7 will show a prepayment for the full amount of the insurance cost (as it all relates to 20X8). The amount will also be removed from the 20X7 expenses and recorded as an expense in 20X8. The prepayment is recorded in 20X7 with the following accounting entry:

DEBIT   Prepaid expenses (SOFP)   £1,000

CREDIT   Insurance expenses (SPL)   £1,000

Illustration 2: Prepaid expenses continued

In the year ended 31 December 20X8, there will be a debit balance b/d of £1,000 in the prepaid expenses (SOFP) account. This amount was paid in the prior year so will not appear in the current year's cash book or expenses. However, the expense relates to the current year. The only way to show the expense in the current year is to reverse the balance b/d in the prepaid expenses (SOFP) account:

DEBIT   Insurance expense (SPL)   £1,000

CREDIT   Prepaid expenses (SOFP)   £1,000

4.2 Accounting entry for reversal of prepaid expenses

The balance b/d on the prepaid expenses account is reversed at the start of the year by way of a **journal** entry.

Formula to learn

The journal to reverse prepaid expenses in the general ledger is:

Account name	Debit £	Credit £
Expense account (SPL)	X	
Prepaid expenses (SOFP)		X

A suitable narrative for the above journal entry is:

'Being: an adjustment to reverse the prior period prepaid expenses.'

This journal will always be dated as at the first day of the accounting period.

4.3 Approach to tasks with reversals of prepaid expenses

If you are required to update the expense and prepaid expenses ledger accounts:

(1) Read through the task to identify whether there is a prepaid expense balance brought down from the previous year.

(2) Reverse any balance b/d on the prepaid expenses account:

DEBIT   Expenses (SPL)

CREDIT   Prepaid expenses (SOFP)

(3) Record all invoices paid in the current year:

DEBIT   Expenses (SPL)

CREDIT   Bank (SOFP)

(4) Review the invoices paid in the current year to see if any relate to next year (if only part of the invoice relates to next year, pro-rate accordingly).

(5) Record the year-end prepaid expense by:

DEBIT   Prepaid expenses (SOFP)

CREDIT   Expenses (SPL)

(6) Balance off the expenses account by transferring the balancing figure to profit or loss and balance off the prepaid expenses account by carrying the balance down.

Activity 6: Reversal of prepaid expenses

Following on from Activity 4, Fiona made the following rent payment in the year to 31 December 20X8:

	Date paid	Amount £	Period
Rent			
	05.04.X8	1,680	12 months to 31 March 20X9

Required

Prepare the rent expense and prepaid expenses accounts for the year ended 31 December 20X8. Show clearly:

- **The reversal of the opening prepayment**
- **The cash book figures**
- **The year-end closing prepayment**
- **The balance to be carried down or transferred to the statement of profit or loss, as appropriate**

Rent expense (SPL)

	£			£
▼		▼		
▼		▼		

Prepaid expenses (SOFP)

	£			£
Balance b/d	396		▼	
▼			▼	

Picklist:

Accrued expenses
Accrued expenses (reversal)
Balance c/d
Bank
Electricity expense
Prepaid expenses
Prepaid expenses (reversal)
Profit or loss account
Rent expense
Statement of financial position

5 Accrued income

So far we have considered the situation where we are making accruals and prepayments for **expenses** (when they are paid in arrears or advance).

Income may also be received in arrears or advance and so the same principles apply.

Remember, though, that here we are considering income rather than expense. Income and expenses are opposite items and so the entries for accruals and prepayments for income will also be the other way round.

Key term

> **Accrued income** is income which **has been earned** during the accounting period **but not invoiced or received**, ie income in arrears.

> **Illustration 3: Accrued income**
>
> Fred owns a property which he rents out for £3,000 per quarter. The property was occupied all year; however, Fred only received £9,000 in rent because he forgot to send out the final invoice of the year.
>
> As the property was let for 12 months, Fred's statement of profit or loss should show income of £12,000 (4 × £3,000) as this is what he has **earned**. This means there will be accrued income of £3,000 in the statement of financial position at the year end.

5.1 Accounting entry for accrued income

Accrued income has a dual effect that needs to be accounted for by:

(a) **Increasing** the relevant **income** account in the statement of profit or loss as the income has been earned in the year but not yet recorded

(b) Recording a **current asset** called **'accrued income'** in the statement of financial position as the income is owed to the business

As for accrued and prepaid expenses, the adjustments for accrued income tend to be carried out at the end of the year and are made by way of a **journal** entry.

> **Formula to learn**
>
> | Account name | Debit £ | Credit £ |
> |---|---|---|
> | Accrued income (SOFP) | X | |
> | Income account (SPL) | | X |

A suitable narrative for the above journal entry is:

'Being: an adjustment to record the xx accrued income for the year ended xx.'

5.2 Statement of financial position presentation

Accrued income is an asset of the business and is shown in the statement of financial position within the **current assets** section.

5.3 Approach to tasks

Read the requirement to the task carefully to identify what you are being asked to do.

Calculate the income for the year:

(1) Review all the invoices or cash receipts listed in the question and identify which amounts relate to the current year.

(2) If the invoice/cash receipt relates to the current year, include the full amount in income.

(3) If the invoice has been raised or the cash has been received after the year end, check whether some or all of it relates to the current year and add that amount to income (pro-rate where necessary).

Calculate the accrued income at the end of the year:

(1) Review the task for any invoices raised/cash received after the year end.

(2) Check whether some or all of that invoice/cash relates to the current year; if so, calculate the portion of the invoice/cash that relates to the current year – this is the accrued income.

Record the accounting entries:

(1) Record cash received in the year by:

DEBIT   Bank (SOFP)

CREDIT   Income (SPL)

(2) Record accrued income by:

DEBIT   Accrued income (SOFP)

CREDIT   Income (SPL)

(3) Balance off the Bank and Accrued income accounts by showing the balance c/d (and b/d if required) and balance off the income account by showing the transfer to profit or loss.

Activity 7: Accrued income

A business has a year end of 31 December 20X1.

A client has paid commission income of £17,000. A further £4,000 is also due; however, a bill has not yet been sent out for this amount nor recorded in the accounting records.

Required

(a)   Calculate the income in respect of commission for the year ended 31 December 20X1.

£ [   ]

(b)   State the amount of accrued income due at the end of the year.

£ [   ]

Activity 8: Accrued income – journal

Following on from Activity 7:

Required

Show the journal entry required to record the year-end accrued income in the general ledger. Include a narrative.

Account name	Debit £	Credit £
▼		
▼		
Being:		▼

Picklist for account name:

Accrued expenses
Accrued income
Commission income
Prepaid expenses
Prepaid income

Picklist for narrative:

an adjustment to accrue the commission income for the year ended December 20X1

an adjustment to record the prepaid commission income for the year ended December 20X1

6 Reversal of accrued income

6.1 Reason for reversal of accrued income

As with accrued and prepaid expenses, the balance b/d on the accrued income (SOFP) account must be reversed at the start of the following year.

This is because this income will be invoiced and received in this following year and recorded in the income account in this following year. However, as it relates to income earned in the prior year, it must be removed from income. This is achieved by reversing the balance b/d on the accrued income account.

6.2 Accounting entry for reversal of accrued income

The journal which would be posted in the general ledger is:

Formula to learn		
Account name	**Debit £**	**Credit £**
Income account (SPL)	X	
Accrued income (SOFP)		X

A suitable narrative for the above journal entry is:

'Being: an adjustment to reverse the prior period accrued income.'

This journal should always be dated as at first day of the accounting period.

6.3 Approach to tasks with reversals of accrued income

If you are required to update the income and accrued income ledger accounts:

(1) Read through the task to identify whether there is an accrued income balance brought down from the previous year.

(2) Reverse any balance b/d on the accrued income account:

DEBIT   Income (SPL)

CREDIT   Accrued income (SOFP)

(3) Record all receipts in the current year:

DEBIT   Bank (SOFP)

CREDIT   Income (SPL)

(4) Review the cash received and invoices raised after the year end to see if any amounts relate to the current year (pro-rate where necessary).

(5) Record the year-end accrued income by:

DEBIT   Accrued income (SOFP)

CREDIT   Income (SPL)

(6) Balance off the income account by transferring the balancing figure to profit or loss and balance off the accrued income account by carrying the balance down.

Activity 9: Reversal of accrued income

Following on from Activity 7, in the year ended 31 December 20X2, the business received commission income from the client of £23,000. This amount includes the £4,000 owing from the year ended 31 December 20X1.

On 10 February 20X3, the business receives £7,200 commission from the client for the three months ended 31 January 20X3.

Required

Prepare the commission income and accrued income accounts for the year ended 31 December 20X2 (you do not need to include dates). Show clearly:

- **The reversal of the opening accrued income**
- **The cash book figure**
- **The year-end closing accrued income**
- **The balance to be carried down or transferred to the statement of profit or loss, as appropriate**

Commission income (SPL)

	£		£
▼		▼	
▼		▼	

Accrued income (SOFP)

	£		£
Balance b/d	4,000	▼	
▼		▼	

Picklist:

Accrued income
Accrued income (reversal)
Balance c/d
Bank
Commission income
Prepaid income
Prepaid income (reversal)
Profit or loss account
Statement of financial position

7 Prepaid income

Key term

> **Prepaid income** is income that has been **received** but **relates to the following accounting period**, ie income in advance.

You may also hear this referred to as deferred income.

> **Illustration 4: Prepaid income**
>
> Fred has a year end of December and rents out his property for £1,000 per month. His tenant normally pays the rent due to Fred on a monthly basis.
>
> However, during December 20X7 the tenant paid £2,000 as he would be on holiday when the January 20X8 payment was due.
>
> In 20X7 Fred has received income of £13,000 but only £12,000 of this relates to the current year. Therefore, there is £1,000 prepaid income as at 31 December 20X7.

7.1 Accounting entry for prepaid income

As the income has been received in the current year but it relates to next year, it needs to be removed from income.

Prepaid income has a dual effect that needs to be accounted for by:

(a) **Decreasing** the relevant **income** account in the statement of profit or loss as the cash has been received in the current year but the income relates to next year

(b) Recording a **current liability** called **'prepaid income'** in the statement of financial position as the business has not earned the income yet so owes it back again

The adjustments for prepaid income tend to occur at the end of the year and are made by way of a **journal** entry.

The journal which would be posted in the general ledger is:

 Formula to learn

Account name	Debit £	Credit £
Income account (SPL)	X	
Prepaid income (SOFP)		X

A suitable narrative for the above journal entry is:

'Being: an adjustment to record the xx prepaid income for the year ended xx.'

7.2 Statement of financial position presentation

Prepaid income is a liability of the business and shown in the statement of financial position within the **'current liabilities'** section.

7.3 Approach to tasks

Read the requirement to the task carefully to identify what you are being asked to do.

Calculate income for the year:

(1) Review all the cash receipts listed in the question and identify which relate to the current year.

(2) If all of the cash receipt relates to the current year, include the full amount in income.

(3) If some or all of the cash receipt relates to the next year, only add to income the portion relating to the current year (pro-rate where necessary).

Calculate prepaid income at the end of the year:

(1) Review the task for any cash receipts in the current year which relate to the next year.

(2) Calculate (where necessary) the portion of that cash receipt which relates to the next year – this is the prepaid income.

Record the accounting entries:

(1) Record cash receipts in the year by:

DEBIT   Bank (SOFP)

CREDIT   Income (SPL)

(2) Record prepaid income by:

DEBIT   Income (SPL)

CREDIT   Prepaid income (SOFP)

(3)   Balance off the prepaid income account by showing the balance c/d (and b/d if required) and balance off the income account by showing the transfer to profit or loss.

Activity 10: Prepaid income

A business has a year end of 31 March 20X3. It earns income from providing maintenance services.

The cash book for the year shows receipts for maintenance services income of £52,965. This includes the following receipts:

Maintenance for the period:	£
1 January 20X3–31 December 20X3	1,032
1 April 20X3–31 March 20X4	810

Required

(a)   Calculate the maintenance services income for the year ended 31 March 20X3.

£ [   ]

(b)   Calculate the amount of prepaid income at 31 March 20X3.

£ [   ]

Workings:

Activity 11: Prepaid income – journal

Following on from Activity 10:

Required

Show the journal entry required to record the year-end prepaid income in the general ledger. Include a narrative.

Account name		Debit £	Credit £
▼			
▼			
Being:			▼

Picklist for account name:

Accrued expenses
Accrued income
Maintenance services expense
Maintenance services income
Prepaid expenses
Prepaid income

Picklist for narrative:

an adjustment to accrue the maintenance services income as at 31 March 20X3

an adjustment to record the prepaid maintenance services income as at 31 March 20X3

8 Reversal of prepaid income

8.1 Reason for reversal of prepaid income

As with accrued and prepaid expenses, the balance b/d on the prepaid income (SOFP) account must be reversed at the start of the following year. The balance b/d is a credit balance because it is a liability account. Cash has been received for income that has not yet been earned so this cash is owed back again. However, in the following period, this income is now earned and therefore the balance b/d in the prepaid income account must be reversed and recorded as income.

8.2 Accounting entry for reversal of prepaid income

The journal which would be posted in the general ledger is:

Formula to learn

Account name	Debit £	Credit £
Prepaid income (SOFP)	X	
Income account (SPL)		X

A suitable narrative for the above journal entry is:

'Being: an adjustment to reverse the prior period prepaid income.'

This journal should always be dated as at the first day of the current accounting period.

8.3 Approach to tasks with reversals of prepaid income

If you are required to update the income and prepaid income ledger accounts:

(1) Read through the task to identify whether there is a prepaid income balance brought down from the previous year

(2) Reverse any balance b/d on the prepaid income account:

DEBIT   Prepaid income (SOFP)
CREDIT   Income (SPL)

(3) Record all receipts in the current year:

DEBIT   Bank (SOFP)
CREDIT   Income (SPL)

(4) Review the cash receipts in the current year to see if any relate to next year (pro-rate where necessary)

(5) Record the year end prepaid income by:

DEBIT   Income (SPL)
CREDIT   Prepaid income (SOFP)

(6) Balance off the income account by transferring the balancing figure to profit or loss and balance off the prepaid income account by carrying the balance down

Activity 12: Reversal of prepaid income

You are working on the accounting records of a business for the year ended 30 June 20X5.

You are looking at licence fee income. Licence fee income of £3,470 was prepaid on 30 June 20X4.

Required

Complete the following statements:

The reversal of this prepaid income is dated [▼]

The reversal is on the [▼] side of the licence fee income account.

Picklist:

1 July 20X4
1 July 20X5
30 June 20X4
credit
debit

9 Preparing an extract from the trial balance

In the Level 2 accounting courses we prepared a trial balance. The trial balance is also tested in *Advanced Bookkeeping* and this topic is explained in detail in Chapter 11 *The trial balance, errors and the suspense account.*

Assessment tasks may ask you to prepare a trial balance, taking into account accrued expenses and income or prepaid expenses and income.

Therefore, it is useful to complete relevant extracts from the trial balance in this chapter.

Activity 13: Extract from a trial balance – accrued income and expenses

This task is about preparing an extract from a trial balance.

Required

Enter the figures given in the table into the appropriate trial balance columns.

Do NOT enter zeros into unused column cells. Do NOT enter any figures as negatives.

Extract from the trial balance as at 31 July 20X9:

Account	Ledger balances £	Trial balance Dr £	Trial balance Cr £
Accrued expenses	110		
Accrued income	489		
Office costs	2,637		
Discounts received	1,535		

Activity 14: Extract from a trial balance – prepaid income and expenses

This task is about preparing an extract from a trial balance.

Required

Enter the figures given in the table into the appropriate trial balance columns.

Do NOT enter zeros into unused column cells. Do NOT enter any figures as negatives.

Extract from the trial balance as at 31 July 20X9:

Account	Ledger balances £	Trial balance Dr £	Cr £
General expenses	8,626		
Prepaid expenses	2,017		
Prepaid income	1,111		
Sundry income	36,535		

9.1 Further preparation for the CBT

Having looked at accruals and prepayments in some detail, it is important to work through assessment standard questions.

Activity 15: Accounting for accrued and prepaid income and expenses

This task is about ledger accounting, including accruals and prepayments, and applying ethical principles.

Required

(a) **Enter the figures given in the table below into the appropriate trial balance columns.**

Do not enter zeros into unused column cells. Do not enter any figures as negatives.

Extract from the trial balance as at 31 March 20X2:

Account	Ledger balances £	Trial balance Dr £	Cr £
Accrued income	2,925		
Commission income	6,720		
Discounts allowed	4,260		
Prepaid expenses	2,550		

You are working on the accounting records of a business for the year ended 31 March 20X2.

In this task, you can ignore VAT.

You are looking at the advertising expenses for the year.

- The cash book for the year shows payments for advertising expenses of £9,110.

- This includes £660 relating to the period 01/03/X2 to 31/08/X2.

Required

(b) **Calculate the value of the adjustment required for advertising expenses as at 31 March 20X2 (show an increase as a positive number and a decrease as a negative number).**

£	

Update the advertising expenses account. Show clearly:

- **The cash book figure**
- **The year-end adjustment**
- **The transfer to the statement of profit or loss for the year**

Advertising expenses

	£			£
Prepaid expenses (reversal)	320		▼	
		▼		▼	

Picklist:

Accrued expenses
Accrued income
Advertising expenses
Balance b/d
Balance c/d
Bank
Prepaid expenses
Prepaid income
Profit or loss account
Purchases
Purchases ledger control account
Rental income
Sales
Sales ledger control account

You are now looking at rental income for the year.

Rental income of £5,880 was accrued on 31 March 20X1.

Required

(c)   Complete the following statements:

The reversal of this accrual is dated [▼]

The reversal is on the [▼] side of the rental income account.

Picklist:

1 April 20X1
1 April 20X2
31 March 20X1
debit
credit

The cash book for the year shows receipts for rental income of £73,865.

Rental income of £3,590 for the month ended 31 March 20X2 was received into the bank on 10 April 20X3.

Required

(d)   Taking into account all the information you have, calculate the rental income for the year ended 31 March 20X2.

£ [   ]

Your junior colleague asks why you are considering the receipt dated 10 April when the financial year ended on 31 March.

Required

(e)   Which of the following can use to explain this?
You must choose ONE answer for each row.

Reason for considering the receipt dated 10 April	Acceptable reason ✓	Not acceptable reason ✓
The proprietor wishes to sell the business and has asked you to maximise profit to obtain the best price		
The transaction is income relevant to the year ended 31 March 20X2		
The figure is a current liability at 31 March 20X2		

10 Knowledge test preparation

The *Advanced Bookkeeping* assessment will include short-form, objective-style requirements on any area of the syllabus. If the requirements are based on accruals and prepayments, they could be structured as follows.

Activity 16: Advanced bookkeeping – knowledge

This task is to test your knowledge.

A business has a year end of 31 December 20X8. On 25 December the accountant pays rent for the quarter ended 31 March 20X9.

Required

(a) **Identify how it will be shown in the statement of financial position. Choose the ONE most suitable option.**

	✓
Accrued expenses (current liability)	
Accrued income (current asset)	
Prepaid expenses (current asset)	
Prepaid income (current liability)	

(b) **Indicate whether the following statements are true or false.**

	True ✓	False ✓
Application of the accruals concept means accounting on a cash basis.		
Prepaid income is accounted for on the debit side of the trial balance.		
A customer owed £400 rent at the year end. This will be adjusted as a credit to the statement of profit or loss and a debit to the accrued income account, in the SOFP.		

11 Double entry summary for the chapter

Accrued expenses adjustment:

Account name	Debit £	Credit £
Expense account (SPL)	X	
Accrued expenses (SOFP)		X

Reversal of accrued expenses:

Account name	Debit £	Credit £
Accrued expenses (SOFP)	X	
Expense account (SPL)		X

Prepaid expenses adjustment:

Account name	Debit £	Credit £
Prepaid expenses (SOFP)	X	
Expense account (SPL)		X

Reversal of prepaid expenses:

Account name	Debit £	Credit £
Expense account (SPL)	X	
Prepaid expenses (SOFP)		X

Accrued income adjustment:

Account name	Debit £	Credit £
Accrued income (SOFP)	X	
Income account (SPL)		X

Reversal of accrued income:

Account name	Debit £	Credit £
Income account (SPL)	X	
Accrued income (SOFP)		X

Prepaid income adjustment:

Account name	Debit £	Credit £
Income account (SPL)	X	
Prepaid income (SOFP)		X

Reversal of prepaid income:

Account name	Debit £	Credit £
Prepaid income (SOFP)	X	
Income account (SPL)		X

11.1 Summary of statement of financial position presentation

If you are asked to include accruals and prepayments in a trial balance, remember this:

Current assets	Current liabilities
Accrued income	Accrued expenses
Prepaid expenses	Prepaid income

Assessment focus point

Accruals and prepayments are an important area of the syllabus. You could be tested on preparing ledger accounts, calculating the accrual or prepayment, or determining the amount to be shown in the statement of profit or loss.

Chapter summary

- Accounts should be prepared according to the **accruals concept** which means that the **income and expenses** that are recognised should be those that have been **earned or incurred** in the period, not just the amounts of cash that have been received or paid.

- By setting up **control accounts** for **sales and purchases on credit**, these sales and purchases are automatically **recorded** according to the **accruals concept** – the sale and purchase is recognised when it is made, not when the cash is received or paid.

- Expenses are however treated differently – some **expenses** will only be **recorded** in the expense ledger account **when** they are actually **paid**; therefore, at the **end of each accounting year** each **expense account must be reviewed** carefully to ensure that the balance represents the **full amount of that expense** that has been incurred in the period.

- **Accrued expenses** are expenses that have been **incurred** but **not yet been invoiced for or paid** and are therefore not yet recorded in the expense ledger account – the accrued expenses must be **added to the expense** ledger account balance and shown in the statement of financial position as a **current liability**, called 'accrued expenses'.

- **Prepaid expenses** are the opposite of accrued expenses – they are expenses that have been **paid** and therefore appear in the ledger account but **relate to the following accounting period**. They must be **removed from the expense** ledger account balance and shown in the statement of financial position as a **current asset**, called 'prepaid expenses'.

- Many businesses will have sources of miscellaneous income – these can also be either accrued or prepaid.

- **Accrued income** is an amount that is **due** for the period but has **not been received** – this must be **added to the income** account balance and included in the statement of financial position as a form of **current asset**, called 'accrued income'.

- **Prepaid income** is where income has been **received** but it actually **relates to the following accounting period** – this must be **deducted from the income** account balance and shown in the statement of financial position as a **liability**, called 'prepaid income'.

- At the **beginning of the following accounting period**, the **balance b/d** on the accrued expenses, prepaid expenses, accrued income and prepaid income accounts must be **reversed** through the corresponding expense or income account.

- **Accrual:** Expense or income that has been incurred or earned during the period but that has not yet been invoiced or paid/received

- **Accruals concept:** Fundamental accounting concept that states that income and expenses shown in the statement of profit or loss should be those that were earned or incurred during the period rather than simply the cash received or paid

- **Accrued expenses:** Expenses that have been incurred during the period but that have not yet been invoiced or paid, ie expenses in arrears

- **Accrued income:** Income that has been earned but that has not yet been invoiced or received, ie income in arrears

- **Prepaid expenses:** Expenses that have been paid for but relate to the following accounting period, ie expenses in advance

- **Prepaid income:** Income that has been received but relates to the following accounting period, ie income in advance

- **Prepayment:** Expense that has been paid for or income that has been received but that relates to the following accounting period

Test your learning

1 **(a)** Rent paid in advance for the following accounting period would appear as

[▼] in the statement of financial position.

(b) Motor expenses owing to the local garage at the year end would appear as

[▼] in the statement of financial position.

Picklist:

accrued expenses
accrued income
prepaid expenses
prepaid income

2 **State what effect each of the following would have in the statement of profit or loss and the statement of financial position of a business with an accounting year end of 31 March 20X5:**

(a) The balance on the heat and light expense account of £670 does not include the latest bill which shows £200 of heat and light expenses for January 20X5 to March 20X5

In the statement of profit or loss the heat and light expense would be:

£ [   ]

In the statement of financial position there would be [▼] of:

£ [   ]

Picklist:

accrued expenses
accrued income
prepaid expenses
prepaid income

(b) The rental income account balance of £380 includes £40 of rent received for April 20X5.

In the statement of profit or loss the rental income would be:

£ [340]

In the statement of financial position there would be [prepaid income ▼] of:

£ [40]

Picklist:
accrued expenses
accrued income
prepaid expenses
prepaid income

(c) The insurance account balance of £1,400 includes £300 for insurance for April 20X5 to June 20X5.

In the statement of profit or loss the insurance expense would be:

£ [1,100]

In the statement of financial position there would be [prepaid expenses ▼] of:

£ [300]

Picklist:
accrued expenses
accrued income
prepaid expenses
prepaid income

(d) The commissions income account balance of £180 does not include £20 of commission due for March 20X5.

In the statement of profit or loss the commissions income would be:

£ [200]

In the statement of financial position there would be [accrued income ▼] of:

£ [20]

Picklist:
accrued expenses
accrued income
prepaid expenses
prepaid income

3   A business has an accounting year end of 30 June 20X3. The cash book for the year ended 30 June 20X3 shows payments for motor expenses of £845. This includes £150 of road fund licences for the year from 1 January 20X3.

Required

Update the motor expenses account. Show clearly:

- **The cash book figure**
- **The year-end adjustment**
- **The balance to be carried down or transferred to the statement of profit or loss, as appropriate**

Motor expenses

		£			£
	▼			▼	
	▼			▼	

Picklist:

Accrued expenses
Accrued income
Balance b/d
Balance c/d
Bank
Motor expenses
Motor income
Prepaid expenses
Prepaid income
Profit or loss account
Statement of financial position

4   A business has an accounting year end of 31 March 20X7. Electricity expenses of £470 were accrued at 31 March 20X6. In the cash book for the year ended 31 March 20X7, payments of £8,950 were paid for electricity expenses. On 7 April 20X7 a further electricity bill is received for January to March 20X7 totalling £180. This bill is then paid on 25 April 20X7.

Required

Update the electricity expenses account. Show clearly:

- **The reversal of the opening accrued expenses**
- **The cash book figure**
- **The year-end adjustment**
- **The balance to be carried down or transferred to the statement of profit or loss, as appropriate.**

Electricity expenses

	£		£
▼		▼	
▼		▼	

Picklist:

Accrued expenses
Accrued expenses (reversal)
Accrued income
Accrued income (reversal)
Balance b/d
Balance c/d
Bank
Motor expenses
Motor income
Prepaid expenses
Prepaid expenses (reversal)
Prepaid income
Prepaid income (reversal)
Profit or loss account
Statement of financial position

Inventories

7

Learning outcomes

1.5	**Carry out financial period end routines**
	• That income or expense accounts will carry a balance prior to closing off to the statement of profit or loss at the end of the financial period
	• Which account balances to carry forward and which to close off to the statement of profit or loss at the end of a financial period.
	• Verify general ledger balances by using other sources of information and performing reconciliations where appropriate: physical checks, inventory records
	• Resolve discrepancies, or refer them to the appropriate person
	• Identify and make corrections in the general ledger, including the journal
4.3	**Record inventory**
	• That IFRS exist that are relevant to inventory valuation
	• The meaning of net realisable value
	• That valuation must be at the lower of cost and net realisable value on an individual item basis
	• The principles of different methods of valuation (calculations not required)
	• What can and cannot be included in the valuation of inventory
	• That accounting for inventory is an application of the accrual basis of accounting
	• Determine the correct closing inventory figure in accordance with current accounting standards
	• Calculate the cost of inventory from selling price when VAT or an element of profit is included (calculations involving an understanding of mark-up or sales margin will not be required)
	• Make entries in the journal
	• Use the following accounts: closing inventory – statement of profit or loss, closing inventory – statement of financial position

Assessment context

Questions on inventory are likely to focus on areas such as how inventory should be valued, what can be included in the cost of inventory and how the net realisable value of inventory is calculated. Also, and as you will see in Chapter 12 *The extended trial balance*, you need to know how to record inventory in the accounting records.

Qualification context

Accounting for inventory is tested in the Level 4 unit *Financial Statements of Limited Companies*. Here, you will need to record inventory in the statement of financial position and statement of profit or loss.

Business context

For businesses such as retailers, which buy and sell goods, the inventory figure in a set of accounts is significant. Businesses will seek to minimise the amount of inventory they hold, partly so that they reduce the amount of money tied up in them, but also to reduce the risk of their inventory becoming obsolete as tastes and fashions change.

Chapter overview

- Closing inventory:

DEBIT	Closing inventory	(SOFP)
CREDIT	Closing inventory	(SPL)

Accounting adjustment

Inventories

- Inventory shall be measured at the lower of cost and net realisable value
- This is on a line-by-line basis

Valuation

Cost

- Cost of purchase, including delivery
- Costs of conversion including direct labour
- Other costs to bring the inventory to its present location and condition

Net realisable value

- Net realisable value includes:

Selling price	X
Less completion costs	(X)
Less selling costs	(X)
	X

Methods of estimating cost

FIFO

First in, first out

- The first goods purchased will be the first sold
- Year-end inventory relates to the most recent purchases

AVCO

Average cost

- Simple average cost calculation or
- Weighted average cost calculation

LIFO

Last in, first out

- The last goods will be the first sold
- Year-end inventory relates to the oldest purchases
- **Not a reliable method**

Introduction

Inventory (stock) are items which are:

- Held for sale in the ordinary course of business, or
- In the process of production for such a sale   (IAS 2, para. 6)

For many businesses, inventory is an important asset. The accounting standard IAS 2 *Inventories* gives detailed rules on how inventory should be valued.

Inventories affect the accounts in two ways:

(a) Statement of financial position: a potentially large balance within current assets

(b) Statement of profit or loss: opening and closing inventory have a direct impact on cost of goods sold and therefore profit

As inventory is a significant balance, businesses must ensure that it is recorded completely and accurately in the general ledger.

1 Cost of goods sold

1.1 Current period inventory expense

Inventory is recognised as an expense in the period in which the item is sold.

As was seen in Chapter 2 *Accounting principles*, two of the main components of cost of goods sold are opening inventory and purchases. Opening inventory is brought forward from the prior period and purchases are items acquired in the current period. They are recognised as expenses in the statement of profit or loss under the cost of goods sold heading.

Statement of profit of loss (extract)

	£
Sales	X
Cost of goods sold:	
Opening inventory	X
Purchases	X
Carriage inwards	X
Less closing inventory	(X)
	(X)
Gross profit	X

Carriage inwards (ie the cost of transporting inventory to the businesses premises) also forms part of cost of goods sold.

Note that carriage outwards (ie the cost of transporting inventory to customers) is excluded from cost of goods sold. Instead, it is part of selling expenses which sit below the gross profit line.

1.2 Closing inventory adjustment

At the end of the accounting period, businesses will have unsold inventory. This will be sold in the next accounting period and therefore should not form part of the current year cost of goods sold expense.

Inventory is generally accounted for as a year-end adjustment via a **journal** entry. As with all journals, a narrative should be provided.

The goods held by the business at the end of the period must be included as an asset in the statement of financial position and as a reduction in the cost of goods sold in the statement of profit or loss. Therefore, closing inventory has a dual effect on the general ledger.

The accounting entry and an appropriate narrative are:

Account name	Debit £	Credit £
Closing inventory (SOFP)	X	
Closing inventory (SPL)		X
Being: a year-end adjustment to record closing inventory		

Assessment focus point

In the assessment you may need to record closing inventory as an adjustment in the extended trial balance and record it in the correct SOFP or SPL column. Therefore, it is important to learn the accounting entry to record inventory. Although you will not be required to prepare a statement of financial position or statement or profit or loss, it is useful to understand the relationship between inventory and the other components of the accounts. This process is demonstrated in Activity 1, part (b).

Activity 1: Recording inventory in the accounts

During the year ended 31 December 20X7, Colin opened a business selling telephones. He bought 50 phones for £20 each, and sold 15 for £30 each. Ignore VAT.

Required

(a) Prepare the journal for closing inventory and include a narrative.

Account name		Debit £	Credit £
	▼		
	▼		
Being:			▼

Workings:

Picklist:

Closing inventory (SOFP)
Closing inventory (SPL)
the year-end adjustment to record closing inventory
the year-end adjustment to record opening inventory

(b) Complete the financial statement extracts.

Statement of profit or loss for the year ended 31 December 20X7

	£
Sales	
Cost of goods sold:	
Purchases	
Less closing inventory	
Gross profit	

Statement of financial position as at 31 December 20X7

Non-current assets	Cost £	Depreciation £	Carrying amount £
Property, plant and equipment	1,900	400	1,500
Current assets			
Inventory			
Receivables		200	
Bank		100	
Total current assets			
Total assets			

2 Inventory: quantity and valuation

The inventory figure comprises two elements, quantity and valuation.

2.1 Quantity

Quantity can be ascertained from an **inventory count** at the end of the accounting period. This is a physical check of the number of items held for each product. The information is listed on period-end inventory records.

Alternatively, the quantity of inventory held will be established from continuous inventory records. Under this system, the business maintains an up-to-date record of the number of items held for each product line.

For each item, inventory records show the product name, product code, the cost of the items and the quantity they are held in, at a point in time.

2.2 Valuation

Valuation is much more subjective, so guidance is provided in the international accounting standard, IAS 2 *Inventories.*

Under this accounting standard, a key rule is that:

'Inventories shall be measured at the **lower of cost** and **net realisable value**.'

In other words,

(a) If inventories are expected to be sold at a profit:

    (i)   Value at **cost**
    (ii)   Do not **anticipate** profit

(b)   If inventories are expected to be sold at a loss:

   (i)   Value at net realisable value
   (ii)   Do provide for the future loss

We will consider the definitions of 'cost' and 'net realisable value' in this context.

2.2.1 Cost

The cost of an item of inventory includes:

- Cost of purchase, including delivery
- Cost of conversion, including direct labour
- Other costs to bring inventory to its present location and condition

The following costs cannot be included in the **cost of inventory**:

- Storage costs of finished goods
- Selling costs

(IAS 2, para. 10–18)

Assessment focus point

You may be required to identify items which are included or excluded from the cost of inventory.

Abnormal costs and administration overheads will not be tested in the assessment.

Activity 2: Determining the cost of inventory

According to IAS 2 *Inventories*, which of the following should not be included in determining the cost of the inventory of an entity?

	✓
Storage costs of finished goods	
Cost of conversion including direct labour	
Selling costs	
Cost of purchase, including delivery	

2.2.2 Net realisable value (NRV)

The **net realisable value (NRV)** of an item is essentially its net selling proceeds after deducting all further costs to be incurred in order for the inventory to be sold.

Formula to learn

NRV is calculated as:

	£
Estimated selling price	X
Less estimated costs of completion	(X)
Less estimated selling and distribution costs	(X)
	X

Activity 3: Net realisable value

Jessie is trying to value her inventory. She has the following information available:

	£
Selling price	35
Costs of purchase	20
Cost of work to complete item	12
Selling costs per item	1

(a) What is the net realisable value of Jessie's inventory?

£ [   ]

(b) At what amount will the inventory be valued in Jessie's accounts?

£ [   ]

Workings:

2.2.3 No netting off

Formula to learn

The IAS 2 rule **'lower of cost and net realisable value'** (para. 9) should be applied as far as possible on an item-by-item (or line-by-line) basis.

Illustration 1: No netting off

An entity has four items of inventory on hand at the year end. Their costs and NRVs are as follows:

Inventory item	Cost	NRV	Lower of cost and NRV
	£	£	£
1	27	32	27
2	14	8	8
3	43	55	43
4	29	40	29
	113	135	107

It would be incorrect to compare the total cost of £113 with the total NRV of £135 and state inventories as £113.

A loss on item 2 of £6 can be foreseen and should therefore be recognised.

The comparison should be made for each item of inventory and thus a value of £107 would be attributed to inventories.

This would be accounted for by the journal entry:

Account name	Debit £	Credit £
Closing inventory (SOFP)	107	
Closing inventory (SPL)		107

Activity 4: Calculating closing inventory

Badger Boy makes widgets and has not made any entries for closing inventory for the year ended 31 August 20X9. Closing inventory has been valued at cost, giving a value of £14,700. Included in this figure is a widget costing £1,800 that will be sold for £1,500.

Required

Give the journal entry needed to record closing inventory. Provide a narrative for the journal entry.

Account name		Debit £	Credit £
	▼		
	▼		
Being:			▼

Workings:

Picklist:

Closing inventory (SOFP)
Closing inventory (SPL)
the year-end adjustment to record closing inventory
the year-end adjustment to record opening inventory

3 Calculating the cost of inventory from the selling price

Assessment focus point

It is possible that a task scenario will give you the selling price of inventory which includes a profit element. From this you may be required to calculate the cost of inventory.

The selling price may or may not include VAT.

This will be explained through illustrations 2 and 3.

Illustration 2: Calculate the cost of inventory when an element of profit is included in the selling price of goods by a business which is not registered for VAT

At the year end, McGregor had inventory in the warehouse which it expected to sell for £20,000 in the next financial period. Included within this is profit of £6,000. McGregor is not VAT registered.

What is the cost of closing inventory?

£	14,000

Workings:

Sales price £20,000 minus profit £6,000

Illustration 3: Calculate the cost of inventory when an element of profit is included in the selling price of goods by a VAT-registered business

At the year end, Passey & Sons has inventory in the warehouse which it expects to sell for £36,000 including VAT in the next financial period.

Included within the selling price is profit of £14,000. Passey & Sons is VAT registered.

What is the cost of closing inventory?

£	16,000

Workings:

	£
Gross selling price	36,000
Less VAT: 36,000 × 20/120	(6,000)
Net amount	30,000
Less profit	(14,000)
Closing inventory at cost	16,000

4 Theoretical methods of estimating cost

4.1 Issue

Most businesses will acquire various batches of inventory at different times during the year and at different prices. Periodically items will be selected by warehouse staff to be sold to customers.

It is not always possible to determine precisely which items are still held at the year end and therefore the actual purchase cost of these goods. Accounting standards therefore allow an entity to approximate the cost of its inventory.

Assessment focus point

In the *Advanced Bookkeeping* assessment you must be aware of the theoretical methods of estimating cost (explained below). **You will not, however, be asked to perform calculations in relation to these methods.**

The methods are:

- First in, first out (FIFO)
- Average cost
- Last in, first out (LIFO)

(a) **First in, first out (FIFO)**

Under FIFO it is assumed that:

(i) The first goods purchased or produced will be the first to be sold.

(ii) Remaining inventories are therefore the most recent purchases or production (IAS 2, para. 27).

This is a sensible approximation method, especially if the business sells perishable items!

(b) **Weighted average cost (AVCO)**

There are various averaging methods available by which a business can approximate the cost of its inventories. These range from a **simple average cost** whereby the cost of all purchases or production during the year is divided by the total number of units to a **weighted average cost** whereby a new average is calculated every time new items are purchased or produced (IAS 2, para. 27).

This is a good approximation method where the inventory items are interchangeable, for example in a timber merchant's.

(c) **Last in, first out (LIFO)**

Under LIFO it is assumed that:

(i) The last goods purchased or produced will be the first to be sold.

(ii) Remaining inventories are therefore the earliest purchases or production.

Note that the **LIFO method is prohibited by international accounting standards** because it is unlikely to produce a cost figure which is a close approximation to actual costs.

5 Closing inventory reconciliation

We mentioned that a business may work out the **quantity** of inventory it holds either by performing an inventory count at the year end or by maintaining continuous inventory records on a computer system.

Where a business maintains inventory records, the computer system will generate a figure at the year end for the quantity of each inventory item held. However, as with any computer system, errors can occur. For example:

- Incorrect entries regarding quantities received

- Inventories damaged and not recorded

- Inventories stolen

- Inventory sold but included in inventory counts as it has not yet been despatched

Due to these risks all businesses should perform periodic inventory counts to ensure that the information held by the computerised records agrees with the actual inventory levels in the warehouse.

Where discrepancies are noted, the computerised inventory records should be corrected and updated.

6 Knowledge test preparation

The *Advanced Bookkeeping* assessment may include short-form, objective-style requirements on any area of the syllabus. If the requirements are based on inventories, they could be structured as follows.

Activity 5: Advanced bookkeeping – knowledge

This task is to test your knowledge.

(a)   Which of these statements is true? Choose ONE.

	✓
The first in, first out method of inventory valuation is the only method acceptable under accounting standards.	
Advertising costs may be included in the cost of inventory.	
Inventory costs may include direct labour relating to the production of goods for sale.	
Inventory is always valued at cost.	

A business estimates the cost of its inventory at the year end by assuming that the last goods purchased will be the first to be sold.

(b) What is this method of inventory valuation known as?

	✓
First in, first out	
Lower of cost and net realisable value	
Average cost	
Last in, first out	

Assessment focus point

Inventories are an important item in the accounts. In the assessment you may be asked to calculate the value of inventories and to record them correctly.

Chapter summary

- At the end of the year, and often at other times during the year, inventory must be counted and the quantity of each item listed in inventory records; alternatively, computerised continuous inventory records may be maintained.

- An inventory reconciliation should be performed, comparing the warehouse's record of the quantity of each item held with the actual quantity counted.

- Once the quantity of each item is known, the inventory must then be valued – IAS 2 states that each line of inventory should be valued at the lower of cost and net realisable value (NRV).

- A method of estimating cost must also be chosen – the most common methods are FIFO and AVCO (weighted average cost).

- LIFO is not permitted under accounting standards.

- Once closing inventory has been valued, it must be included in the final accounts as a current asset in the statement of financial position and as a reduction in cost of goods sold in the statement of profit or loss.

Keywords

- **Cost of inventory:** Cost of purchase, including delivery; cost of conversion including direct labour and other costs to bring the inventory to its present location and condition

- **First in, first out (FIFO):** Method of inventory valuation that assumes that items sold are the earliest purchases so closing inventory contains the most recent purchases

- **Inventories:** Items which are held for sale in the ordinary course of business or in the process of production for such a sale

- **Inventory count:** The process of counting each line of inventory and comparing that quantity to the inventory records

- **Inventory reconciliation:** Comparison of the quantity of each item shown in the inventory records to the actual quantity counted

- **Last in, first out (LIFO):** Method of inventory valuation that assumes that the items sold are the most recent purchases so closing inventory contains the earliest purchases

- **Net realisable value (NRV):** The expected selling price of the item less any further costs to be incurred such as costs to completion and selling or distribution expenses

- **Weighted average cost (AVCO):** Method of inventory valuation that operates by calculating a weighted average cost for the inventory after each new purchase

1 A business has 120 units of an item at the year end which cost £25 each plus delivery charges of £2 per unit. This item can be sold for £43 per unit but must be delivered to the customer at a further cost to the business of £3 per unit.

Required

Complete the following statements.

Statements	£
The cost of each item is	
The net realisable value of each item is	
In the statement of financial position the 120 units will be shown at a value of	

2 During the year ended 31 December 20X2, a business bought 250 units of product K at £6 per unit. 60 items were sold at £11 each. Assume that net realisable value is higher than cost at the year end.

Required

Prepare the journal for closing inventory and include a narrative.

Account name		Debit £	Credit £
	▼		
	▼		
Being:			▼

Picklist:

Closing inventory (SOFP)
Closing inventory (SPL)
the year-end adjustment to record closing inventory
the year-end adjustment to record opening inventory

3 Edgar is trying to value his inventory. He has the following information available:

	£
Selling price	4,000
Costs of conversion, including direct labour	1,400
Cost of work to complete the items	1,100
Selling costs	400

What is the net realisable value of Edgar's inventory?

£

4   A business values inventories by assuming that the first goods purchased are the first goods to be sold. Remaining inventories are therefore the most recent purchases.

What is this method of inventory valuation known as?

	✓
First in, first out	
Lower of cost and net realisable value	
Average cost	
Last in, first out	

5   At the year end, a business which is not VAT registered has inventory in the warehouse which it expected to sell for £60,000 in the next financial period. This includes profit on this inventory of £26,000.

What is the cost of closing inventory?

£	

Irrecoverable and doubtful debts

8

Learning outcomes

4.2	Record irrecoverable debts and allowances for doubtful debts
	• The differences between irrecoverable debts, allowances for specific doubtful debts and general allowances
	• That allowances for doubtful debts are an application of the accrual basis of accounting (recognition only)
	• Calculate new allowances for doubtful debts in accordance with organisational policy
	• Calculate adjustments for an existing general allowance for doubtful debts
	• Account for the recovery of an irrecoverable debt previously written off
	• Use the journal to record irrecoverable debts and allowances for doubtful debts (VAT implications are not required)
	• Use the following accounts: irrecoverable debts (statement of profit or loss), sales ledger control account, allowance for doubtful debts account (statement of financial position), allowance for doubtful debts adjustment account (statement of profit or loss)

Assessment context

This topic could be examined in several ways. You may be asked to calculate the doubtful debt balances or complete journal entries to record the irrecoverable and doubtful debt adjustments. Also, the irrecoverable and doubtful debt accounts may feature in an extended trial balance task (studied later in the course).

Qualification context

Irrecoverable debts is a topic you covered in Level 2 *Bookkeeping Controls*. The *Advanced Bookkeeping* assessment extends this knowledge and requires you to be able to account for doubtful debts as well. This area is assumed knowledge for the Level 4 unit, *Financial Statements of Limited Companies*.

Business context

Irrecoverable and doubtful debts is always a topical area and no more so than in today's economic climate. Nowadays, most businesses sell on credit and this immediately exposes them to the risk that the customer will not pay. This will inevitably mean that a business's year-end receivables figure will need to be reduced for any amounts that may not be recoverable.

Chapter overview

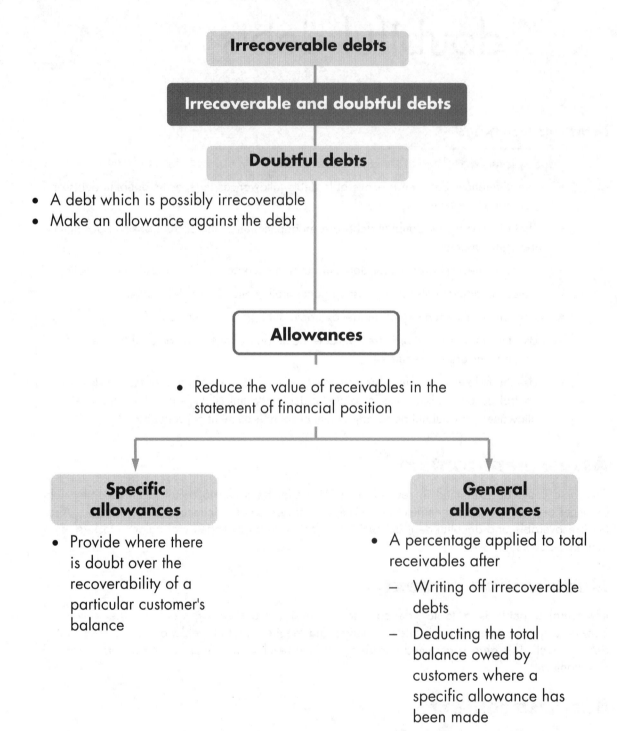

- A debt which is definitely irrecoverable
- Write off to the statement of profit or loss
- Remove from the sales ledger control account

Irrecoverable debts

Irrecoverable and doubtful debts

Doubtful debts

- A debt which is possibly irrecoverable
- Make an allowance against the debt

Allowances

- Reduce the value of receivables in the statement of financial position

Specific allowances

- Provide where there is doubt over the recoverability of a particular customer's balance

General allowances

- A percentage applied to total receivables after
  - Writing off irrecoverable debts
  - Deducting the total balance owed by customers where a specific allowance has been made
- The general allowance is increased or decreased as necessary at each year end

Introduction

Businesses offer credit facilities to customers in order to encourage them to buy products and services. Goods or services sold on credit result in an asset being recorded in the sales ledger control account of the seller's books (with a corresponding liability in the purchases ledger control account in the buyer's books).

The amount owed by credit customers should only be classed as an asset (trade receivable) if it is probable that it is recoverable (ie that the customer will pay the amount due). Consequently, if it becomes apparent that a customer will not pay, the item no longer meets the definition of an asset.

In this chapter we consider the adjustments that may be made in respect of irrecoverable debts and allowances for doubtful debts.

Remember, the term 'sales ledger control account' is used to refer to the general ledger account that forms part of the accounting records. In the statement of financial position, the term 'trade receivables' is often used.

Assessment focus point

There are two main ways in which this topic could be tested:

(a) It could form part of a task on 'accounting adjustments', with calculations required.

(b) You may be asked to include irrecoverable and doubtful debts in the trial balance.

VAT implications are not required.

1 Irrecoverable debts

If a debt is definitely irrecoverable it should be written off to the statement of profit or loss as an **irrecoverable debt**.

Recording an irrecoverable debt

Account name	Debit £	Credit £
Irrecoverable debts (SPL)	X	
Sales ledger control account (SOFP)		X

Activity 1: SND Trading (part I)

SND Trading has a balance on its sales ledger control account at 31 December 20X1 of £105,000. A review of customer files indicates that two customers, A and B, who owe £15,000 and £22,000 respectively, have gone bankrupt and their debts are considered irrecoverable.

Required

(a) **Update the sales ledger control account and the irrecoverable debts account.**

As appropriate, on each account show clearly the:

- **Balance to be carried down and brought down**
- **Balance transferred to the statement of profit or loss**

Sales ledger control account (SOFP)

	£		£
Balance b/d	105,000	▼	
▼		▼	
▼		▼	

Irrecoverable debts (SPL)

	£		£
▼		▼	

Picklist:
Balance b/d
Balance c/d
Irrecoverable debts
Profit or loss account
Sales ledger control account

184

(b) **Complete the trial balance extract by entering the figures calculated in part (a) in the correct places.**

Trial balance (extract)

Ledger account	Ledger balance	
	Dr £	Cr £
Sales ledger control account		
Irrecoverable debts		

Activity 2: GEN Trading (part I)

GEN Trading has a balance on its sales ledger control account at 31 July 20X2 of £50,000. As part of its year-end procedures, it has reviewed its customer files and realised that one customer, Pat Co, which owes £8,000, has severe financial difficulties and is unlikely to be able to pay its debt.

(a) **What will be the accounting entries to write off the debt in the general ledger?**

Account name	Debit £	Credit £
▼		
▼		

Picklist:

Bank
Irrecoverable debts
Sales
Sales ledger control account

(b) **What will be the closing balance on the trade receivables account in GEN Trading's financial statements?**

£ [   ]

2 Recovery of an irrecoverable debt previously written off

From time to time, an irrecoverable debt that has been written off might unexpectedly be paid (in some cases, in subsequent financial periods).

As the debt has already been written off, it is no longer listed in the sales ledger and so the cash received cannot be offset against it in the usual way.

Therefore, the cash received is offset against the irrecoverable debts expense.

Recording the recovery of an irrecoverable debt previously written off

Account name	Debit £	Credit £
Bank	X	
Irrecoverable debts (SPL)		X

Activity 3: GEN Trading (part II)

In December 20X3, GEN Trading unexpectedly receives £8,000 from Pat Co. This relates to the amount written off in the previous financial period.

What will be the accounting entries to record the recovery of the irrecoverable debt previously written off in the general ledger?

Account name	Debit £	Credit £
▼		
▼		

Picklist:

Bank
Irrecoverable debts
Sales
Sales ledger control account

3 Doubtful debts

As well as writing off irrecoverable debts, a business may make an allowance for receivables as a prudent precaution to account for the fact that some receivables balances might not be collectable.

Doubtful debts may occur, for example, when invoices are in dispute, customers are late paying or when customers are in financial difficulty.

In this situation, such debts are not written off, as it is not certain that they are irrecoverable. But because there is doubt over whether they will be paid, an allowance for receivables is made against the doubtful debts.

A new account is created, called the **allowance for doubtful debts** account.

This account is offset against the sales ledger control account balance in the statement of financial position (following the accruals basis of accounting) and the expense taken to the statement of profit or loss.

> **Assessment focus point**
>
> In the assessment you will need to calculate and account for doubtful debts in accordance with the policy of the organisation stated in the task.

3.1 Types of allowance

There are two types of allowances to consider:

(a) **Specific**: provided against a particular customer

(b) **General**: percentage applied to the total on the sales ledger control account **after**:

  (i) Writing off irrecoverable debts

  (ii) Deducting the full balance owed by any customers for whom a **specific allowance** has been created

Each business will have a specific policy regarding general allowances.

3.2 Creating a specific doubtful debt allowance

Account name	Debit £	Credit £
Allowance for doubtful debts – adjustments (SPL)	X	
Allowance for doubtful debts (SOFP)		X

Activity 4: SND Trading (part II)

Following on from SND Trading (part I), a further review of SND Trading's customer files indicates there is some uncertainty as to whether a debt of £18,000 owed by customer C is recoverable.

Required

(a) **Update the allowance for doubtful debts (SOFP) and allowance for doubtful debts – adjustments (SPL) accounts.**

As appropriate, on each account show clearly the:

- **balance to be carried down and brought down or**
- **balance transferred to the profit or loss account**

(b) **Complete the trial balance extract by entering the figures calculated in part (a) in the correct places.**

Solution

(a)

Allowance for doubtful debts (SOFP)

	£			£
▼			▼	
▼			▼	

Allowance for doubtful debts – adjustments (SPL)

	£			£
▼			▼	

Picklist:

Allowance for doubtful debts
Allowance for doubtful debts – adjustments
Balance b/d
Balance c/d
Irrecoverable debts
Profit or loss account
Sales ledger control account

(b) Trial balance (extract)

Ledger account	Ledger balance	
	Dr £	Cr £
Allowance for doubtful debts		
Allowance for doubtful debts – adjustment		

3.3 Creating a general allowance

When creating a **general allowance**, the steps are as follows:

Step 1 Identify the receivables balance (after irrecoverable debts written off and excluding the full amounts of debts on which a specific allowance has been made).

Step 2 Apply the general allowance percentage (%) to the receivables balances identified in step 1.

Illustration 1: Creating a general allowance

PH Trading has a balance on its sales ledger control account at 31 December 20X4 of £40,000. Included within this balance is £1,500 irrecoverable debts to write off and a specific allowance to be made of £500.

This year, a general allowance for doubtful debts will be made. The allowance for doubtful debts will be 2% of the outstanding trade receivables.

Complete the trial balance extract by entering the figures in the correct places.

Trial balance (extract)

Ledger account	Ledger balance	
	Dr £	Cr £
Sales ledger control account		
Irrecoverable debts		
Allowance for doubtful debts		
Allowance for doubtful debts – adjustment		

Workings:

	£	Trial balance – Reference
Opening balance per sales ledger control account	40,000	
Less irrecoverable debts	(1,500)	Row 2
Adjusted balance per sales ledger control account	38,500	Row 1
Less specific allowance	(500)	
	38,000	
General allowance (£38,000 × 2%)	(760)	
∴ **Total allowance:**		
Specific	500	
General	760	
Total closing allowance	1,260	Rows 3 & 4

Solution

Trial balance (extract)

	Ledger balance	
Ledger account	Dr £	Cr £
Sales ledger control account	38,500	
Irrecoverable debts	1,500	
Allowance for doubtful debts		1,260
Allowance for doubtful debts – adjustment	1,260	

Explanation

Sales ledger control account: this is the £40,000 unadjusted balance less the irrecoverable debts of £1,500

Irrecoverable debts: this is given in the scenario as £1,500

Allowance for doubtful debts: this is the amount where recoverability is uncertain; it is a statement of financial position item and will reduce the sales ledger control account balance in the accounts

Allowance for doubtful debts – adjustment: this is the expense which will be transferred to the profit or loss account; it is made up of the specific allowance (£500) and general allowance (£760)

3.4 Adjusting the general allowance

Once a business has created an allowance for doubtful debts, this will be adjusted each year, in line with organisational policy.

> **Assessment focus point**
>
> In the assessment the organisational policy will be stated in the scenario. For example, you may be told that:
>
> 'The allowance for doubtful debts needs to be adjusted to 1% of outstanding trade receivables.'

When there is an opening allowance for doubtful debts, to calculate the closing balance you need to:

Step 1: Identify the opening balance for doubtful debts.

Step 2: Calculate the closing balance. This is the 'Allowance for doubtful debts (SOFP)'.

Step 3: Compare the opening and closing balances. The difference is the balancing figure (β) and equates to the 'Allowance for doubtful debts – adjustments (SPL)'.

In summary:

	£
Opening allowance for doubtful debts (per scenario)	X
Allowance for doubtful debts – adjustments (β)	X/(X)
Closing allowance for doubtful debts (calculated)	X

At the end of each accounting period, the business will establish whether it needs to increase or decrease the allowance for doubtful debts. In other words, the closing allowance for doubtful debts may be higher or lower than the opening balance.

Adjusting the opening allowance for doubtful debts to INCREASE the closing allowance:

Account name	Debit £	Credit £
Allowance for doubtful debts – adjustments (SPL)	X	
Allowance for doubtful debts (SOFP)		X

An increase in the closing allowance gives rise to an expense and therefore a debit entry in respect of the 'allowance for doubtful debts – adjustments'.

Adjusting the opening allowance for doubtful debts to DECREASE the closing allowance:

Account name	Debit £	Credit £
Allowance for doubtful debts (SOFP)	X	
Allowance for doubtful debts – adjustments (SPL)		X

A decrease in the closing allowance gives rise to a decrease in expenses and therefore a credit entry in respect of the 'allowance for doubtful debts – adjustments'.

Activity 5: ND Trading

ND Trading has a balance on its sales ledger control account at 31 December 20X5 of £60,000. Included within this balance is £3,000 of irrecoverable debts to write off and a specific allowance to be made of £600.

At 31 December 20X4, the allowance for doubtful debts was £2,000. At 31 December 20X5, the allowance for doubtful debts will be 3% of the outstanding trade receivables.

Required

Complete the trial balance extract by entering the figures in the correct places.

Trial balance (extract)

Ledger account	Ledger balance Dr £	Ledger balance Cr £
Sales ledger control account		
Irrecoverable debts		
Allowance for doubtful debts		
Allowance for doubtful debts – adjustments		

Workings:

Activity 6: JM Trading

JM Trading has a balance on its sales ledger control account at 31 December 20X5 of £100,000. Included within this balance is £4,000 of irrecoverable debts to write off and a specific allowance to be made of £1,000.

At 31 December 20X4, the allowance for doubtful debts was £2,500. At 31 December 20X5, the allowance for doubtful debts will be 1% of the outstanding trade receivables.

Required

Complete the trial balance extract by entering the figures in the correct places.

Trial balance (extract)

Ledger account	Ledger balance	
	Dr £	Cr £
Sales ledger control account		
Irrecoverable debts		
Allowance for doubtful debts		
Allowance for doubtful debts – adjustments		

Workings:

4 Knowledge test preparation

The *Advanced Bookkeeping* assessment may test your knowledge of any area of the syllabus. If the task is based on irrecoverable and doubtful debts, it could be as follows.

Activity 7: Advanced bookkeeping – knowledge

This task is to test your knowledge.

Which of these statements is true? Choose ONE.

	✓
An irrecoverable debt should remain in the sales ledger control account at the year end.	
Once an organisation has calculated the allowance for doubtful debts it will remain unchanged each year.	
The doubtful debt adjustment will affect the statement of profit or loss and statement of financial position.	

5 Double entry summary for the chapter

Recording an irrecoverable debt:

Account name	Debit £	Credit £
Irrecoverable debts (SPL)	X	
Sales ledger control account (SOFP)		X

Recording the recovery of an irrecoverable debt previously written off:

Account name	Debit £	Credit £
Bank (SOFP)	X	
Irrecoverable debts (SPL)		X

Creating a specific or general doubtful debt allowance:

Account name	Debit £	Credit £
Allowance for doubtful debts – adjustments (SPL)	X	
Allowance for doubtful debts (SOFP)		X

Adjusting the opening allowance for doubtful debts to **increase** the closing allowance:

Account name	Debit £	Credit £
Allowance for doubtful debts – adjustments (SPL)	X	
Allowance for doubtful debts (SOFP)		X

Adjusting the opening allowance for doubtful debts to **decrease** the closing allowance:

Account name	Debit £	Credit £
Allowance for doubtful debts (SOFP)	X	
Allowance for doubtful debts – adjustments (SPL)		X

Chapter summary

- If money owed by a credit customer is unlikely to be paid, then it should not appear as an asset in the statement of financial position.

- Any debts that are not going to be recovered should be written off as irrecoverable debts by debiting the irrecoverable debts expense account and crediting the sales ledger control account.

- If a customer eventually pays a debt that has already been written off as an irrecoverable debt then the bank account is debited with the receipt and the irrecoverable debts expense account is credited.

- A doubtful debt is one where there is concern about its recoverability – this is dealt with by making allowance for doubtful debts accounts in the general ledger.

- The doubtful debt allowance may comprise specific and general allowances.

- Once the allowance for doubtful debts has been set up, each year the balance must be increased or decreased to the amount that is required – this is done by debiting or crediting the allowance for doubtful debts adjustment account by the difference between the opening and closing doubtful debt allowance.

Keywords

- **Allowance for doubtful debts:** An amount that will be deducted from the sales ledger control account balance in the statement of financial position to reduce the balance for amounts that are possibly irrecoverable

- **Allowance for doubtful debts – adjustments:** The account used to record the setting up and then adjustment of the allowance for doubtful debts

- **Doubtful debts:** Amounts over which there is some doubt as to their recoverability

- **General allowance:** An allowance set up as a percentage of the receivables balance to reflect the fact that on average a certain percentage of debts will be doubtful

- **Irrecoverable debt:** A debt that it is believed will not be paid

- **Irrecoverable debts expense account:** The expense account used to record the irrecoverable debts that are written off – the balance appears as an expense in the statement of profit or loss

- **Specific allowance:** An allowance against particular debts that are recognised as doubtful

1   A business must write off an irrecoverable debt of £3,000.

What is the journal entry to record this in the general ledger?

Account name	Debit £	Credit £
▼		
▼		

Picklist:

Allowance for doubtful debts
Allowance for doubtful debts – adjustments
Irrecoverable debts
Sales ledger control account

2   A business has a draft closing balance on the sales ledger control account of £60,000. Irrecoverable debts of £4,000 are to be written off and a specific allowance of £1,000 is to be made.

Required

Complete the trial balance extract by entering the figures in the correct places.

Trial balance (extract)

Ledger account	Ledger balance	
	Dr £	Cr £
Sales ledger control account		
Irrecoverable debts		
Allowance for doubtful debts		
Allowance for doubtful debts – adjustments		

3   A business wrote off an irrecoverable debt of £2,500 last year. In the current financial period, this amount owed has unexpectedly been paid.

What is the journal entry to record this in the general ledger?

Account name	Debit £	Credit £
▼		
▼		

Picklist:

Allowance for doubtful debts
Allowance for doubtful debts – adjustments
Bank
Irrecoverable debts
Sales ledger control account

4   On 1 January 20X9 a business has a balance brought down in the allowance for doubtful debts account of £1,200.

On 31 December 20X9, the sales ledger control account has a balance of £30,000. The business needs a specific allowance of £600 and a general allowance of 2% of remaining receivables.

Required

Complete the trial balance extract by entering the figures in the correct places.

Trial balance (extract)

| Ledger account | Ledger balance | |
	Dr £	Cr £
Sales ledger control account		
Allowance for doubtful debts		
Allowance for doubtful debts – adjustments		

Workings:

5 On 1 January 20X7 a business has a balance brought down in the allowance for doubtful debts account of £1,200.

On 31 December 20X7, the sales ledger control account has a balance of £45,000. The business needs a specific allowance of £900 and a general allowance of 1% of remaining receivables.

Required

Complete the trial balance extract by entering the figures in the correct places.

Trial balance (extract)

Ledger account	Ledger balance	
	Dr £	Cr £
Sales ledger control account		
Allowance for doubtful debts		
Allowance for doubtful debts – adjustments		

Workings:

Bank reconciliations

Learning outcomes

1.5	Carry out financial period end routines
	• Verify general ledger balances by using other sources of information and performing reconciliations where appropriate: bank statements
	• Resolve discrepancies, or refer them to the appropriate person
	• Identify and make corrections in the general ledger, including the journal

Assessment context

Bank reconciliations, along with control account reconciliations, form an important part of the *Advanced Bookkeeping* syllabus. Questions on bank reconciliations may ask you to identify the cash book adjustments required or identify items that have not yet cleared the bank statement and represent timing differences.

Qualification context

The knowledge covered in this chapter was also examined in the Level 2 unit *Bookkeeping Controls* and so this chapter is a revision chapter. However, in *Advanced Bookkeeping* the topic is likely to be tested as part of a task on period-end routines. Therefore, you will not be asked to perform a full bank reconciliation.

Business context

Cash flow is of great importance to all businesses and so it is imperative that a business reconciles its bank account on a regular basis (at least monthly). This will ensure that the business knows exactly what level of cash resources it has available at any point in time.

Chapter overview

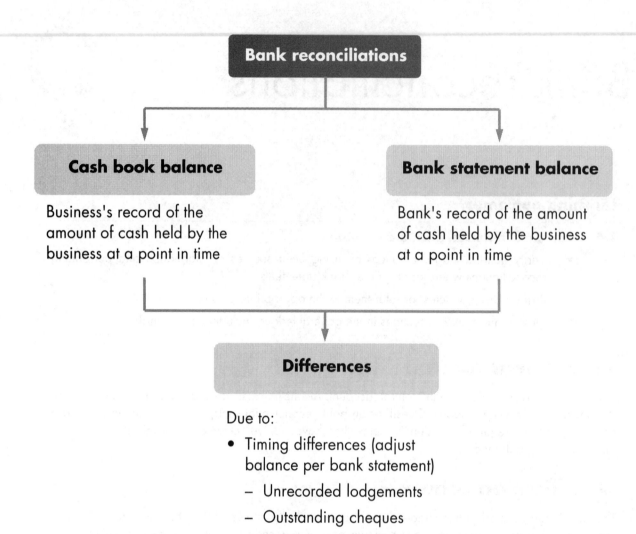

Bank reconciliations

Cash book balance

Business's record of the amount of cash held by the business at a point in time

Bank statement balance

Bank's record of the amount of cash held by the business at a point in time

Differences

Due to:
- Timing differences (adjust balance per bank statement)
  - Unrecorded lodgements
  - Outstanding cheques
- Cash book needs to be updated (adjust cash book) eg
  - Standing orders
  - Direct debits
  - BACS transfers
  - Bank charges
  - Interest
  - Counter credits
  - Faster payments
- Bank errors

Introduction

Bank reconciliations were tested in the Level 2 unit *Bookkeeping Controls* and so you should already have an understanding of the purpose of the bank reconciliation and the process by which the balance on the business's cash book is reconciled to the balance per the bank statement.

The cash book is used to record the detailed transactions of receipts and payments into and out of the bank account. Cash is a very important asset for the business and the owner of the business must be able to see how much money the business has. As a security measure, the balance shown in the accounting records (prepared by the accountant) must be agreed to the bank statement.

Bank statements provide an independent record of the balance on the bank account **but** this balance is unlikely to agree exactly to the cash book balance – therefore a reconciliation is required.

1 Differences between the cash book balance and the bank statement

Differences occur for three main reasons:

(a) **Timing differences**

When a business receives a cheque from a customer or sends a cheque to a supplier, it will update the cash book. This means the cash book balance includes this receipt or payment.

However, cheques will clear and appear on the bank statement at a later date, which results in a temporary difference in the balance per the cash book and the balance on the bank statement.

The main timing differences are:

- **Unrecorded lodgements** (money paid into the bank by the business which have not yet appeared as a receipt on the bank statement)

- **Unpresented cheques** (cheques paid out by the business which have not yet appeared on the bank statement)

(b) **The cash book has not yet been updated to include items that already appear on the bank statements**

Typical examples include:

- Standing orders (SO)

- Direct debits (DD)

- BACS direct credits (eg payments made to staff for salaries, monies received electronically from credit customers)

- Bank charges

- Interest (received or charged)

- **Counter credit** (cash and cheques paid into the business's bank account at the bank's counter by someone from the business)

- **Faster payments** (a system that allows customers to make small and medium-sized payments online almost instantaneously)

Often, when a business receives the monthly bank statement the person responsible will then update the cash book to include these items.

(c) **Bank errors**

If the business becomes aware of a bank error, they must notify the bank so that any necessary adjustments can be processed.

Dishonoured cheques

Another point to note is that some cheques received by the business may be dishonoured because, for example, there are insufficient funds in the payer's account. A **dishonoured cheque** is sent back to the payee so that payment can be pursued in some other way. The cash book must be updated to recognise dishonoured cheques.

2 Updating the cash book and performing a bank reconciliation

When updating the cash book and performing a bank reconciliation, the steps are as follows:

(1) Compare the debit side of the cash book to the paid in amounts shown on the bank statement – for each paid in amount that agrees, tick the item both in the cash book and on the bank statement.

(2) Compare the credit side of the cash book to the paid out amounts shown on the bank statement – for each paid out amount that agrees, tick the item both in the cash book and on the bank statement.

(3) Any unticked items on the bank statement (other than errors made by the bank) are items that should have been entered into the cash book but have been omitted for some reason. Enter these into the cash book and then the adjusted balance on the cash book can be calculated as usual.

(4) Finally, any unticked items in the cash book are timing differences – **outstanding lodgements** (debit side) and unpresented cheques (credit side) – that are used to reconcile the bank statement closing balance to the correct, adjusted cash book closing balance.

Before attempting questions on this topic, it is useful to review a typical cash book and **bank reconciliation statement**.

Illustration 1: Cash book and bank reconciliation statement

This is a typical cash book (with the bold items representing possible adjustments as a result of performing a bank reconciliation):

Cash book

Date 20XX	Details	Bank £	Date 20XX	Cheque no.	Details	Bank £
01 July	Balance b/d	12,597	06 July	248952	Cash payment	6,250
16 July	Cash received	5,349	10 July	248953	Cash payment	1,164
28 July	Cash received	2,147	17 July	248954	Cash payment	2,250
			23 July	248955	Cash payment	275
			29 July	248956	Cash payment	76
XX July	**Bank interest received**		**XX July**		**Bank interest paid**	
XX July	**Counter credit**		**XX July**		**Bank charges**	
			XX July		**Standing orders**	
			XX July		**Direct debits**	
			XX July		**BACS**	
			31 July		**Balance c/d**	
	Total				Total	
1 August	Balance b/d					

This is a typical bank reconciliation statement:

Bank reconciliation statement

Bank reconciliation statement as at 31 July 20XX	£
Balance per bank statement	
Add:	
Name:	
Name:	
Total to add	
Less:	
Name:	
Name:	
Total to subtract	
Balance as per adjusted cash book	

A word of warning

Note that the bank statement shows the balance from the bank's point of view whereas the cash book is from the business's point of view.

Therefore, should a task state the bank account is in credit, this means that there is a **debit** balance in the business's records.

Conversely, should a question state that the bank account balance is overdrawn, then there is a **credit** balance in the business's records.

Assessment focus point

The *Advanced Bookkeeping* assessment will test your understanding of bank reconciliations through a short-form, objective-style question. This will be set in the context of a task on period-end routines.

However, to answer this type of question successfully, you need to understand the full process of preparing a bank reconciliation. This is recapped in Activity 1.

Activity 1: Bank reconciliation (recap)

A business received the following bank statement for April 20X3.

Date 20X3	Details	Paid out £	Paid in £	Balance £	
01 April	Balance b/f			32,637	C
03 April	Cheque 5678	8,880		23,757	C
09 April	Cheque 5679	14,700		9,057	C
10 April	Bank interest		180	9,237	C
10 April	Cheque 5672	3,900		5,337	C
15 April	Direct Debit – Power Ltd	1,950		3,387	C
16 April	Cheque 5680	3,000		387	C
18 April	Counter Credit – QTK Ltd		20,550	20,937	C
22 April	Bank charges	150		20,787	C
22 April	BACS – RDC Ltd	891		19,896	C
26 April	Counter Credit – R57 Ltd		1,350	21,246	C
27 April	Cheque 5681	8,100		13,146	C
	D = Debit C = Credit				

The cash book as at 30 April 20X3 is shown below.

Cash book

Date 20X3	Details	Bank £	Date 20X3	Cheque no.	Details	Bank £
01 April	Balance b/f	28,737	01 April	5678	ABC Ltd	8,880
18 April	QTK Ltd	20,550	05 April	5679	SRG Ltd	14,700
26 April	KT Ltd	1,770	12 April	5680	HAL Ltd	3,000
	▼		15 April	DD	Power Ltd	1,950
	▼		21 April	5681	ERT Ltd	8,100
	▼		24 April	5682	TGN Ltd	2,280
	▼				▼	
	▼				▼	
	▼				▼	
	▼				▼	

Required

(a) **Check the items on the bank statement against the items in the cash book.**

(b) **Enter any items into the cash book as needed.**

(c) **Total the cash book and clearly show the balance carried down at 30 April 20X3 and brought down at 1 May 20X3.**

(d) **Identify the TWO transactions that are included in the cash book but missing from the bank statement and complete the bank reconciliation statement below as at 30 April 20X3.**

Bank reconciliation statement	£
Balance per bank statement	
Add:	
Name:	
Total to add	
Less:	
Name:	
Total to subtract	
Balance as per cash book	

Picklist:

Balance b/d
Balance c/d
Bank charges
Bank interest
KT Ltd
R57 Ltd
RDC Ltd
TGN Ltd

3 Assessment questions

As has been mentioned, the *Advanced Bookkeeping* assessment will test your understanding of bank reconciliations through a short-form, objective-style question.

> **Assessment focus point**
>
> In the assessment, it is likely that you will:
>
> - Either be asked to adjust the cash book
> - Or identify the items that have yet to clear the bank statement
>
> It is important to read the task information carefully and ensure you follow the instructions.

However, as a check that you have understood all of the adjustments, the following steps are useful.

(1) On scrap paper, set up two columns. Label one column 'cash book adjustments' and the other column 'bank statement – timing differences'.

(2) Read the scenario and enter the relevant opening balance at the top of each column.

(3) Work through the items described in the scenario. For each item, determine whether it:

    (a) Affects the cash book or bank statement
    (b) Increases or decreases that balance

    On paper, note the correct treatment in the appropriate column.

(4) Once you have addressed all the items, add the columns. If you have processed the items correctly, the adjusted cash book and bank statement balances will reconcile.

(5) To answer the task requirement, ensure that the relevant items are included in your on-screen solution.

We will see how this process works in the activities that follow.

Activity 2: Adjustments to the cash book (example 1)

The balance showing on the bank statement is a credit of £7,150 and the balance in the cash book is a debit of £4,190.

The bank statement has been compared with the cash book and the following differences identified:

(1) Bank interest received of £90 was not entered into the cash book.

(2) Cash sales totalling £200 have been entered into the cash book but are not yet banked.

(3) A cheque received for £620 has been incorrectly entered into the cash book as £260.

(4) Cheques received from a customer for £400 have been entered into the cash book but are not showing on the bank statement.

(5) A BACS payment of £1,100 to a supplier has not been entered into the cash book.

(6) Cheques totalling £4,210 sent to suppliers at the end of the month are not showing on the bank statement.

Required

Use the following table to show the THREE adjustments you need to make to the cash book.

Adjustment	Amount £	Debit ✓	Credit ✓
▼			
▼			
▼			

Picklist:

Adjustment (1)
Adjustment (2)
Adjustment (3)
Adjustment (4)
Adjustment (5)
Adjustment (6)

Activity 3: Adjustments to the cash book (example 2)

The balance showing on the bank statement is a debit of £12,056 and the balance in the cash book is a credit of £7,871.

The bank statement has been compared to the cash book and the following differences identified:

(1) Cheques received from customers of £2,956 are not showing on the bank statement.

(2) An automated payment to a supplier of £550 has been correctly recorded in the cash book but delayed by the bank due to an error in the account number given.

(3) A BACS payment of £950 has been incorrectly entered into the cash book as £980.

(4) A standing order payment of £1,919 has not been entered into the cash book.

(5) An automated receipt from a credit customer for £844 has been incorrectly entered into the cash book as £484.

(6) Cash receipts totalling £250 have been entered into the cash book but are not yet banked.

Required

Use the following table to show the THREE adjustments you need to make to the cash book.

Adjustment	Amount £	Debit ✓	Credit ✓
▼			
▼			
▼			

Picklist:

Adjustment (1)
Adjustment (2)
Adjustment (3)
Adjustment (4)
Adjustment (5)
Adjustment (6)

Activity 4: Bank statement

The balance showing on the bank statement is a credit of £19,750 and the balance in the cash book is a debit of £21,434.

The bank statement has been compared to the cash book and the following differences identified:

(1) Bank charges of £46 have not yet been entered into the cash book.

(2) Cheques totalling £4,210 sent to suppliers at the end of the month are not showing on the bank statement.

(3) Cheques received from customers of £6,543 are not showing on the bank statement.

(4) A refund in respect of an overpayment of rates of £135 has not yet been entered into the cash book.

(5) A cheque from a customer for £440 has been dishonoured by the bank. This has not yet been reflected in the cash book.

(6) An automated payment to a supplier of £1,000 has been correctly recorded in the cash book but delayed by the bank due to an error in the account number given.

Required

Use the following table to show the THREE items you would expect to appear on the next bank statement. Indicate whether they will be debit or credit entries on the bank statement.

Adjustment	Amount £	Debit ✓	Credit ✓
▼			
▼			
▼			

Picklist:

Adjustment (1)
Adjustment (2)
Adjustment (3)
Adjustment (4)
Adjustment (5)
Adjustment (6)

4 Knowledge test preparation

The *Advanced Bookkeeping* assessment may include short-form, objective-style requirements on any area of the syllabus. If the requirements are based on bank reconciliations, they could be structured as follows.

Activity 5: Advanced bookkeeping – knowledge

This task is to test your knowledge.

While preparing a bank reconciliation statement at 31 December, the following items caused a difference between the bank statement balance and the cash book balance.

Required

(a) Identify the items that WILL be shown in the bank reconciliation as an adjustment to the balance per the bank statement.

	✓
Bank interest charged to the account in error	
Direct debit for £500 for insurance	
Bank charges of £70	
Cheque paid to a supplier on 29 December and included in the cash book but not yet received and cashed by the supplier	
Receipt from a credit customer by electronic transfer (BACS)	

(b) Indicate whether the following statements are true or false.

	True ✓	False ✓
A bank reconciliation should be performed on a regular basis (eg monthly).		
The bookkeeper may have to update the cash book for items on the bank statement which are not yet included in the business's general ledger.		
Outstanding lodgements are normally a cash book adjustment.		
Cheques sent to suppliers which have not yet cleared the bank statement are normally a cash book adjustment.		

Chapter summary

- When updating the cash book and performing a bank reconciliation, the steps are as follows:

  (1) Compare the debit side of the cash book to the paid in amounts shown on the bank statement – for each paid in amount that agrees, tick the item both in the cash book and on the bank statement.

  (2) Compare the credit side of the cash book to the paid out amounts shown on the bank statement – for each paid out amount that agrees, tick the item both in the cash book and on the bank statement.

  (3) Any unticked items on the bank statement (other than errors made by the bank) are items that should have been entered into the cash book but have been omitted for some reason. Enter these into the cash book and then the adjusted balance on the cash book can be calculated as usual.

  (4) Finally, any unticked items in the cash book are timing differences – outstanding lodgements (debit side) and unpresented cheques (credit side) – that are used to reconcile the bank statement closing balance to the correct, adjusted cash book closing balance.

- The closing balance on the bank statement is reconciled to the correct, adjusted closing cash book balance in the bank reconciliation statement.

Keywords

- **Bank reconciliation statement:** A statement reconciling the bank statement balance to the corrected cash book balance

- **Counter credit:** Cash and cheques paid into the business's bank account at the bank's counter by someone from the business

- **Dishonoured cheque:** Cheque that is paid into a business's bank account and then is returned by the drawer's bank unpaid

- **Faster payments:** A system that allows customers to make small and medium-sized payments online almost instantaneously

- **Outstanding lodgements:** Cheques that have been received and recorded in the cash book – debit side but do not yet appear on the bank statement

- **Unpresented cheques:** Cheque payments that have been recorded in the cash book – credit side but do not yet appear on the bank statement

Test your learning

1   A standing order payment of £150 for electricity has cleared the bank statement but has not yet been entered into the cash book.

Required

Answer the following questions.

Questions	Answer
When the electricity payment is entered into the cash book, will it be a debit or credit item?	▼
Will the electricity payment be included on the debit or credit side of the bank statement?	▼

Picklist:

Debit
Credit

2   Money received from a credit customer by the faster payments method has cleared the bank statement but has not yet been entered into the cash book.

Required

Answer the following questions.

Questions	Answer
When the receipt is entered into the cash book, will it be a debit or credit item?	▼
Is the receipt included on the debit or credit side of the bank statement?	▼

Picklist:

Debit
Credit

3   **Enter the term which is explained in each of the descriptions.**

Description	Term
Cheques paid out by the business which have not yet appeared on the bank statement.	▼
Money paid into the bank by the business but which has not yet appeared as a receipt on the bank statement.	▼

Picklist:

Unpresented cheques
Unrecorded lodgements

4 **Answer the following questions.**

Questions	Answer
If the bank statement shows a credit balance, does the business have a positive or negative cash balance?	▼
If the bank statement shows a debit balance, does the business have a positive or negative cash balance?	▼

Picklist:

Positive

Negative

5 A BACS payment of £1,000 has been incorrectly entered into the cash book as £100.

What adjustment will be made to the cash book?

Adjustment	Amount £	Debit ✓	Credit ✓
BACS payment			

Control account reconciliations 10

Learning outcomes

1.3	Demonstrate the purpose and use of books of prime entry and ledger accounting
	• The different books and records that make up the accounting system: books of prime entry: sales and purchases daybooks (sales, sales returns, purchase and purchase returns), cash book, general ledger accounts, memorandum ledgers, control accounts: sales ledger, purchases ledger, payroll
1.5	Carry out financial period end routines
	• Income or expense accounts will carry a balance prior to closing off to the statement of profit or loss at the end of the financial period
	• Which account balances to carry forward and which to close off to the statement of profit or loss at the end of a financial period
	• Verify general ledger balances by using other sources of information and performing reconciliations where appropriate: supplier statements, sales and purchases ledgers (memorandum ledger accounts)
	• Resolve discrepancies, or refer them to the appropriate person
	• Identify and make corrections in the general ledger, including the journal

Assessment context

Control accounts and payroll are topics that were examined in your Level 2 *Bookkeeping Controls* studies and are also examinable in *Advanced Bookkeeping*.

Questions on control account reconciliations may ask you to determine the adjustments needed to correct the control account balance and the individual subsidiary sales or purchases ledger balance.

Questions on payroll may test your knowledge of the general ledger accounts used to include payroll transactions in the accounting records.

Qualification context

The knowledge covered in this chapter was also examined in *Bookkeeping Controls* and so this chapter is partly revision. However, control accounts are an area which students often find challenging and so this chapter will be taught from first principles, with some revision of the Level 2 control accounts chapters. Contra entries are not studied at Level 2 and so are new to this course.

Business context

Cash flow is of great importance to all businesses. One of the major cash inflows for a business is monies received from customers, and significant cash outflows are supplier payments and wages.

Recording these transactions accurately helps businesses manage cash flow, and control account reconciliations are an important part of this process.

Chapter overview

The SLCA and the SL, and the PLCA and the PL show the same information and so the balances should reconcile

Reconciliations

**Sales ledger control account (SLCA)
Purchases ledger control account (PLCA)**

**Subsidiary sales ledger (SL)
Subsidiary purchases ledger (PL)**

- **SLCA:** The total owed by all credit customers at a particular point in time
- **PLCA:** The total owed to all credit suppliers at a particular point in time

Control account reconciliations

- **SL:** Individual accounts listing transactions with each credit customer
- **PL:** Individual accounts listing transactions with each credit supplier

Other considerations

Contra entries

- May be made when a business has a customer which is also a supplier
- A contra will always be for the lower of the two amounts owed
- Contra entries reduce the balances in the sales ledger control account and purchases ledger control account

Discounts allowed and received

- Discounts allowed are offered by a business to their credit customer (an expense)
- Discounts received are received by a business from their suppliers (sundry income)

Payroll

- Payroll transactions are recorded using the usual principles of double entry
- The general ledger accounts used to record payroll transactions include:
  - Wages control account
  - Wages expense
  - HMRC
  - Pension

Introduction

This chapter examines the process of reconciling the sales ledger (SL) with the sales ledger control account (SLCA), and purchases ledger (PL) with the purchases ledger control account (PLCA), and the adjustments that may arise from the process.

Note that in the *Advanced Bookkeeping* assessment, the following terms may be used interchangeably:

- Sales ledger control account and receivables ledger control account
- Memorandum (subsidiary) sales ledger and memorandum (subsidiary) receivables ledger
- Purchases ledger control account and payables ledger control account
- Memorandum (subsidiary) purchases ledger and memorandum (subsidiary) payables ledger

The chapter then moves on to look at payroll. Payroll is a key expense for businesses and the wages control account is used to help ensure all transactions are recorded accurately.

1 Books of prime entry (recap)

In your Level 2 studies we saw how a business's individual transactions were categorised in the books of prime entry.

Transaction	Book of prime entry
Sales invoices, in respect of credit sales	Sales day book
Sales credit notes, in respect of credit sales returns	Sales returns day book
Sales credit notes, in respect of prompt payment discounts taken up by customers	Discounts allowed day book
Cash receipts	Cash book – debit side
Purchases invoices, in respect of credit purchases	Purchases day book
Purchases credit notes, in respect of credit purchases returns	Purchases returns day book
Purchase credit notes, in respect of prompt payment discounts from suppliers taken up by the business	Discounts received day book
Cash payments	Cash book – credit side

Periodically, the books of prime entry are totalled.

The totals will be posted to the general ledger accounts using the double entry bookkeeping system with which we are familiar.

2 Controls accounts and memorandum accounts

2.1 Control accounts

Control accounts contain summarised totals of all the individual transactions affecting their respective ledgers. They contain the same information that is in the memorandum sales and purchases ledgers; however, they show the totals rather than the individual transactions.

The sales ledger control account is an account in which records are kept of transactions involving all credit customers in total.

A purchases ledger control account is an account in which records are kept of transactions involving all credit suppliers in total.

2.2 Memorandum (subsidiary) accounts

While the closing balances in the control accounts are important as they are included in the period-end accounts, the business also needs a detailed analysis of transactions with credit customers and suppliers.

Subsidiary ledger accounts are prepared so that the business can see the amount owed from credit customers or to credit suppliers at a point in time. The sales ledger contains separate accounts for each credit customer and the purchases ledger contains separate accounts for each credit supplier. The separate accounts list all transactions (invoices, credit notes, payments etc) relating to individual credit customers and suppliers.

If the double entry in the general ledger and the entries in the subsidiary ledger have all been entered correctly, the total of the list of balances in the ledgers will always equal the balance on the respective control account.

2.3 Reconciling the sales ledger and the sales ledger control account

In Chapter 1 the day books for a business called 'G Mason' were introduced. There were the following day books.

For credit sales:

- Sales day book
- Sales returns day book
- Discounts allowed day book
- Cash book – debit side

For credit purchases:

- Purchases day book
- Purchases returns day book
- Discounts received day book
- Cash book – credit side

This chapter takes the example a stage further by posting the transactions from the day books to the memorandum accounts and then reconciling the memorandum accounts with the relevant control account.

Illustration 1 considers accounting for credit sales.

Illustration 1: The accounting system for credit sales

G Mason has two credit customers, H and I. On 1 July 20X1, customer H owes £200 on one outstanding invoice and customer I owes £150 (therefore £350 in total).

In July the following transactions occur and are recorded in the day books.

The sales day book is used to record all invoices sent to customers buying on credit.

Sales day book (extract)

Date 20X1	Details	Invoice number	Total £	VAT £	Net £
4 July	H	0015	192	32	160
10 July	I	0016	96	16	80
15 July	H	0017	120	20	100
29 July	I	0019	144	24	120
	Totals		552	92	460

If items are returned by customers, credit notes are recorded in the sales returns day book.

Sales returns day book (extract)

Date 20X1	Details	Credit note number	Total £	VAT £	Net £
18 July	I	CN041	96	16	80
25 July	H	CN042	120	20	100
	Totals		216	36	180

Money received from credit customers is entered into the debit side of the cash book. Customer H takes advantage of a 6% prompt payment discount and pays £188 to settle the £200 owing on 1 July. Customer I pays the full amount of £150 owing on 1 July.

Cash book – debit side (extract)

Date 20X1	Details	Bank £	Trade receivables £
15 July	H	188	188
20 July	I	150	150
	Totals	338	338

Where the customer decides to take a prompt payment discount, the business issues a credit note which is recorded in the discounts allowed day book. The £12 entry for the prompt payment discount was calculated on H's outstanding invoice of £200 as 6% x £200. This is shown below:

Discounts allowed day book (extract)

Date 20X1	Details	Credit note number	Total £	VAT £	Net £
15 July	H	CN035	12	2	10
	Totals		12	2	10

The individual transactions are then posted to the sales ledger:

Sales ledger

The subsidiary sales ledger for G Mason in July will be as follows:

Customer H – Sales ledger account

	£		£
Balance b/d	200	Bank	188
Invoice	192	Credit note	120
Invoice	120	Discounts allowed	12
		Balance c/d	192
	512		512
Balance b/d	192		

Customer I – Sales ledger account

	£		£
Balance b/d	150	Bank	150
Invoice	96	Credit note	96
Invoice	144	Balance c/d	144
	390		390
Balance b/d	144		

To complete the reconciliation, the sales ledger control account for G Mason in July will be as follows:

Sales ledger control account

	£		£
Balance b/d	350	Bank	338
Sales	552	Sales returns	216
		Discounts allowed	12
		Balance c/d	336
	902		902
Balance b/d	336		

Reconciliation

Details	Amount £
Customer H	192
Customer I	144
Total of the sales ledger account balances	336
Balance b/d at the end of July in the sales ledger control account	336
Difference	Nil

This suggests that the transactions have been correctly recorded in the accounting records.

Tutorial note. In your *Advanced Bookkeeping* assessment, you are likely to have to identify whether reconciling items affect the memorandum accounts or control account or both. You will not have to post books of prime entry to memorandum accounts and control accounts. This illustration is to assist your understanding. Therefore, the approach has been simplified and the sales, sales returns and discounts allowed amounts have been entered gross of VAT in the sales ledger control account in a single line for each. The amounts could have been split out into the net amount and the corresponding VAT amount in two separate lines with separate narratives.

2.4 Reconciling the purchases ledger and the purchases ledger control account

This next illustration looks at reconciling the purchases ledger and the purchases ledger control account.

Illustration 2: The accounting system for credit purchases

G Mason purchases goods on credit from suppliers J and K. On 1 July 20X1, G Mason owes supplier J £120 on one outstanding invoice and owes supplier K £70 (therefore £190 in total).

In July the following transactions occur and are recorded in the day books.

The purchases day book is used to record all invoices received from suppliers when purchasing on credit.

Purchases day book (extract)

Date 20X1	Details	Invoice number	Total £	VAT £	Net £
6 July	J	JC24	168	28	140
11 July	J	JC25	72	12	60
20 July	K	K93	108	18	90
29 July	K	K104	60	10	50
	Totals		408	68	340

If items are returned to suppliers, credit notes are recorded in the purchases returns day book.

Purchases returns day book (extract)

Date 20X1	Details	Credit note number	Total £	VAT £	Net £
17 July	J	CN045	72	12	60
31 July	K	CN159	60	10	50
	Totals		132	22	110

Money paid to credit suppliers is entered into the credit side of the cash book. G Mason takes advantage of a 5% prompt payment discount from supplier J and pays £114 as full settlement of the £120 owing at 1 July. G Mason pays the full £70 due to supplier K on 1 July.

Cash book – credit side (extract)

Date 20X1	Details	Bank £	Trade payables £
11 July	J	114	114
16 July	K	70	70
	Totals	184	184

Where the business decides to take a prompt payment discount, the supplier issues a credit note which is recorded in the discounts received day book. The entry for the prompt payment discount of £6 (5% × £120) on supplier J's invoice is shown below.

Discounts received day book (extract)

Date 20X1	Details	Credit note number	Total £	VAT £	Net £
11 July	J	CN243	6	1	5
	Totals		6	1	5

Purchases ledger

The subsidiary purchases ledger for G Mason in July will be as follows:

Supplier J – Purchases ledger account

	£		£
Bank	114	Balance b/d	120
Credit note	72	Invoice	168
Discount received	6	Invoice	72
Balance c/d	168		
	360		360
		Balance b/d	168

Supplier K – Purchases ledger account

	£		£
Bank	70	Balance b/d	70
Credit note	60	Invoice	108
Balance c/d	108	Invoice	60
	238		238
		Balance b/d	108

To complete the reconciliation, the purchases ledger control account for G Mason in July will be as follows:

Purchases ledger control account

	£		£
Bank	184	Balance b/d	190
Purchases returns	132	Purchases	408
Discounts received	6		
Balance c/d	276		
	598		598
		Balance b/d	276

Reconciliation

Details	Amount £
Supplier J	168
Supplier K	108
Total of the purchases ledger account balances	276
Balance b/d at the end of July in the purchases ledger control account	276
Difference	Nil

This suggests that the transactions have been correctly recorded in the accounting records.

Tutorial note. As per Illustration 1, a simplified approach has been taken and the purchases, purchases returns and discounts received amounts have been entered gross of VAT into the purchases ledger control account in a single line for each. The amounts could have been split out into the net amount and the corresponding VAT amount in two separate lines with separate narratives.

2.5 Reconciling the purchases ledger with a supplier statement

Supplier statements (also known as 'statements of account') were studied in Level 2 *Bookkeeping Transactions*. It is useful to recap this topic and see how supplier statements can be used as a check that the purchases ledger is correct.

A business may have many transactions with a particular supplier. On a monthly basis, the supplier should send a supplier statement listing the invoices, credit notes, discounts and payments that have arisen that month.

In theory, the supplier statement should agree to the memorandum purchases ledger account for that supplier. However, it is important to check this with a reconciliation.

Illustration 3: Reconciling the supplier statement and the purchases ledger

This is G Masons's July supplier statement from Supplier J.

| | | | Supplier J
X Street
X Town
Supplier Statement | | | |
		To: G Mason				
Date 20X1	Invoice/credit note number	Details	Invoice amount £	Credit note amount £	Payment amount £	Balance £
1 July		Balance b/d	120			120
6 July	JC24	Invoice	168			288
11 July	JC25	Invoice	72			360
11 July		Payment			114	246
11 July	CN243	Credit note		6		240
17 July	CN045	Credit note		72		168
30 July		Balance c/d				168

The details listed on the supplier statement match the information recorded in G Mason's accounting records for Supplier J. This provides further confirmation that G Mason's purchases ledger is accurate.

3 Other aspects of accounting for credit sales and purchases

Two important considerations are prompt payments discounts and contra entries.

3.1 Prompt payment discounts (recap)

As we saw in the Level 2 accounting units, many businesses offer discounts to their customers.

When a credit customer takes advantage of a prompt payment discount, this must be recorded in the ledgers. The entries are as follows.

Discounts allowed

General ledger – discounts allowed

Account name	Debit £	Credit £
Discounts allowed	X	
VAT	X	
Sales ledger control account		X

The credit entry to the sales ledger control account is for the gross amount as the full amount settled by way of the discount is no longer owed by the customer. The VAT element is posted to the VAT account cancelling out the VAT which arose on the original sale. The net amount is posted as a debit to the discounts allowed account, being an increase in expenses.

In terms of control account reconciliations, the key point to note is that discounts allowed reduce the amount owed by credit customers. Therefore, they are entered on the credit side of the sales ledger control account. The relevant subsidiary sales ledger account should also be updated for discounts allowed.

Discounts received

General ledger – discounts received

Account name	Debit £	Credit £
Purchases ledger control account	X	
VAT		X
Discounts received		X

The debit entry to the purchases ledger control account is for the gross amount because the full amount settled by way of the discount is no longer owed to the supplier. The VAT element is posted to the VAT account thus cancelling out the VAT which arose on the original purchase. The net amount is posted as a credit to the discounts received account, being an increase in income.

In terms of control account reconciliations, the key point to note is that discounts received reduce the amount owed to credit suppliers. Therefore, they are entered on the debit side of the purchases ledger control account. The relevant subsidiary purchases ledger account should also be updated for discounts received.

3.2 Contra entries

Another transaction which may be tested in *Advanced Bookkeeping* is contra entries.

Sometimes a business will have a customer who also supplies the business with goods.

Illustration 4: Contra entries

P is a printing business which sells stationery to F, a florist. F supplies P with flowers and plants for its offices.

During October, P sells stationery worth £200 to F and F delivers flowers and plants to P worth £70.

P has the following amounts in its books:

Receivables (owing from F):   £200
Payables (owed to F):   £70

The two businesses agree to offset the balances receivable and payable via a contra.

The contra will be for the lower of the two amounts: £70. This will decrease both receivables and payables by £70 and the remaining £130 can then be paid in cash.

A **contra entry** is always recorded as:

Account name	Debit £	Credit £
Purchases ledger control account	X	
Sales ledger control account		X

This will **reduce** both the sales ledger control account balance and the purchases ledger control account balance.

Note that the subsidiary sales and purchases ledgers will also need to be updated for the contra entry.

4 Performing a control reconciliation – T-account format

The next activities recap your knowledge of control account reconciliations and also test your understanding of contra entries.

They are preparation questions for this unit and therefore T-account format is used.

Activity 1: Sales ledger control account reconciliation

This is a summary of Silver's transactions with credit customers during August 20X1.

Transactions	£
Balance of sales at 1 August 20X1	18,234
Goods sold on credit	29,211
Money received from credit customers	16,321
Discount allowed	2,421
Goods returned by credit customers	5,311
Contra entries	500
Irrecoverable debts written off	360

Required

(a) **Enter the following items into the sales ledger control account. Show the balance c/d and the balance b/d.**

Sales ledger control account

	£		£
▼		▼	
▼		▼	
▼		▼	
▼		▼	
▼		▼	
▼		▼	
▼		▼	

Picklist:

Balance b/d
Balance c/d
Bank
Discounts allowed
Irrecoverable debts
Purchases ledger control account
Sales
Sales returns

The following balances were in Silver's sales ledger on 1 September 20X1.

Transactions	£
Edward	2,690
Emily Co	5,321
Henry	1,273
Gordon	9,408
Rosie Co	3,840

Required

(b) Reconcile the balances shown above with the sales ledger control account balance you have calculated in part (a).

	£
Sales ledger control account balance as at 1 September 20X1	
Total of sales ledger accounts as at 1 September 20X1	
Difference	

Activity 2: Purchases ledger control account reconciliation

This is a summary of Silver's transactions with credit suppliers during August 20X1.

Transactions	£
Balance of purchases at 1 August 20X1	12,325
Goods bought on credit	22,573
Payments made to credit suppliers	10,325
Discount received	3,721
Goods returned to credit suppliers	2,811
Contra entries	500

Required

(a) Enter the following items into the purchases ledger control account. Show the balance c/d and the balance b/d.

Purchases ledger control account

	£			£
▽			▽	
▽			▽	
▽			▽	
▽			▽	
▽			▽	
▽			▽	

Picklist:

Balance b/d
Balance c/d
Bank
Discounts received
Purchases
Purchases returns
Sales ledger control account

The total of the balances on the purchases ledger on 1 September 20X1 is £18,041.

(b) Reconcile the balances shown above with the purchases ledger control account balance you have calculated in part (a).

	£
Purchases ledger control account balance as at 1 September 20X1	
Total of purchases ledger accounts as at 1 September 20X1	
Difference	

5 Control account reconciliations in the assessment

> **Assessment focus point**
>
> In the assessment, it is likely that you will:
>
> - **Either** be asked to adjust the control account
> - **Or** adjust the total of the ledger balances
>
> It is important to read the task information carefully and ensure you follow the instructions.

However, as a check that you have understood all of the adjustments, the following steps are useful:

(1) On scrap paper, set up two columns. Label one column 'control account' and the other column 'subsidiary balance total'.

(2) Read the scenario and enter the relevant opening balance at the top of each column.

(3) Work through the errors given in the scenario. For each error, determine whether the error:

    (i) Affects the control account or the ledger balance
    (ii) Increases or decreases that balance

    On paper, note the correct treatment in the appropriate column.

(4) Once you have addressed all the errors, add the columns. If you have processed the errors correctly, the control account and ledger balance will reconcile.

(5) To answer the task requirement, ensure that the relevant adjustments are included in your on-screen solution.

We will see how this process works in the activities that follow.

235

Activity 3: Reconciling the sales ledger control account and the sales ledger

This task is about preparing reconciliations.

The individual balances of the accounts in the subsidiary sales ledger have been listed and totalled to £16,600. The total has been compared with the £10,674 balance on the sales ledger control account. After investigation the following errors were found:

(1) A total in the sales day book of £3,500 was recorded as £3,050.

(2) A sales invoice of £763 has been posted to customer A's account in the subsidiary sales ledger, rather than customer B's.

(3) Cheques of £5,492 received from customers have not been recorded in the subsidiary accounts.

(4) A customer account with a debit balance of £3,200 has been listed in the subsidiary sales ledger as £3,020.

(5) A contra for £200 was only recorded in the sales ledger.

(6) A credit note issued for £182 has been debited to a customer account in the subsidiary sales ledger.

Required

Use the following table to show the THREE adjustments required to the listing of subsidiary sales ledger balances.

Adjustment	Amount £	Add ✓	Deduct ✓
▼			
▼			
▼			

Picklist:

Adjustment (1)
Adjustment (2)
Adjustment (3)
Adjustment (4)
Adjustment (5)
Adjustment (6)

Activity 4: Reconciling the purchases ledger control account and the purchases ledger

This task is about preparing reconciliations.

The individual balances of the accounts in the purchases ledger have been listed and totalled to £4,406. The total has been compared with the £6,426 balance on the purchases ledger control account. After investigation the following errors were found:

(1) Purchases credit notes received from suppliers totalling £760 had been entered as a credit entry in the purchases ledger control account.

(2) A supplier's account with a balance of £390 had been omitted from the purchases ledger listing.

(3) Cheques paid to suppliers totalling £1,460 had been omitted from the purchases ledger control account.

(4) A page in the purchases day book had been understated by £900.

(5) A purchases credit note for £300 had been omitted from supplier X's account in the subsidiary purchases ledger.

(6) Returns to a supplier of £150 had not been recorded in the purchases ledger account.

Required

Use the following table to show the THREE adjustments required to the purchases ledger control account.

Adjustment	Amount £	Debit ✓	Credit ✓
▼			
▼			
▼			

Picklist:

Adjustment (1)
Adjustment (2)
Adjustment (3)
Adjustment (4)
Adjustment (5)
Adjustment (6)

6 Knowledge test preparation

The *Advanced Bookkeeping* assessment may include short-form, objective-style requirements on any area of the syllabus. If the requirements are based on control account reconciliations, they could be structured as follows.

Activity 5: Advanced bookkeeping – knowledge

This task is to test your knowledge. A reconciliation is performed between the sales ledger control account and the subsidiary sales ledger.

(a) Which items will be adjusted in the sales ledger control account?

	✓
Cheques received from customers omitted from the sales ledger control account.	
A credit note entered on the debit side of a customer's account in the subsidiary sales ledger.	
A sales invoice omitted from a customer's account in the subsidiary sales ledger.	
A purchases day book total posted to the sales ledger control account.	
A BACS receipt recorded on the debit side of the customer's account in the subsidiary sales ledger.	

(b) Which items will be adjusted in the subsidiary sales ledger accounts?

	✓
Cheques received from customers omitted from the sales ledger control account.	
A credit note entered on the debit side of a customer's account in the subsidiary sales ledger.	
A sales invoice omitted from a customer's account in the subsidiary sales ledger.	
A purchases day book total posted to the sales ledger control account.	
A BACS receipt recorded on the debit side of the customer's account in the subsidiary sales ledger.	

7 Payroll

Salaries and wages usually form a substantial part of a business's expenditure, especially in service organisations. However, salaries and wages expenditure does not arise in the same way as other cash and credit purchases.

The entries in the accounting system that are made in respect of salaries and wages are known as **payroll transactions**. This topic was studied in detail in the Level 2 *Bookkeeping Controls* unit. Here, we will recap the key general ledger accounts used when recording payroll transactions and payroll accounting entries.

Note that in *Bookkeeping Controls*, payroll transactions are recorded using a **wages control account**. Therefore, when payroll expenses occur, the liability is initially credited to this account.

7.1 Payroll terminology

Gross pay

Gross pay is the total amount that the employer owes the employee before any deductions have been made.

Statutory deductions

Income tax (pay-as-you-earn or PAYE) and employees' **national insurance contributions (NIC)** are known as statutory deductions from gross pay, because the law (statute) requires employers to make these deductions from individuals' salaries.

NIC is just another form of tax, calculated differently from income tax. An individual employee's NIC is deducted from the employee's wages and paid over to **Her Majesty's Revenue & Customs (HMRC)**, together with the employee's income tax.

Voluntary deductions

An employee may choose to have other (voluntary) deductions made from gross pay. These items can only be deducted from an employee's gross salary **if** the employer has the employee's written permission to do so.

For example, if an employee chooses to make **pension contributions**, this money is deducted from gross pay and transferred to a pension administrator to provide a pension for the employee on retirement. Other voluntary deductions include trade union fees and give-as-you-earn (GAYE).

Net pay

Once all deductions have been made, the amount paid to the employee is called net pay. It is sometimes referred to as 'take home pay'.

Employer's national insurance contribution (statutory)

The employer is also required to pay an additional amount of NIC for each employee, known as the **employer's NIC**. This is yet another form of tax, but the difference is that it is only borne by the employer. There is no deduction from the employee's gross pay for the employer's NIC. Employer's NIC is paid by the employer to HMRC.

Employer's pension contribution (voluntary)

The employer may make a voluntary contribution to the employee's pension. Again, this is in addition to the gross pay. Therefore, it increases the 'total cost' of employing individuals. However, it is not deducted from the gross pay.

Full cost of employing an employee

Therefore, gross pay plus employer's NIC plus employer's pension contribution is the cost of employing an employee and the total of these is what appears as the wages expense for the business.

7.2 Accounting for payroll

Payroll is accounted for using the double entry bookkeeping rules that we are familiar with. There are, however, some new general ledger (or T) accounts which are used for this purpose.

Account name	Purpose
Wages control account (also known as the '**net pay control account**')	This is like any other control account and helps to ensure that the double entry is made correctly. All payroll liabilities are initially credited to this control account. They are subsequently transferred to the relevant general ledger account (such as HMRC, pension and bank). At the end of a period, once all the necessary payroll entries have been made, this account will have a balance of zero.
Wages expense	This expense account shows the total cost to the business of employing workers (ie the gross salary **plus** the employer's NIC and, if applicable, the employer's pension contribution).
HM Revenue & Customs	This liability account shows the amount of income tax and NIC owed to the tax authorities.
Pension	This liability account shows the amount of pension that must be paid over to the pension scheme. It will include both the employees' and employer's contributions.

If further voluntary deductions are made by employees, other payable accounts are used.

There are a number of double entries to be made:

(i) **Gross pay is recorded:**

Account name	Debit £	Credit £
Wages expense	X	
Wages control account		X

(ii) **Net pay is paid to employees:**

Account name	Debit £	Credit £
Wages control account	X	
Bank		X

(iii) **Income tax and employees' NIC is allocated to the HM Revenue and Customs account:**

Account name	Debit £	Credit £
Wages control account	X	
HM Revenue and Customs		X

(iv) **Employees' pension contributions are allocated to the pension account:**

Account name	Debit £	Credit £
Wages control account	X	
Pension		X

(v) **Employer's NIC is recorded:**

Account name	Debit £	Credit £
Wages expense	X	
Wages control account		X

(vi) **Employer's NIC is transferred to the HMRC account:**

Account name	Debit £	Credit £
Wages control account	X	
HM Revenue and Customs		X

(vii) **Employer's pension contributions are recorded:**

Account name	Debit £	Credit £
Wages expense	X	
Wages control account		X

(viii) **Employer's pension contribution is transferred to the pension account:**

Account name	Debit £	Credit £
Wages control account	X	
Pension		X

Illustration 5: Recording payroll in the ledger accounts

Reeves pays its employees by BACs direct credit every month and maintains a wages control account. A summary of last month's payroll transactions is shown below:

Item	Amount £
Gross pay	30,000
Employees' NI	5,000
Income tax	8,000
Employer's NI	3,000

(a) Record the wages expense

Account name	Amount £	Debit ✓	Credit ✓
Wages expense	33,000	✓	
Wages control account	33,000		✓

Workings:

£30,000 + £3,000 = £33,000

(b) Record the HMRC liability

Account name	Amount £	Debit ✓	Credit ✓
Wages control account	16,000	✓	
HM Revenue and Customs	16,000		✓

Workings:

£5,000 + £8,000 + £3,000 = £16,000

(c) Record the net wages paid to the employees

Account name	Amount £	Debit ✓	Credit ✓
Wages control account	17,000	✓	
Bank	17,000		✓

Workings:

£30,000 – £5,000 – £8,000 = £17,000

Picklist:

Bank
HM Revenue and Customs
Pension
Wages control account
Wages expense

Chapter summary

- If all of the entries are correctly recorded then the total of the closing balances on the memorandum sales ledger accounts should agree to the balance on the sales ledger control account.

- Likewise, if all of the entries are correctly recorded then the total of the closing balances on the memorandum purchases ledger accounts should agree to the balance on the purchases ledger control account.

- If errors are identified, then they must be corrected.

- Accounting for payroll involves the use of several general ledger accounts:
  - Wages control account
  - Wages expense account
  - HM Revenue and Customs account
  - Pension account
  - Other payable accounts if further voluntary deductions are made

Keywords

- **Contra entry:** An amount owed by a customer which is set off against an amount owed to the customer as a supplier

- **Gross pay:** The salary or wages payable to an employee before any statutory or voluntary deductions

- **Her Majesty's Revenue & Customs (HMRC):** The UK government department responsible for collecting tax

- **Income tax:** A tax that is paid by individuals on all sources of income, including salary and wages

- **National insurance contributions (employees' NIC):** A tax on employees' income deducted from gross pay

- **National insurance contributions (employer's NIC):** An additional tax, suffered by the employer, based on an employee's gross pay

- **Payroll transactions:** Payments to employees in respect of salaries and wages

- **Pension contribution:** A form of voluntary deduction from employees, and a contribution from employers which is paid to the pension administrator to provide a pension for employees on retirement

- **Purchases ledger control account reconciliation:** An exercise which agrees the balance on the purchases ledger control account to the total of the list of balances in the purchases ledger

- **Sales ledger control account reconciliation:** An exercise which agrees the balance on the sales ledger control account to the total of the list of balances in the sales ledger

- **Wages control account (or 'net pay control account'):** This is like any other control account and helps to ensure that the double entry is made correctly

1   BG has a credit customer, WT & Sons. WT & Sons is also a credit supplier of BG.

The following sales transactions relate to WT & Sons for the month of August.

Transactions	£
Sales invoices	5,400
Credit notes	798
Discount allowed	120
Contra entry	200
Bank receipt	3,042

Required

Enter the items into the WT & Sons subsidiary sales ledger account, in the books of BG. Show the balance c/d and the balance b/d.

WT & Sons – Sales ledger account

	£			£
Balance b/d	2,600		▼	
▼			▼	
▼			▼	
▼			▼	
▼			▼	
▼			▼	

Picklist:

Balance b/d
Balance c/d
Bank
Discounts allowed
Purchases ledger control account
Sales
Sales returns

2 The balance on a business's sales ledger control account at the end of June was £41,774 and the total of the list of balances from the sales ledger came to £41,586.

The following errors were discovered:

(1) The sales day book was undercast by £100 on one page.

(2) A page from the sales returns day book with a total of £450 had not been posted to the control account although the individual returns had been recorded in the memorandum ledger.

(3) An invoice from the sales day book had been posted to the individual account of the customer as £769 instead of the correct figure of £679.

(4) A discount allowed to one customer of £16 had been posted to the wrong side of the customer's account in the sales ledger.

(5) An irrecoverable debt of £210 had been written off in the account in the sales ledger but not in the general ledger.

(6) A credit balance in the memorandum ledger of £125 had been included in the list of balances as a debit balance.

Required

Use the following table to show the THREE adjustments you need to make to the sales ledger control account.

Adjustment	Amount £	Debit ✓	Credit ✓
▼			
▼			
▼			

Picklist:

Adjustment (1)
Adjustment (2)
Adjustment (3)
Adjustment (4)
Adjustment (5)
Adjustment (6)

3   The balance on a business's purchases ledger control account at the end of June is £38,694 and the total of the list of balances in the memorandum purchases ledger comes to £39,741.

The following errors were noted for the month:

(1)   A page in the purchases returns day book was overcast by £300.

(2)   A total from the cash book – credit side (payments to suppliers) of £3,145 was posted in the general ledger as £3,415.

(3)   Prompt payment discounts received from suppliers of £267 were omitted from both the general ledger and the purchases ledger.

(4)   A credit note from a supplier for £210 was entered into the supplier's account in the purchases ledger as £120.

(5)   A debit balance on an account in the purchases ledger of £187 was omitted from the list of balances.

(6)   A credit balance in the purchases ledger should have been included in the list as £570 but instead was recorded as £770.

Required

Use the following table to show the THREE adjustments you need to make to the purchases ledger control account.

Adjustment	Amount £	Debit ✓	Credit ✓
▼			
▼			
▼			

Picklist:

Adjustment (1)
Adjustment (2)
Adjustment (3)
Adjustment (4)
Adjustment (5)
Adjustment (6)

4 Gross wages for a business in August are £62,500. Employer's NIC is £7,500 and employees' NIC is £8,300. Income tax is £9,900.

Required

Answer the following questions.

Questions	£
What is the total wages expense for August?	
What is the total amount to be paid to HMRC in respect of the August payroll?	

5 **Indicate whether the following statements about the net pay control account are true or false.**

Statements	True ✓	False ✓
It is a record of how much is paid to each individual employee each month.		
It should have a balance of zero at the end of the period once all payroll entries have been made.		
It is debited with gross pay.		
It is credited when net pay is paid to employees.		
It is where all payroll liabilities are initially recorded with a credit entry.		

The trial balance, errors and the suspense account

11

Learning outcomes

1.5	Carry out financial period end routines
	• Income or expense accounts will carry a balance prior to closing off to the statement of profit or loss at the end of the financial period
	• Which account balances to carry forward and which to close off to the statement of profit or loss at the end of a financial period
	• Resolve discrepancies or refer them to the appropriate person
	• Identify and make corrections in the general ledger, including the journal
4.4	Record period end adjustments
	• When making period end adjustments, there is scope to significantly affect the reported results of the organisation
	• The effects of including misleading or inaccurate period end adjustments (non-compliance with regulations, misinformed decision making by users of the final accounts)
	• Respond appropriately to period end pressures (time pressure, pressure to report favourable results, pressure from authority)
5.1	Prepare a trial balance
	• Certain accounts can carry either a debit or a credit balance (in particular: VAT, disposals, allowance for doubtful debts adjustment, bank, loan, irrecoverable debts)
	• The importance of the trial balance for the preparation of final accounts
	• Transfer balances from ledger accounts, a list of balances or written data into correct debit or credit columns of the trial balance
	• Correct any errors that are not shown by the trial balance
	• Use and clear the suspense account
5.2	Carry out adjustments to the trial balance
	• Place the following adjustments correctly in the extended trial balance: closing inventory, accruals, prepayments, corrections of errors/omissions, depreciation, irrecoverable debts, allowances for doubtful debts

Assessment context

You are likely to be presented with the situation where adjustments need to be entered into a trial balance extract. The adjustments may relate to items introduced in this unit (including doubtful debts, depreciation, accruals and prepayments). They may also relate to the correction of errors, including clearing a suspense account.

Qualification context

Correcting errors and redrafting the trial balance was introduced in the Level 2 *Bookkeeping Controls* unit. You may also be required to make adjustments to a trial balance in your Level 4 *Financial Statements of Limited Companies* unit.

Business context

At the period end all businesses must prepare a trial balance which is complete, accurate and includes valid business transactions. This will provide both internal and external users with useful information. This may then assist a business in assessing its performance, raising finance and meeting its statutory requirements.

Chapter overview

A suspense account is a temporary account which never appears in the financial statements
- Used when:
  - An accountant is unsure of a double entry
  - A preliminary trial balance does not balance
- Must be cleared out
- Steps:
  (1) What entry **was** made?
  (2) Decide what entry **should** have been made
  (3) Make the required **adjustment**

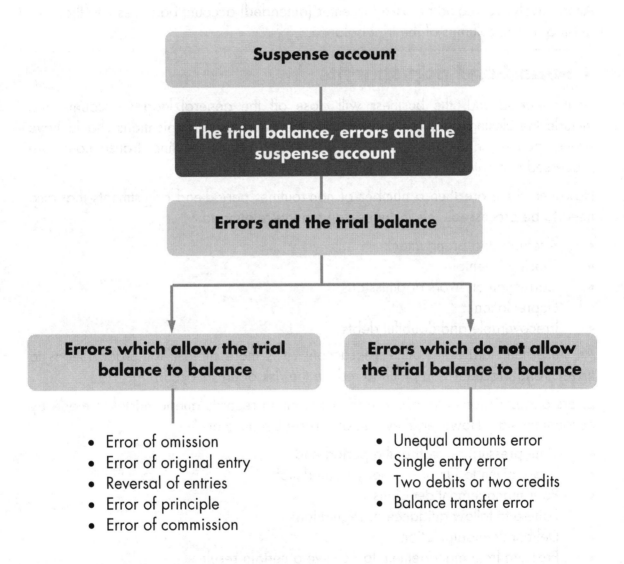

Suspense account

The trial balance, errors and the suspense account

Errors and the trial balance

Errors which allow the trial balance to balance	**Errors which do not allow the trial balance to balance**
• Error of omission	• Unequal amounts error
• Error of original entry	• Single entry error
• Reversal of entries	• Two debits or two credits
• Error of principle	• Balance transfer error
• Error of commission	

Introduction

The Level 2 *Bookkeeping Controls* unit explained how to redraft a trial balance following the correction of errors.

We now move on to process the more complex period-end adjustments which have been studied in this unit. The journal entries will then be in included in a **trial balance**.

> **Assessment focus point**
>
> In the assessment, the scenario may present you with a trial balance extract and adjustments to process.
>
> You could be asked to record the necessary adjustments in the 'Adjustments' columns of the trial balance.
>
> Alternatively, you could be asked to enter (amended) account balances into the debit or credit columns of the trial balance.

1 Period-end adjustments

At the period end, the business will close off the general ledger accounts and include the closing balances in an initial trial balance. Organisations should have strong policies and procedures in place that ensure routine transactions are processed accurately.

However, there are then a number of non-routine, period-end adjustments that also need to be processed. This includes adjustments relating to:

- Accruals and prepayments
- Closing inventory
- Correction of errors or omissions
- Depreciation
- Irrecoverable and doubtful debts

As these items are non-routine transactions, it is more difficult for organisations to have strong procedures in place to reduce the risk of errors occurring.

Errors and omissions can occur in the accounting records due to mistakes made by accounting staff. However, they can also arise because of:

- Time pressure on staff at the period end
- Work given to junior or poorly trained staff
- Poor management decisions
- Failure to follow guidance or regulations
- Deliberate manipulation
- Pressure from management to achieve a certain result

Mis-stated period-end adjustments will have an:

- Effect on profit
- Effect on assets and liabilities

- Impact on the evaluation of management performance
- Impact on stakeholder decisions based on the business's financial performance (eg whether a bank should lend or a supplier should offer credit)

Where junior members of staff become aware of discrepancies that they cannot resolve, the organisation should have procedures in place to enable them to report the errors to an appropriate person. They should either report concerns to their immediate line manager or another senior member of the organisation. It is important that discrepancies are resolved.

Furthermore, at all times accountants must maintain their integrity and professional conduct in the work environment, and not be influenced or pressurised into manipulating financial information. As was discussed in Chapter 2 *Accounting principles*, there is an ethical dimension to this.

Illustration 1: Supplier's invoice

ABC has deliberately omitted a substantial supplier's invoice from its records at the period end.

What effect will this have on ABC's profit for the period?

	✓
Profit will be overstated	
Profit will be understated	

Solution

	✓
Profit will be overstated	✓
Profit will be understated	

Explanation

The amount omitted is a significant expense. If recorded it would reduce profit and increase liabilities. Therefore, its omission means that the profit figure is overstated and liabilities are understated.

2 Errors and the suspense account

As was mentioned above, this is a topic you are familiar with from *Bookkeeping Controls* in Level 2.

Assessment focus point

It is likely that the task on accounting adjustments and journals will include the correction of errors. This may include clearing a suspense account.

To recap, there are two categories of errors that can affect the accounting records:

- Errors which still allow the trial balance to balance
- Errors which cause an imbalance in the trial balance

The following errors will still **allow the trial balance to balance**.

Type of error	Detail
Error of omission	Both sides of a transaction have been completely left out. For example, a rent payment of £800 is not recorded in the general ledger.
Error of original entry	An entry has been made so that debits = credits but the amount is incorrect. For example, a credit sale of £1,000 is posted as: DEBIT Sales ledger control account £150 CREDIT Sales £150
Reversal of entries	A transaction has been recorded at the correct amount but the debit and credit entries have been reversed. For example, posting the credit sale above as: DEBIT Sales £1,000 CREDIT Sales ledger control account £1,000
Error of principle	Here debits = credits; however, one of the entries has been made to the wrong type of account. For example, £500 spent on repairing a motor vehicle has been recorded as: DEBIT Motor vehicles at cost £500 CREDIT Bank £500 Repairs are an item of expense which should be shown in the statement of profit or loss whereas the item has been recorded as a non-current asset.
Error of commission	Here debits = credits; however, one of the entries has been made to the wrong account, but not the wrong type of account. For example, £200 spent on telephone costs has been recorded as: DEBIT Insurance expense £200 CREDIT Bank £200 Both accounts (telephone and insurance costs) are expenses and so this is an error of commission rather than an error of principle.

These errors will be corrected through a journal.

The trial balance will not balance if total debits do not equal total credits. The following errors **cause an imbalance in the trial balance**:

Type of error	Detail
Unequal amounts error	Here an entry has been posted where debits ≠ credits. A common example of this is where a transposition error has been made and figures have been reversed. For example, £450 of rent costs have been posted as follows: DEBIT Rent £450 CREDIT Bank £540 Here debits ≠ credits and so the trial balance will not balance.
Single entry error	Here a debit entry has been posted with no corresponding credit made or vice versa. For example, a credit sale of £300 has been posted as: DEBIT Sales ledger control account £300 or as: CREDIT Sales £300 Here debits ≠ credits and so the trial balance will not balance.
Two debits or two credits error	Here two debit entries or two credit entries have been posted. For example, the credit sale of £300 above has been posted as: DEBIT Sales ledger control account £300 DEBIT Sales £300 or as: CREDIT Sales ledger control account £300 CREDIT Sales £300 Here debits ≠ credits and so the trial balance will not balance.
Balance transfer error	Here the final balance on the general ledger account is incorrectly transferred to the trial balance. For example, a balance of £560 on the sales account was recorded in the trial balance as £650 or £400. Note that this type of error also includes the situation where the £560 balance on the sales account was completely omitted from the trial balance. Here debits ≠ credits and so the trial balance will not balance.

These errors will be corrected by creating a **suspense account** so that the trial balance will balance and then making a journal entry to correct the error.

3 Suspense accounts

A suspense account is a **temporary** account. It **never** appears in the final accounts.

It is used for two main reasons:

(a) To account for a debit or credit entry when the accountant is unsure as to where it should go

(b) To make a preliminary trial balance balance when an error has been detected

Steps to clear a suspense account:

(1) Determine the original accounting entry which **was** made.
(2) Decide what entry **should** have been made.
(3) Make the required **adjustment.**

Illustration 2: Suspense account

W sold goods with a value of £2,500 to James, a credit customer. When recording the sale W posted the transaction to the correct accounts but made two debit entries.

Steps:

(1) Entry made was:

Account name	Debit £	Credit £
Sales ledger control account	2,500	
Sales	2,500	
Suspense β		5,000*

*As there were two debit entries of £2,500 each, the suspense account must have been credited with the balancing figure (β) of £5,000.

(2) Entry should have been:

Account name	Debit £	Credit £
Sales ledger control account	2,500	
Sales		2,500

(3)   Make the required adjustment:

Account name	Debit £	Credit £
Suspense	5,000	
Sales		5,000

The entry to the sales ledger control account was correct in the original entry but sales had been debited by £2,500 when they should have been credited by that amount. The correction is therefore twice the original error.

Activity 1 provides useful preparation for identifying the errors that have been made in the accounting records and recording the journals to correct these errors and clear the suspense account. This is excellent practice for the assessment-standard activities which follow.

Activity 1: Journals and the suspense account

This task is about accounting adjustments and journals.

You are working on the accounting records of a business with a year end of 31 August. A trial balance has been drawn up and a suspense account opened. You now need to make some corrections and adjustments for the year ended 31 August 20X9.

You may ignore VAT in this task.

Required

Record the journal entries needed in the general ledger to deal with the items below.

You do not need to give narratives. Do NOT enter zeros into unused cells.

Picklist:

Capital
Discounts allowed
Machinery accumulated depreciation
Rent
Sales ledger control account
Stationery expense
Suspense

(a) **A rent payment of £350 has been debited to the sales ledger control account.**

Journal

Account name		Debit £	Credit £
	▼		
	▼		

(b) **Depreciation of £1,900 was charged on the machinery during the year. The only entry made was to record the expense.**

Journal

Account name		Debit £	Credit £
	▼		
	▼		

(c) **Discounts allowed of £500 have not been recorded in the books.**

Journal

Account name		Debit £	Credit £
	▼		
	▼		

(d) **The purchase of stationery for £1,460 cash has been correctly entered into the bank account, but no entry has been made to the appropriate expense account.**

Journal

Account name		Debit £	Credit £
	▼		
	▼		

(e) **Capital of £35,000 was recorded incorrectly as £53,000. The posting to bank was made correctly.**

Journal

Account name		Debit £	Credit £
	▼		
	▼		

Workings (NB: not part of the assessment answer):

Suspense account

Details	Amount £	Details	Amount £
Balance b/f	17,560		

This example has revised the process of correcting errors and clearing a suspense account. Activity 2 takes this a stage further by requiring adjustments to be made and then recorded in an extended trial balance.

4 Adjustments and the extended trial balance

This task is about recording **adjustments** in the extended trial balance and closing off accounts.

Activity 2: Adjustments and the extended trial balance

You are working on the accounts of a business with a year end of 31 August.

A trial balance has been drawn up and a suspense account opened.

You now need to make some corrections and adjustments for the year ended 31 August 20X9.

You may ignore VAT in this task.

Required

(a) **Record the adjustments needed in the extract from the extended trial balance to deal with the items below. You will not need to enter adjustments on every line. Do NOT enter zeros into unused cells.**

(i) A bank payment of £950 made on 25 August 20X9 for buildings insurance for the year ended 31 August 20Y0 is included in the insurance expenses figures as at 31 August 20X9.

(ii) Travel expenses of £230 paid by business debit card have been correctly entered into the travel expenses account but no other entries were made.

(iii) The allowance for doubtful debts needs to be adjusted to 5% of the outstanding trade receivables.

(iv) Discounts allowed of £100 were omitted from the discounts allowed expense account. The other entries were made correctly.

Extract from the extended trial balance

Ledger account	Ledger balance		Adjustment	
	Debit £	Credit £	Debit £	Credit £
Accrued expenses		1,050		
Administration expenses	14,039			
Allowance for doubtful debts		1,400		
Allowance for doubtful debts – adjustment				
Bank		1,970		
Discounts allowed	2,100			
Insurance expenses	2,400			
Irrecoverable debts	300			
Prepaid expenses				
Purchases	106,032			
Purchases ledger control account		21,324		
Sales		179,323		
Sales ledger control account	25,840			
Suspense		130		
Travel expenses	8,245			

The ledgers are now ready to be closed off for the year ended 31 August 20X9.

(b) Show the correct journal entries to close off the administration expenses account and select an appropriate narrative.

Journal entries	Debit £	Credit £
▼		
▼		
Narrative:		
Being:		▼

Picklist – journal entries:

Accrued expenses
Administration expenses
Insurance expenses
Prepaid expenses
Profit or loss account
Statement of financial position
Suspense

Picklist – narrative:

Transfer of administration expenses for the year ended 31 August 20X9 to the bank account

Transfer of administration expenses for the year ended 31 August 20X9 to the profit or loss account

Transfer of administration expenses for the year ended 31 August 20X9 to the statement of financial position

Transfer of administration expenses for the year ended 31 August 20X9 to the suspense account

5 Completing the debit and credit columns in a trial balance extract

Instead of entering adjustments in the 'Adjustments' columns of a trial balance, you could be given a trial balance extract and asked to include the correct figures in the debit or credit column, as appropriate.

Approach to preparing a trial balance

This type of task should be approached as follows:

(1) Read the requirement and review the extract from the trial balance.

(2) Transfer any ledger balances already included in the trial balance extract to the debit or credit column, as appropriate.

(3) Work through the ledger accounts transferring the balances brought forward to the debit or credit columns of the trial balance, as appropriate.

(4) Review your answer. Does it make sense?

Note that if it is an extract from the trial balance, you will not be required to total the debit and credit columns.

We will practise this approach in the activity which follows.

Activity 3: Extract from the trial balance

This task is about preparing a trial balance.

You are working on the accounting records of a business with a year end of 31 August.

You have five extracts from the ledger accounts as at 31 August 20X9:

Office costs

		£			£
31.08.X9	Balance b/d	6,321			

Purchases returns

		£			£
			31.08.X9	Balance b/d	775

Recycling rebates

		£			£
			31.08.X9	Balance b/d	11,550

Sales returns

		£			£
31.08.X9	Balance b/d	4,367			

VAT

		£			£
			31.08.X9	Balance b/d	9,440

You need to start preparing the trial balance as at 31 August 20X9.

Required

Using all the information given above and the figures given in the table below, enter amounts into the appropriate trial balance columns for the accounts shown.

Do NOT enter zeros into unused column cells.

Extract from the trial balance as at 31 August 20X9:

Account	Ledger balances £	Trial balance Debit £	Trial balance Credit £
Office costs			
Purchases	30,100		
Purchases returns			
Recycling rebates			
Salaries	13,500		
Sales	58,304		
Sales returns			
VAT			

6 Knowledge test preparation

The *Advanced Bookkeeping* assessment may include short-form, objective-style requirements on any area of the syllabus. If the requirements are based on the trial balance, errors and the suspense account, they could be structured as follows.

Activity 4: Advanced bookkeeping – knowledge

This task is to test your knowledge.

There is an error in the accounting records. The accountant has recorded discounts received by debiting the discounts received account and crediting the purchases ledger control account. Ignore VAT.

Required

(a) What type of error is this? Choose the ONE most suitable description.

	✓
Error of commission	
Reversal of entries	
Error of omission	
One-sided entry	

(b) Indicate whether the following statements are true or false.

	True ✓	False ✓
The suspense account can appear in the financial statements.		
All errors cause an imbalance in the trial balance.		
A trial balance is prepared before the financial statements.		
A trial balance includes the closing balances of the subsidiary sales ledgers.		

Chapter summary

- After the initial trial balance has been prepared, there may be further adjustments to process.

- This may include adjustments relating to accruals, prepayments, closing inventory, depreciation, and irrecoverable and doubtful debts.

- Some adjustments will relate to the correction of errors which allow the trial balance to balance.

- Others will relate to the correction of errors which do not allow the trial balance to balance and therefore require a suspense account to be cleared.

- The correcting journals are posted to an extended trial balance.

- The affected ledger balances are then revised.

- As a final year-end adjustment all income and expense balances must be cleared out to the profit or loss account.

Keywords

- **Balance transfer error:** A balance on a general ledger account is transferred incorrectly into the trial balance

- **Error of commission:** The double entry is arithmetically correct but one of the entries has been made to the wrong account, though an account of the correct type

- **Error of omission:** Both the debit and credit entries have been omitted from the ledger accounts

- **Error of original entry:** Both the debit and credit entries in the ledgers have been made at the wrong amount

- **Error of principle:** The double entry is arithmetically correct but one of the entries has been to the wrong type of account

- **Reversal of entries:** The debit and credit entries have been reversed in the ledger accounts

- **Single entry error:** Only one side of the double entry has been made

- **Suspense account:** An account opened in order to make the balances on a trial balance equal whilst the reason for the imbalance is discovered and corrected

- **Two debits or two credits error:** Instead of a debit and a credit entry, either two debits or two credits have been made

- **Unequal amounts error:** Debit and credit entries have been made for different amounts

1 **Indicate whether the following statements are true or false.**

Statements	True ✓	False ✓
An error of principle will be detected by an imbalance in the trial balance.		
A one-sided entry will be detected by an imbalance in the trial balance.		

2 An electricity expense of £8,500 is posted as a debit to the electricity expense account of £8,400 and a credit to bank of £8,400.

Required

Complete the following sentence.

This is an error of	▼

Picklist:

commission
original entry
principle
reversal

A picklist for questions 3 to 5 can be found below question 5.

3 A purchases returns credit note of £1,100 has been omitted from the accounting records. Ignore VAT.

What is the journal to correct the error?

Journal

Account name		Debit £	Credit £
	▼		
	▼		

4   The journal to record depreciation charges of £4,000 has been reversed.

What is the journal to correct the error?

Journal

Account name		Debit £	Credit £
	▼		
	▼		

5   When the sales day book totals were posted to the general ledger, the sales account was correctly credited with £10,000 and the VAT account was correctly credited with £2,000. The debit entry was omitted.

What is the journal to remove the error?

Journal

Account name		Debit £	Credit £
	▼		
	▼		

Picklist (for questions 3 to 5):

Accumulated depreciation
Depreciation charges
Purchases ledger control account
Purchases returns
Sales ledger control account
Suspense

6   **Show how each of the following account balances will appear in an initial trail balance. Draw a line from the account balance to 'Credit' or 'Debit', as appropriate.**

Account balance   **Trial balance**

| Accumulated depreciation |

| Discounts allowed | | Credit |

| Interest paid | | Debit |

| Prepaid income |

The extended trial balance

12

Learning outcomes

5.3	Complete the extended trial balance
	• Extend figures in the ledger balances and adjustments columns correctly into the statement of profit or loss and statement of financial position columns
	• Make the extended columns balance
	• Correctly label the balancing figure line as profit or loss

Assessment context

Questions are likely to provide you with an extended trial balance that includes the closing balances from the general ledger accounts and various adjustments. You then need to add across each row and include the relevant figures in the statement of profit or loss or statement of financial position columns.

You are also likely to need to show the profit or loss for the year and to include this as a balancing figure in one of the statement of financial position columns.

Qualification context

This topic is only tested in the *Advanced Bookkeeping* assessment. However, it is a useful extension of the knowledge you acquired on the preparation of a trial balance in the Level 2 accounting units and provides a strong foundation for the Level 3 unit, *Final Accounts Preparation*.

Business context

For businesses using a manual accounting system, the extended trial balance allows them to see all the journal adjustments they have posted after the initial trial balance has been extracted. These adjustments can then be added to or deducted from the original trial balance amounts to provide the final figures which will then be shown in the statement of profit or loss and statement of financial position.

Nowadays, however, most businesses keep their accounting records on a computerised system. It is important to note that the computer still uses the same techniques, although it may be that the only output reviewed by the owners is the final statement of profit or loss and statement of financial position.

Chapter overview

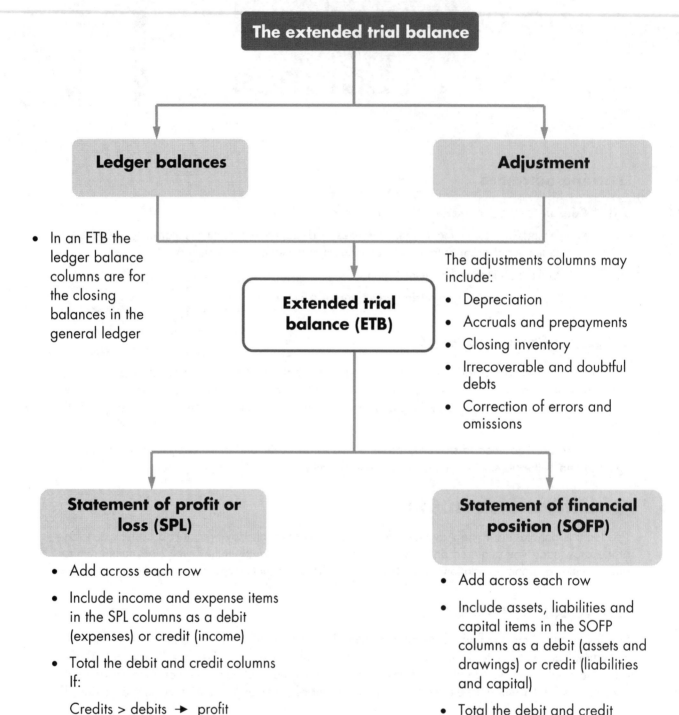

The extended trial balance

Ledger balances

Adjustment

- In an ETB the ledger balance columns are for the closing balances in the general ledger

Extended trial balance (ETB)

The adjustments columns may include:
- Depreciation
- Accruals and prepayments
- Closing inventory
- Irrecoverable and doubtful debts
- Correction of errors and omissions

Statement of profit or loss (SPL)

- Add across each row
- Include income and expense items in the SPL columns as a debit (expenses) or credit (income)
- Total the debit and credit columns If:

  Credits > debits ➔ profit
  Debits > credits ➔ loss

Statement of financial position (SOFP)

- Add across each row
- Include assets, liabilities and capital items in the SOFP columns as a debit (assets and drawings) or credit (liabilities and capital)
- Total the debit and credit columns
- Include the profit or the loss for the year to complete the double entry and balance the columns

Introduction

An initial trial balance contains a list of the closing balances extracted from the general ledger at the period end. This forms the starting point for an extended trial balance. However, an extended trial balance also has debit and credit columns for:

- Adjustments (ie non-routine journals)
- Statement of profit or loss balances
- Statement of financial position balances

An extended trial balance is a very useful way of enabling a business to keep track of any post trial balance adjustments. Therefore, the preparation of an extended trial balance is an important final step which occurs before the accounts are drafted.

In *Advanced Bookkeeping* you will be required to complete the statement of profit or loss columns and statement of financial position columns of an extended trial balance. This includes calculating the profit or loss for the year and totalling the columns.

1 Approach to preparing an extended trial balance

This type of task should be approached as follows:

(1) Read the requirement and review the proforma **extended trial balance**.

(2) Work down the ledger accounts line by line. Identify whether they relate to the statement of profit or loss or statement of financial position and insert the ledger account balances into the appropriate boxes.

(3) Include the adjustments where relevant. Think carefully whether they increase or decrease the final balance in the statement of profit or loss or statement of financial position.

(4) Once you have completed step (3) add up the totals of the debit and credit columns in the statement of profit or loss columns.

These two columns should not balance and the difference will be the profit or loss for the period.

(5) Insert the profit or loss on the debit or credit side of the statement of profit or loss, as appropriate:

Statement of profit or loss columns	During the period:	Post to:
Total of the credit column is higher than the total of the debit column	Profit	Debit side statement of profit or loss
Total of the debit column is higher than the total of the credit column	Loss	Credit side statement of profit or loss

The statement of profit or loss columns will now balance.

(6) This is a double entry and so you need to insert a corresponding debit or credit balance into the statement of financial position.

(7) Once you have transferred the profit or loss to the statement of financial position, total both of the statement of financial position columns. **These should balance.**

The next activity provides practice in these steps. It is a preparation activity designed to familiarise you with the process of:

(a) Identifying whether the ledger balances should be included on the statement of profit or loss or statement of financial position

(b) Adding across (and correctly deciding whether the adjustments increase or decrease the opening ledger balance)

(c) Completing the double entry with the profit or loss for the year

In addition, the activity requires you to calculate and record the adjustment journals in the extended trial balance. This is **not** something you will be asked to do in the *Advanced Bookkeeping* assessment. However, it is useful in illustrating how the extended trial balance is prepared.

Activity 1: Adjustments and the extended trial balance

An extended trial balance has been drawn up and a suspense account opened with a debit balance of £900. You now need to make some corrections and adjustments for the year ended 31 December 20X9.

(1) The annual depreciation of plant has yet to be accounted for. Plant is depreciated at the rate of 10% using the straight-line method.

(2) Inventories were valued at £1,500 on 31 December 20X9.

(3) Wages of £900 were not entered into the wages expense account. The other side of the double entry was correctly made.

(4) A rates payment of £250 has been charged to the rent expense account.

Required

(a) Record the journals which need to be entered into the adjustments column in the extended trial balance.

(1) Plant depreciation

Account name		Debit £	Credit £
	▼		
	▼		

(2) Closing inventory

Account name		Debit £	Credit £
	▼		
	▼		

(3) Wages

Account name		Debit £	Credit £
	▼		
	▼		

(4) Rates

Account name		Debit £	Credit £
	▼		
	▼		

Picklist:

Closing inventory (SOFP)
Closing inventory (SPL)
Depreciation charges
Plant accumulated depreciation
Rates
Rent
Suspense
Wages expense

(b) **Enter the journals you have recorded in part (a) into the adjustments column.**

Then, extend the figures into the statement of profit or loss and statement of financial position columns.

Do NOT enter zeros into unused column cells.

Complete the extended trial balance by entering figures and a label in the correct places.

Picklist (for penultimate row, first column only):

Gross profit/loss for the year
Profit/loss for the year
Suspense

Extended trial balance

Ledger account	Ledger balances		Adjustments		Statement of profit or loss		Statement of financial position	
	Dr £	Cr £	Dr £	Cr £	Dr £	Cr £	Dr £	Cr £
Bank		7,435						
Plant at cost	20,000							
Closing inventory								
Depreciation charges								
Opening inventory	800							
Purchases	20,301							
Purchases ledger control		5,755						
Plant accumulated depreciation								
Rates	1,600							
Rent	2,866							
Sales		49,126						
Sales ledger control	8,325							
Suspense	900							
Wages expense	7,524							
▼								
TOTAL	62,316	62,316						

2 Balances to watch out for

You will be familiar with most ledger account balances you see on the extended trial balance.

For example, you know that sales is always on the credit side of the statement of profit or loss column. Machinery is always on the debit side of the extended trial balance in the statement of financial position column.

Other balances require more detailed consideration.

Remember that the opening position of each balance (ie whether it is in the debit or credit column) gives important information about the type of balance it is.

Balance	Considerations
Accumulated depreciation	The accumulated depreciation is on the credit side of the SOFP column.
Allowance for doubtful debts	The allowance for doubtful debts is on the credit side of the SOFP column.
Allowance for doubtful debts – adjustment	If the doubtful debt allowance has increased since the prior period, the adjustment is a debit balance in the SPL column, being an increase in expenses. If the doubtful debt allowance has decreased since the prior period, the adjustment is a credit balance in the SPL column, being a decrease in expenses.
Bank	A debit balance indicates the business has an asset (ie a positive cash balance). It is included in the debit column of the SOFP.
Bank overdraft or loan	A credit balance indicates this is a liability (ie an overdraft). It is included in the credit column of the SOFP.
Depreciation charges	This is an expense to the statement of profit or loss and therefore a debit balance.
Disposal of non-current assets	If the proceeds are lower than the carrying amount on disposal, this will be included in the debit column of the SPL (being a loss on disposal). If the proceeds exceed the carrying amount on disposal, this will be included in the credit column of the SPL (being a gain on disposal).
Drawings	This is a reduction in the owners' capital and is included in the debit column of the SOFP.

Balance	Considerations
Irrecoverable debts	This is an expense to the statement of profit or loss and therefore a debit balance.
Purchases returns	This will be on the credit side of the statement of profit or loss column (a reduction in expenses).
Sales returns	This will be on the debit side of the statement of profit or loss column (a reduction in income).
VAT	A **credit** balance indicates VAT is due **to** HMRC and is included in the SOFP credit column. A **debit** balance indicates VAT is due **from** HMRC and is included in the SOFP debit column.
Suspense	This will be cleared in the adjustment columns and therefore does not appear in the SPL or SOFP columns.

2.1 Inventories in the extended trial balance

It is likely that the preliminary extended trial balance will include **opening inventory**. The phrase 'opening inventory' just means it was held by the business at the start of the accounting period.

It is also probable that the adjustments columns will include **closing inventory**.

We need to ensure inventory (and purchases) are recorded correctly in the statement of profit or loss and statement of financial position columns.

Remember:

Cost of goods sold = Opening inventory + Purchases – Closing inventory

Opening inventory will be an expense this year as it will be used up by the business as part of cost of goods sold. Therefore, this balance is included as a debit entry to the statement of profit or loss.

From Chapter 7 *Inventories*, we know that closing inventory is accounted for via the following journal entry:

Account name	Debit £	Credit £
Closing inventory (SOFP)	X	
Closing inventory (SPL)		X

Assessment focus point

In an extended trial balance opening inventory, purchases and closing inventory may be shown on separate rows.

Alternatively, cost of goods sold (SPL) may be shown on one row and then closing inventory on a separate row.

Although the presentation can vary, the principles are the same.

Illustration 1: Closing inventory in the extended trial balance

Scenario (a) RB Trading

In the extended trial balance RB Trading shows cost of goods sold on three separate rows.

It has opening inventory of £3,000, purchases of £11,000 and then closing inventory of £2,000.

How is this shown on the extended trial balance?

Ledger account	Ledger balances		Adjustments		SPL		SOFP	
	Debit £	Credit £	Debit £	Credit £	Debit £	Credit £	Debit £	Credit £
Opening inventory	3,000				3,000			
Purchases	11,000				11,000			
Closing inventory (SOFP)			2,000	2,000		2,000	2,000	

Scenario (b) PT Trading

In the extended trial balance PT Trading has one row for cost of goods (SPL) and a separate row for closing inventory.

It has cost of goods sold (SPL) of £14,000 and then closing inventory of £2,000.

How is this shown on the extended trial balance?

Ledger account	Ledger balances		Adjustments		SPL		SOFP	
	Debit £	Credit £	Debit £	Credit £	Debit £	Credit £	Debit £	Credit £
Cost of goods sold (SPL)	14,000			2,000	12,000			
Closing inventory (SOFP)			2,000				2,000	

Activity 2: Completing the extended trial balance

This task is about the extended trial balance.

You have the following extended trial balance. The adjustments have already been correctly entered.

Required

Extend the figures into the statement of profit or loss and statement of financial position columns.

Do NOT enter zeros into unused column cells.

Complete the extended trial balance by entering figures and a label in the correct places.

Picklist: (for penultimate row, first column only)

Gross profit/loss for the year
Profit/loss for the year
Suspense

Extended trial balance

Ledger account	Ledger balances		Adjustments		Statement of profit or loss		Statement of financial position	
	Dr £	Cr £	Dr £	Cr £	Dr £	Cr £	Dr £	Cr £
Allowance for doubtful debts		4,243	400					
Allowance for doubtful debts – adjustments				400				
Bank	80,213			2,600				
Capital		80,000						
Closing inventory			36,000	36,000				
Depreciation charges			20,000					
Office expenses	50,000			1,000				
Opening inventory	31,000							
Payroll expenses	30,632			250				
Purchases	210,422		750					
Purchases ledger control account		43,221						
Sales		433,764						
Sales ledger control account	50,323							
Selling expenses	5,068							
Suspense		3,100	3,850	750				
VAT		18,330						
Vehicles at cost	155,000							
Vehicles accumulated depreciation		30,000		20,000				
▼								
TOTAL	612,658	612,658	61,000	61,000				

3 Final steps

3.1 The profit or loss account in the general ledger

At the end of the period any balances on the income and expenditure general ledger (or 'T') accounts are closed off and transferred to the profit or loss account in the general ledger.

This leaves a nil balance on those ledger accounts ready for the next period.

3.2 Completing the statement of financial position

The statement of financial position:

(a)   Lists all ledger accounts with balances remaining (ie all assets and liabilities)
(b)   Is **not** part of a double entry system so these balances are not transferred out

3.3 Completing the capital account

At the end of the period the profit or loss general ledger account is cleared out with the balance being transferred to the capital account. The double entry is as follows.

If the business makes a profit for the year:

Account name	Debit £	Credit £
Profit or loss account	X	
Capital		X

If the business makes a loss for the year:

Account name	Debit £	Credit £
Capital	X	
Profit or loss account		X

The overall effect is to leave the profit or loss account with no balance at the start of the following period and to adjust the capital account to reflect the increase or decrease in the amount owed to the owner by the business as a result of any profit or loss made during the period.

The amount owed to the owner by the business is also affected by drawings, which represent amounts that the owner has effectively received. Therefore, the balance on the drawings account will also be transferred to the capital account using the double entry:

Account name	Debit £	Credit £
Capital	X	
Drawings		X

The final balance carried down on the capital account after all adjustments have been made will show the net asset value of the business.

4 Knowledge test preparation

The *Advanced Bookkeeping* assessment may include short-form, objective-style requirements on any area of the syllabus. If the requirements are based on the extended trial balance, they could be structured as in the following activity.

Activity 3: Advanced bookkeeping – knowledge

This task is to test your knowledge.

(a) Which of the following best describes the purpose of an extended trial balance? Select ONE option.

	✓
It ensures the accuracy of the sales and purchases ledger accounts.	
The extended trial balance can form the basis for the preparation of the financial statements.	
It is used in place of the financial statements.	
It ensures that all transactions are recorded in the financial statements.	

(b) **Indicate whether the following statements are true or false.**

	True ✓	False ✓
A bank overdraft will be shown on the debit side of the extended trial balance, in the statement of financial position column.		
The irrecoverable debt expense will be shown in one of the statement of profit or loss columns in the extended trial balance.		
Drawings will be shown in one of the statement of financial position columns in the extended trial balance.		
VAT will be excluded from the extended trial balance.		

Chapter summary

- An extended trial balance contains four debit and four credit columns. These columns are for:
  - Ledger balances (from the closing balances on the general ledger)
  - Adjustments (ie non-routine journals)
  - Statement of profit or loss balances
  - Statement of financial position balances

- Once the ledger balances and adjustments are included in the extended trial balance, each row is totalled and extended into either the statement of profit or loss columns or the statement of financial position columns as a debit or a credit item.

- In the statement of profit or loss there are income and expenses items.

- In the statement of financial position there are entries for assets, liabilities, capital and drawings.

- The statement of profit or loss columns are then totalled and the balancing figure is inserted as a new account line: 'profit/loss for the year'.

- The profit or loss for the year is also inserted in the statement of financial position columns – a debit in the statement of profit or loss column is a credit in the statement of financial position column and vice versa.

- The final stage is to total the statement of financial position columns.

- All pairs of debit/credit column totals should now agree.

Keyword

- **Extended trial balance:** An accounting technique of moving from the initial trial balance, through the year-end adjustments, to the figures for the final accounts

Test your learning

1 Having entered the figures into the statement of profit or loss columns, the debit and credit columns then need to be totalled.

Required

Answer the following questions.

Questions	Solution
In the statement of profit or loss columns, if the total of the debit column is higher than the total of the credit column, has a profit or a loss arisen during the period?	▼
In the statement of profit or loss columns, if the total of the credit column is higher than the total of the debit column, has a profit or loss arisen during the period?	▼

Picklist:

Loss
Profit

2 **In the extended trial balance will the following items be included in the debit or the credit column of the statement of financial position columns?**

Ledger account	Statement of financial position – Debit or Credit column
Bank overdraft	▼
Allowance for doubtful debts	▼
VAT – due from HMRC	▼
Loan to employee	▼
Accumulated depreciation	▼
VAT – owed to HMRC	▼

Picklist:

Debit
Credit

3   **What entries if any are made in the adjustments column for the closing inventory? Choose ONE.**

	✓
Both a debit and a credit	
A debit	
A credit	
No entry	

4   **Complete the following sentence.**

The closing inventory figure is a [▼] entry in the statement of profit or loss columns and a [▼] entry in the statement of financial position columns of the extended trial balance.

Picklist:

debit
credit

5   **In the extended trial balance will the following items be included in the debit or the credit column of the statement of profit or loss columns?**

Ledger account	Statement of profit or loss – Debit or Credit column
Allowance for doubtful debts – adjustment: increase in the allowance	▼
Sales returns	▼
Purchases returns	▼
Depreciation charges	▼
Allowance for doubtful debts – adjustment: decrease in the allowance	▼

Picklist:

Debit
Credit

Activity answers

CHAPTER 1 Bookkeeping transactions

Activity 1: Double entry bookkeeping

GENERAL LEDGER

Bank

	£		£
Capital (1)	30,000	Purchases (2)	800
Sales (4)	400	Rent (3)	500
		Rates (5)	150

Capital

	£		£
		Bank (1)	30,000

Purchases

	£		£
Bank (2)	800		
Purchases ledger control account (7)	450		

Rent

	£		£
Bank (3)	500		

Sales

	£		£
		Bank (4)	400
		Sales ledger control account (6)	1,150

Rates

	£		£
Bank (5)	150		

Sales ledger control account

	£		£
Sales (6)	**1,150**		

Purchases ledger control account

	£		£
		Purchases (7)	450

Activity 2: Balancing off ledger accounts

GENERAL LEDGER

Bank (SOFP)

	£		£
Capital (1)	30,000	Purchases (2)	800
Sales (4)	400	Rent (3)	500
		Rates (5)	150
		Balance c/d	28,950
	30,400		30,400
Balance b/d	28,950		

Capital (SOFP)

	£		£
Balance c/d	30,000	Bank (1)	30,000
	30,000		30,000
		Balance b/d	30,000

Purchases (SPL)

	£		£
Bank (2)	800	Profit or loss account	1,250
Purchases ledger control account (7)	450		
	1,250		1,250

Rent (SPL)

	£		£
Bank (3)	500	Profit or loss account	500
	500		500

Sales (SPL)

	£		£
Profit or loss account	1,550	Bank (4)	400
		Sales ledger control account (6)	1,150
	1,550		1,550

Rates (SPL)

	£		£
Bank (5)	150	Profit or loss account	150
	150		150

Sales ledger control account (SOFP)

	£		£
Sales (6)	1,150	Balance c/d	1,150
	1,150		1,150
Balance b/d	1,150		

Purchases ledger control account (SOFP)

	£		£
Balance c/d	450	Purchases (7)	450
	450		450
		Balance b/d	450

Activity 3: Advanced bookkeeping – knowledge

(a)

	✓
Statement of profit or loss	
Purchases day book	
Trial balance	
Purchases ledger control account	✓

(b)

	✓
The amount of cash injected by the owner of the business	
The ongoing expenses of the business	
Amounts due from other parties	
Amounts owed to other parties	✓

CHAPTER 2 Accounting principles

Activity 1: Classifying items

	Asset, liability, capital, income or expense	SOFP or SPL
Trade receivables (sales ledger control account)	Asset	SOFP
Capital	Capital	SOFP
Sales	Income	SPL
Bank overdraft	Liability	SOFP
Wages expense	Expense	SPL
Intangible assets	Asset	SOFP
Cost of sales	Expense	SPL

Activity 2: Accounting equation

(a)

	True ✓	False ✓
Capital = assets plus liabilities		✓
Assets plus capital = liabilities		✓
Capital plus liabilities = assets	✓	

(b)

Question	Answer £
If liabilities total £39,000 and capital totals £51,000, what is the amount of assets? **Explanation** Assets = Liabilities + Capital Assets = £39,000 + £51,000 = £90,000	90,000
If assets total £86,000 and liabilities total £44,000, what is the amount of capital? **Explanation** Assets – Liabilities = Capital £86,000 – £44,000 = £42,000	42,000
If capital totals £74,000 and assets total £162,000, what is the amount of liabilities? **Explanation** Liabilities = Assets – Capital Liabilities = £162,000 – £74,000 = £88,000	88,000

(c)

	Increase ✓	Decrease ✓	No change ✓
Assets		✓	
Liabilities			✓
Capital		✓	

Explanation

When an owner withdraws the business's cash for personal use, this is known as 'drawings'. The double entry to record cash drawings is:

DEBIT   Drawings

CREDIT   Bank

Capital is calculated as: Opening capital + Profit – Drawings. Therefore, the above entry will cause capital to decrease. Bank is an asset account so crediting it will cause assets to decrease. No liability account is affected by the above accounting entry.

Activity 3: Policies and procedures

(a)

	✓
Physical controls	
Segregation of duties	✓
Authorisation of transactions	
Written record of procedures	

Explanation

This is a medium-sized organisation with six members of staff in the accounts department. Segregation of duties would improve security over the sales ledger. For example, one member of staff could raise sales invoices, and another raise sales returns credit notes and record money received from customers in the accounting records.

(b)

	✓
To learn about changes in accounting standards as part of your continuing professional development	
To allow you to access the records required for your day-to-day work	
To remove the possibility of any numerical errors arising	
To assist in the understanding of both individual responsibilities and team responsibilities	✓

Explanation

In this activity, you need to identify the most appropriate option on the balance of the information provided.

AAT members are required to keep their technical knowledge up to date as part of their continuing professional development and the requirement to do this might well be included in an accounting firm's procedures. However, this alone does not cover the full purpose of the procedures. Nor will the actual changes in accounting standards be covered in the organisational procedures – employees will be expected to attend separate internal or external training on such matters.

Whilst the organisational policies may include guidance on how to access records necessary for your day-to-day work, they will also cover many other areas. Furthermore, you should automatically be able to access records required to do your job without needing authorisation from the organisational procedures.

Whilst organisational policies and procedures are likely to try and minimise numerical errors, it is not possible to entirely eliminate the chance of numerical errors arising.

The overall aim of the organisational policies and procedures should be to help enable both individual and team responsibilities to be understood.

Activity 4: Fundamental principles

Scenarios	Fundamental principle
All accounting estimates (such as depreciation charges) are reviewed independently by two members of staff, to ensure they are fair.	Objectivity
Employees are not permitted to make negative references to competitors when trying to win new business.	Professional behaviour
The new trainee accounting technician receives training from an experienced supervisor before beginning work.	Professional competence and due care
A client has overpaid. The managing partner contacts the client to notify him of this and issue a refund.	Integrity
No client details may be disclosed outside the firm without specific consent from that client.	Confidentiality

Activity 5: Ethical behaviour

Reason for considering the sale	Acceptable reason ✓	Unacceptable reason ✓
The proprietor needs to increase the profit for the year ended 30 June 20X2 to encourage the bank to extend the business's overdraft limit		✓
The transaction is an expense relevant to the year ended 30 June 20X2		✓
The figure is a current asset at 30 June 20X2	✓	

Explanation

As AAT accountants, we must act under the principle of integrity and be aware of threats arising from situations such as pressure from the client to achieve a certain result (including reaching a certain profit level in order to extend an overdraft). We must also show professional competence and prepare accounts which meet accounting standards. Therefore, accounting for an item in a certain way just to please the client is not acceptable.

The second reason listed is not acceptable either because the transaction is income relating to the year ended 30 June 20X2.

The third reason is acceptable. By the 30 June 20X2 year end, the goods have been despatched and an invoice raised. Therefore, a credit sale has taken place resulting in the recognition of a trade receivable. At the year end, the customer has not yet paid for the goods so the trade receivable still exists. Trade receivables are classified as current assets in the accounts.

Activity 6: Professional behaviour

	✓
A client's sales manager wishes you to record in the current accounting period credit sales made in the last month of the year. The bank statement shows that cash was not received from customers until the second month of the next year.	✓
A client wants you to reduce the profit figure in order to pay less tax. She asked you to put back the date of a large sales invoice into the next accounting period.	
Your firm needs to meet its deadline for preparing the accounts. Your supervisor tells you to save time by writing off the same amount for irrecoverable debts as the prior year.	
A client has a VAT-registered business. At the year end there is a credit balance on the business's VAT control account. The client asks you to record the balance as income in the statement of profit or loss.	

Explanation

Accounts should be prepared on an accruals basis (when the transactions occur) rather than a cash basis. Therefore, it would be correct to record credit sales made in the final month of the year in the current accounting period (ie in the period in which the sales took place).

However, to change the date on an invoice so that it is recorded in the subsequent accounting period in order to pay less tax is not acceptable. The original date of the sales invoice should be retained and the sale recorded in the current accounting period.

To write off the same amount of irrecoverable debts as the prior year in order to save time is not acceptable. The current year-end portfolio of trade receivables must be reviewed for recoverability.

A VAT-registered business charges VAT on its sales (output VAT) and collects this tax on behalf of HMRC. It can also recover VAT paid on purchases and expenses (input VAT) from HMRC. The amounts are then netted off and settled net with HMRC. As the VAT control account has a credit balance, output tax exceeds input tax and the business owes money to HMRC. Therefore, the balance should be recorded as a liability in the statement of financial position not income in the statement of profit or loss.

CHAPTER 3 Purchase of non-current assets

Activity 1: Examples of non-current assets

Examples include:

- Land and buildings
- Plant and equipment
- Motor vehicles
- Furniture and fittings
- Computers

Activity 2: Cost of the asset

£	20,700

Explanation

The cost capitalised should include the purchase price (£20,000) plus all directly attributable costs (delivery £200 and installation £500).

Note that although delivery costs are less than the capitalisation threshold of £300, they are still capitalised as they make up part of the cost of the machine, which at £20,000 is greater than the capitalisation threshold.

The cost of the maintenance contract (£800) should be shown as an expense in the statement of profit or loss.

Activity 3: Capital versus revenue expenditure

	Capital expenditure ✓	Revenue expenditure ✓
Cost of the plot	✓	
Surveyor's fees	✓	
Legal fees for drawing up the purchase contract	✓	
Cost of researching alternative buildings to purchase		✓

Explanation

IAS 16 only allows capitalisation of the asset's purchase price and any costs directly attributable to bringing the asset to the location and condition necessary for it to be capable of operating in the manner intended by management. Costs of researching alternative buildings are not costs that relate directly to the purchase of this specific asset and therefore may not be capitalised. However, the cost of the plot is the purchase price and should be capitalised. The surveyor's fees and legal fees are both directly attributable and therefore should also be capitalised.

Activity 4: Recording a machine in the general ledger

Account name	Debit £	Credit £
Machine at cost	12,000	
Bank		12,000

Activity 5: Recording a motor vehicle in the general ledger

Account name	Debit £	Credit £
Bank	18,500	
Loan		18,500

Account name	Debit £	Credit £
Motor vehicle at cost	18,500	
Bank		18,500

Activity 6: VAT and purchase of non-current

Account name	Debit £	Credit £
Computer at cost	1,000	
VAT control account	200	
Bank		1,200

Explanation

As the business is VAT registered, it can recover the VAT on the purchase cost of the asset from HMRC. The VAT is calculated as 20% × £1,000 purchase price = £200. The amount paid from the business bank account will be gross of VAT ie £1,200 (£1,000 + £200).

CHAPTER 4 Depreciation of non-current assets

Activity 1: Straight-line depreciation – machine

(a)

£	750

Workings:

Straight-line method:

$$\text{Depreciation charge} = \frac{£2,500 - £250}{3 \text{ years}}$$

$$= £750 \text{ per annum}$$

(b)

Year	Cost £	Accumulated depreciation £	Carrying amount £
1	2,500	750	1,750
2	2,500	1,500	1,000
3	2,500	2,250	250

Activity 2: Straight-line depreciation – building

(a)

£	2,000

Workings:

£100,000 × 2%

(b)

£	14,000

Workings:

£12,000 + £2,000

Activity 3: Diminishing balance depreciation – machine

Year	Carrying amount b/d £	Depreciation rate	Depreciation charge £	Accumulated depreciation £	Carrying amount c/d £
1	6,000	40%	2,400	2,400	3,600
2	3,600	40%	1,440	3,840	2,160
3	2,160	40%	864	4,704	1,296

Activity 4: Diminishing balance depreciation – vehicle

(a)

£	5,145

Workings:

(£50,000 – £32,850) × 30%

(b)

£	37,995

Workings:

£32,850 + £5,145

Activity 5: Units of production depreciation – machine

Year	Number of units produced	Carrying amount b/d £	Depreciation charge £	Accumulated depreciation £	Carrying amount c/d £
1	10,000	40,000	4,000	4,000	36,000
2	24,000	36,000	9,600	13,600	26,400
3	30,000	26,400	12,000	25,600	14,400

Workings:

Year	Workings	Depreciation charge
1	10,000 / 100,000 × 40,000	4,000
2	24,000 / 100,000 × 40,000	9,600
3	30,000 / 100,000 × 40,000	12,000

Activity 6: Assets acquired part way through the year

(a)

Accumulated depreciation	Carrying amount
£ 600	£ 7,400

Workings:

Depreciation for year = £8,000 × 10% × $^9/_{12}$ = £600
Carrying amount = £8,000 – £600 = £7,400

(b)

Accumulated depreciation	Carrying amount
£ 1,400	£ 6,600

Workings:

Depreciation for year = £8,000 × 10% = £800
Accumulated depreciation = £600 + £800 = £1,400
Carrying amount = £8,000 – £1,400 = £6,600

Activity 7: Depreciation in the financial statements

(a)

Account name	Debit £	Credit £
Depreciation charges	750	
Machine accumulated depreciation		750

(b)

Machine at cost (SOFP)

	£		£
Bank	2,500	Balance c/d	2,500
	2,500		2,500
Balance b/d	2,500		

Bank (SOFP)

	£		£
		Machine at cost	2,500

Depreciation charges (SPL)

	£		£
Machine accumulated depreciation (Year 1)	750	Profit or loss account (Year 1)	750
Machine accumulated depreciation (Year 2)	750	Profit or loss account (Year 2)	750
Machine accumulated depreciation (Year 3)	750	Profit or loss account (Year 3)	750

Machine accumulated depreciation (SOFP)

	£		£
Balance c/d	750	Depreciation charges (Year 1)	750
Balance c/d	1,500	Balance b/d	750
		Depreciation charges (Year 2)	750
	1,500		1,500
Balance c/d	2,250	Balance b/d	1,500
		Depreciation charges (Year 3)	750
	2,250		2,250
		Balance b/d	2,250

(c) **Statement of profit or loss (extracts)**

	Year 1 £	Year 2 £	Year 3 £
Expenses			
Depreciation charges	750	750	750

Statement of financial position (extracts)

Machine	Cost £	Accumulated depreciation £	Carrying amount £
Year 1	2,500	(750)	1,750
Year 2	2,500	(1,500)	1,000
Year 3	2,500	(2,250)	250

Activity 8: Ledger accounting for non-current assets

(a)

£	6,000

Workings:

(£28,000 – £4,000)/4 years = £6,000

(b) and (c)

Vehicles at cost

	£		£
Balance b/d	36,000	Balance c/d	64,000
Bank	28,000		
	64,000		64,000

Depreciation charges

	£		£
Balance b/d	9,000	Profit or loss account	15,000
Vehicles accumulated depreciation	6,000		
	15,000		15,000

Vehicles accumulated depreciation

	£		£
Balance c/d	24,000	Balance b/d	18,000
		Depreciation charges	6,000
	24,000		24,000

CHAPTER 5 Disposal of non-current assets

Activity 1: Disposal of a machine for cash

(a)

	Gain	Loss
£ 840	✓	

Workings:

Gain or loss on disposal working	£
Proceeds	3,000
Less carrying amount at end of year 2*	(2,160)
Gain on disposal	840
Carrying amount at date of disposal:	
Cost	6,000
Less depreciation year 1 (6,000 × 40%)	(2,400)
Carrying amount at end of year 1	3,600
Less depreciation year 2 (3,600 × 40%)	(1,440)
Carrying amount at end of year 2	2,160*

(b)

Machine at cost (SOFP)

	£		£
Balance b/d	6,000	Disposals (1)	6,000

Machine accumulated depreciation (SOFP)

	£		£
Disposals (2)	3,840	Balance b/d	3,840

Disposals (SPL)

	£		£
Machine at cost (1)	6,000	Machine accumulated depreciation (2)	3,840
Profit or loss account (4)	840	Bank (3)	3,000
	6,840		6,840

Activity 2: Disposal of a machine – part exchange

(a)

		Gain	Loss
£	840	✓	

The gain on disposal is still £840; the only difference is that the proceeds were not received in cash, but in the form of a part exchange allowance.

(b)

£	7,000

Cash paid for the new machine is £7,000 (£10,000 – £3,000).

(c)

Old machine at cost (SOFP)

	£		£
Balance b/d	6,000	Disposals (1)	6,000

Old machine accumulated depreciation (SOFP)

	£		£
Disposals (2)	3,840	Balance b/d	3,840

New machine at cost (SOFP)

	£		£
Disposals (3)	3,000	Balance c/d	10,000
Bank (5)	7,000		
	10,000		10,000

Disposals (SPL)

	£		£
Old machine at cost (1)	6,000	Old machine accumulated depreciation (2)	3,840
Profit or loss account (4)	840	New machine at cost (3)	3,000
	6,840		6,840

Activity 3: Vans – part exchange

(a)

£	10,000

Workings:

Depreciation charge per year:

£16,000 – £1,000 (residual value) = £15,000 depreciable amount

£15,000 over 6 years = £2,500 per year

Van held for 4 years: £2,500 × 4 years = £10,000

(b)

Disposals (SPL)

	£		£
Van at cost	16,000	Van accumulated depreciation	10,000
		Van at cost	5,200
		Profit or loss account	800
	16,000		16,000

Activity 4: Part exchange of a machine

(a)

Disposals

	£		£
Machine at cost	10,600	Machine accumulated depreciation	8,480
		Machine at cost	1,250
		Profit or loss account	870
	10,600		10,600

Workings:

Accumulated depreciation = £10,600 × 20% × 4 years = £8,480

(y/e 31.08.X5, 31.08.X6, 31.08.X7, 31.08.X8)

(b)

Bank

	£		£
Balance b/d	9,000	Machine at cost	8,900
		Balance c/d	100
	9,000		9,000

(c)

£	10,150

Workings:

£8,900 + £1,250 = £10,150

(d)

£	6,090

Workings:

W1: Depreciation: $10{,}150 \times 20\% = 2{,}030$ per annum	
W2:	£
Cost	10,150
Depreciation 31.08.X9	(2,030)
Depreciation 31.08.Y0	(2,030)
Carrying amount	6,090

Activity 5: Non-current assets register

(a)

Item	Yes ✓	No ✓
Motor van (reg. no. AT59 CBA), cost £6,000 and funded through a hire purchase agreement. Purchased on 23.09.X9.	✓	
Optional insurance taken out on the above van for a cost of £350 paid in cash.		✓
A Dell laptop (serial number LT405), cost £2,000 and paid in cash. Purchased on 24.05.X9 from Dell on standard commercial credit terms.	✓	
A second-hand scanner and printer, cost £50, purchased on 19.01.X9, paid for in cash. This item has an expected life of approximately 10 months.		✓
A photocopier (serial number CO132), cost £3,525 and funded through a loan. Purchased on 24.03.X9.	✓	

(b)

Description/ Serial number	Acquisition date	Cost £	Depreciation charges £	Carrying amount £	Funding method	Disposal proceeds £	Disposal date
Motor vehicles							
Van AT59 CBA	23.09.X9	6,000			Hire purchase		
Computers							
Dell laptop LT405	24.05.X9	2,000			Cash		
Office equipment							
Photocopier CO132	24.03.X9	3,525			Loan		

Activity 6: MIL Trading

Description/ Serial number	Acquisition date	Cost £	Depreciation charges £	Carrying amount £	Funding method	Disposal proceeds £	Disposal date
Office equipment							
Laptop computer 081	30.06.X6	600.00			Cash		
Year end 31.08.X6			120.00	480.00			
Year end 31.08.X7			**120.00**	**360.00**			
Printer/ scanner BORMK95B	**28.05.X7**	**1,000.00**			**Loan**		
Year end 31.08.X7			**200.00**	**800.00**			
Motor vehicles							
1.6 litre van HG03 YHG	01.08.X5	8,940.00			Hire purchase		
Year end 31.08.X5			2,235.00	6,705.00			
Year end 31.08.X6			1,676.25	5,028.75			
Year end 31.08.X7			**1,257.19**	**3,771.56**			
1.2 litre car MN06 HNF	01.04.X5	6,000.00			Part exchange		
Year end 31.08.X5			1,500.00	4,500.00			
Year end 31.08.X6			1,125.00	3,375.00			
Year end 31.08.X7			**0.00**	**0.00**		**2,250.00**	**23.07.X7**

Workings:

The amount capitalised on the printer/scanner is the purchase price of £950.00 plus the directly attributable costs of £50.00 for pre-delivery testing, coming to a total of £1,000.00. The £75.00 for ink and toner and the £90.00 for insurance both qualify as revenue expenditure and should be expensed to the statement of profit or loss.

Depreciation on the printer/scanner = £1,000.00 cost × 20% = £200.00 (straight-line)

Depreciation on the van = £5,028.75 carrying amount × 25% = £1,257.19 (diminishing balance)

Depreciation on the car is nil (0.00) because the policy is no depreciation in the year on disposal. The carrying amount is cleared to zero on disposal.

Activity 7: Advanced bookkeeping – knowledge

(a)

	✓
Depreciation shows the wear and tear on an asset.	
The systematic allocation of the depreciable amount of an asset over its useful life.	✓
This accounting treatment helps management establish the replacement cost of the asset.	
It results in the asset being expensed to the statement of profit or loss in the period it is acquired.	

(b)

	True ✓	False ✓
Directly attributable costs cannot be capitalised as part of the cost of a new non-current asset.		✓
The depreciable amount of an asset is its cost less residual balance.	✓	
When a non-current asset is disposed of, if the sale proceeds exceed the carrying amount there will be a loss on disposal.		✓
Depreciation is an example of the accruals concept.	✓	

Activity 1: Accrued expenses

(a)

£	521

Workings:

		£
Cash paid:	10.03.X7	96
	12.06.X7	120
	14.09.X7	104
	10.12.X7	145
December expense missing ($1/3 \times £168$)		56
		521

(b)

£	56

(c)

Electricity expense (SPL)

	£		£
Bank	96		
Bank	120		
Bank	104		
Bank	145		
Accrued expenses	56	Profit or loss account	521
	521		521

Bank

	£		£
		Electricity expense	96
		Electricity expense	120
		Electricity expense	104
		Electricity expense	145

Accrued expenses (SOFP)

	£		£
Balance c/d	56	Electricity expense	56
	56		56

Activity 2: Accrued expenses – journal

Account name	Debit £	Credit £
Electricity expense	56	
Accrued expenses		56
Being: an adjustment to accrue the electricity expense for the year ended 31 December 20X7		

Activity 3: Reversal of accrued expenses

Electricity expense (SPL)

	£		£
Bank	168	Accrued expenses (reversal)	56
Bank	134		
Bank	118		
Bank	158		
Accrued expenses (⅓ × £189)	63	Profit or loss account	585
	641		641

Accrued expenses (SOFP)

	£		£
Electricity expense	56	Balance b/d	56
Balance c/d	63	Electricity expense (⅓ × £189)	63
	119		119

Activity 4: Prepaid expenses

(a)

£	1,563

Workings:

Rent expense	£
Cash paid: 01.02.X7	375
06.04.X7	1,584
Less expense relating to Jan–Mar X8 ($^3/_{12} \times$ £1,584)	(396)
	1,563

(b)

£	396

(c)

Rent expense (SPL)

	£		£
Bank	375	Prepaid expenses	396
Bank	1,584	Profit or loss account	1,563
	1,959		1,959

Bank (SOFP)

	£		£
		Rent expense	375
		Rent expense	1,584

Prepaid expenses (SOFP)

	£		£
Rent expense	396	Balance c/d	396
	396		396

Activity 5: Prepaid expenses – journal

Account name	Debit £	Credit £
Prepaid expenses	396	
Rent expense		396
Being: an adjustment to record the rent prepayment for the year ended 31 December 20X7		

Activity 6: Reversal of prepaid expenses

Rent expense (SPL)

	£		£
Prepaid expenses (reversal)	396	Prepaid expenses ($^3/_{12} \times$ £1,680)	420
Bank	1,680	Profit or loss account	1,656
	2,076		2,076

Prepaid expenses (SOFP)

	£		£
Balance b/d	396	Rent expense	396
Rent expense ($^3/_{12} \times$ £1,680)	420	Balance c/d	420
	816		816

Activity 7: Accrued income

(a)

£	21,000

This is calculated as the £17,000 received from the client during the year plus the £4,000 owing from the client at the year end.

(b)

£	4,000

This is a current asset representing the amount due from the client at the year end for work completed in the year.

Activity 8: Accrued income – journal

Account name	Debit £	Credit £
Accrued income	4,000	
Commission income		4,000
Being: an adjustment to accrue the commission income for the year ended December 20X1		

Activity 9: Reversal of accrued income

Commission income (SPL)

	£		£
Accrued income (reversal)	4,000	Bank	23,000
Profit or loss account	23,800	Accrued income ($^2/_3$ × £7,200)	4,800
	27,800		27,800

Accrued income (SOFP)

	£		£
Balance b/d	4,000	Commission income	4,000
Commission income ($^2/_3$ × £7,200)	4,800	Balance c/d	4,800
	8,800		8,800

Activity 10: Prepaid income

(a)

£	51,381

Workings:

	£
Cash received	52,965
Prepaid: 01.04.X3–31.12.X3 (9/12 × £1,032)	(774)
Prepaid: 01.04.X3–31.03.X4	(810)
	51,381

(b)

£	1,584

This is the sum of the two items of prepaid income: £774 + £810 = £1,584.

Activity 11: Prepaid income – journal

Account name	Debit £	Credit £
Maintenance services income	1,584	
Prepaid income		1,584
Being: an adjustment to record the prepaid maintenance income as at 31 March 20X3.		

Activity 12: Reversal of prepaid income

The reversal of this prepaid income is dated | 1 July 20X4 |

The reversal is on the | credit | side of the licence fee income account.

Explanation

Prepaid income is a liability account and therefore a credit balance. To reverse it, prepaid income must be debited with a corresponding credit to the licence fee income account. The reversal of the prepayment is always dated as at first day of the accounting period. As the year end is 30 June 20X5, the first day of the accounting period is 1 July 20X4.

Activity 13: Extract from a trial balance – accrued income and expenses

Extract from the trial balance as at 31 July 20X9:

Account	Ledger balances £	Trial balance Dr £	Cr £
Accrued expenses	110		110
Accrued income	489	489	
Office costs	2,637	2,637	
Discounts received	1,535		1,535

Activity 14: Extract from a trial balance – prepaid income and expenses

Extract from the trial balance as at 31 July 20X9:

Account	Ledger balances £	Trial balance Dr £	Cr £
General expenses	8,626	8,626	
Prepaid expenses	2,017	2,017	
Prepaid income	1,111		1,111
Sundry income	36,535		36,535

Activity 15: Accounting for accrued and prepaid income and expenses

(a)

Extract from the trial balance as at 31 March 20X2:

Account	Ledger balances £	Trial balance Dr £	Cr £
Accrued income	2,925	2,925	
Commission income	6,720		6,720
Discounts allowed	4,260	4,260	
Prepaid expenses	2,550	2,550	

(b)

£	–550

Workings:

Of the £660 paid, only one month relates to the current accounting period (March 20X2) and the remaining five months relate to the next accounting period (April, May, June, July, August 20X2). Therefore, a prepayment of $5/6 \times £660 = £550$ is required with the amount being removed from advertising expenses. The double entry will be:

DEBIT   Prepaid expenses (SOFP)   £550
CREDIT Advertising expenses (SPL)   £550

Advertising expenses

	£		£
Prepaid expenses (reversal)	320	Prepaid expenses	550
Bank	9,110	Profit or loss account	8,880
	9,430		9,430

(c)

The reversal of this accrual is dated | 1 April 20X1 |

The reversal is on the | debit | side of the rental income account.

(d)

£	71,575

Workings:

You might find it easiest to calculate rental income for the year by preparing the rental income ledger account:

Rental income

	£		£
Accrued income (reversal)	5,880	Bank	73,865
Profit or loss account	71,575	Accrued income	3,590
	77,455		77,455

(e)

Reason for considering the receipt dated 10 April	Acceptable reason ✓	Not acceptable reason ✓
The proprietor wishes to sell the business and has asked you to maximise profit to obtain the best price		✓
The transaction is income relevant to the year ended 31 March 20X2	✓	
The figure is a current liability at 31 March 20X2		✓

Under the AAT's *Code of Professional Ethics*, as an accountant you have a duty of professional competence and care. This means that the accounts should comply with accounting standards which includes following the accruals concept. As the rental income relates to the year ended 31 March 20X2, it is correct to record it in this period even though the cash has not been received by the year end. However, the other side of the double entry is a current asset in the form of accrued income not a current liability as the amount is owed to the business from the tenant. The *Code of Professional Ethics* warns of several threats to its fundamental principles and one of these is a self-interest threat which exists here because this adjustment will increase profit which could enable the proprietor to achieve a higher price on selling the business. This is not a justifiable reason for an accounting treatment whereas following accounting standards, concepts and principles is.

Activity 16: Advanced bookkeeping – knowledge

(a)

	✓
Accrued expenses (current liability)	
Accrued income (current asset)	
Prepaid expenses (current asset)	✓
Prepaid income (current liability)	

(b)

	True ✓	False ✓
Application of the accruals concept means accounting on a cash basis.		✓
Prepaid income is accounted for on the debit side of the trial balance.		✓
A customer owed £400 rent at the year end. This will be adjusted as a credit to the statement of profit or loss and a debit to the accrued income account, in the SOFP.	✓	

CHAPTER 7 Inventories

Activity 1: Recording inventory in the accounts

(a)

Account name	Debit £	Credit £
Closing inventory (SOFP)	700	
Closing inventory (SPL)		700
Being: the year-end adjustment to record closing inventory		

Workings:

Phones bought	50
Less phones sold	(15)
Phones held at year end	35 × £20 cost = £700

(b)

Statement of profit or loss for the year ended 31 December 20X7

	£
Sales (15 × £30)	450
Cost of goods sold:	
Purchases (50 × £20)	1,000
Less closing inventory	(700)
	(300)
Gross profit	150

Statement of financial position as at 31 December 20X7

Non-current assets	Cost £	Depreciation £	Carrying amount £
Property, plant and equipment	1,900	400	1,500
Current assets			
Inventory		700	
Receivables		200	
Bank		100	
Total current assets			1,000
Total assets			2,500

Activity 2: Determining the cost of inventory

	✓
Storage costs of finished goods	✓
Cost of conversion including direct labour	
Selling costs	✓
Cost of purchase, including delivery	

Activity 3: Net realisable value

(a)

£	22

(b)

£	20

Workings:

Net realisable value is:

	£
Estimated selling price	35
Less costs of completion	(12)
Less selling costs	(1)
	22

Inventory will be valued at cost of purchase (£20) being lower than NRV (£22).

Activity 4: Calculating closing inventory

Account name	Debit £	Credit £
Closing inventory (SOFP)	14,400	
Closing inventory (SPL)		14,400
Being: the year-end adjustment to record closing inventory		

Workings:

Inventory costing £1,800 can only be sold for £1,500 and so the total closing inventory figure needs to be written down by £300.

	£
Original cost	14,700
Less write down	(300)
Lower of cost and NRV	14,400

Activity 5: Advanced bookkeeping – knowledge

(a)

	✓
The first in, first out method of inventory valuation is the only method acceptable under accounting standards.	
Advertising costs may be included in the cost of inventory.	
Inventory costs may include direct labour relating to the production of goods for sale.	✓
Inventory is always valued at cost.	

(b)

	✓
First in, first out	
Lower of cost and net realisable value	
Average cost	
Last in, first out	✓

Activity 1: SND Trading (part I)

(a)

Sales ledger control account (SOFP)

	£		£
Balance b/d	105,000	Irrecoverable debts	37,000
		Balance c/d	68,000
	105,000		105,000
Balance b/d	68,000		

Irrecoverable debts (SPL)

	£		£
Sales ledger control account	37,000	Profit or loss account	37,000
	37,000		37,000

(b) Trial balance (extract)

Ledger account	Ledger balance	
	Dr £	Cr £
Sales ledger control account	68,000	
Irrecoverable debts	37,000	

Activity 2: GEN Trading (part I)

(a)

Account name	Debit £	Credit £
Irrecoverable debts	8,000	
Sales ledger control account		8,000

(b)

£	42,000

Workings:

£50,000 – £8,000

Activity 3: GEN Trading (part II)

Account name	Debit £	Credit £
Bank	8,000	
Irrecoverable debts		8,000

Activity 4: SND Trading (part II)

(a)

Allowance for doubtful debts (SOFP)

	£		£
Balance c/d	18,000	Allowance for doubtful debts – adjustments	18,000
	18,000		18,000
		Balance b/d	18,000

Allowance for doubtful debts – adjustments (SPL)

	£		£
Allowance for doubtful debts	18,000	Profit or loss account	18,000
	18,000		18,000

(b) Trial balance (extract)

Ledger account	Ledger balance	
	Dr £	Cr £
Allowance for doubtful debts		18,000
Allowance for doubtful debts – adjustment	18,000	

Activity 5: ND Trading

Trial balance (extract)

Ledger account	Ledger balance	
	Dr £	Cr £
Sales ledger control account	57,000	
Irrecoverable debts	3,000	
Allowance for doubtful debts		2,292
Allowance for doubtful debts – adjustments	292	

Workings:

	£
Opening balance per sales ledger control account	60,000
Less irrecoverable debts	(3,000)
Adjusted balance per sales ledger control account	57,000
Less specific allowance	(600)
	56,400
General allowance (£56,400 × 3%)	(1,692)
∴ **Total allowance:**	
Specific	600
General	1,692
Total closing allowance	2,292
Calculating the allowance for doubtful debts – adjustments	
Opening allowance (per scenario)	2,000
Adjustment (to TB – SPL)	292
Closing allowance (to TB – SOFP)	2,292

Activity 6: JM Trading

Trial balance (extract)

Ledger account	Ledger balance	
	Dr £	Cr £
Sales ledger control account	96,000	
Irrecoverable debts	4,000	
Allowance for doubtful debts		1,950
Allowance for doubtful debts – adjustments		550

Workings:

	£
Opening balance per sales ledger control account	100,000
Less irrecoverable debts	(4,000)
Adjusted balance per sales ledger control account	96,000
Less specific allowance	(1,000)
	95,000
General allowance (£95,000 × 1%)	(950)
∴ **Total allowance:**	
Specific	1,000
General	950
Total closing allowance	1,950
Calculating the allowance for doubtful debts – adjustments	
Opening allowance (per scenario)	2,500
Adjustment (to TB – SPL)	(550)
Closing allowance (to TB – SOFP)	1,950

Activity 7: Advanced bookkeeping – knowledge

	✓
An irrecoverable debt should remain in the sales ledger control account at the year end.	
Once an organisation has calculated the allowance for doubtful debts it will remain unchanged each year.	
The doubtful debt adjustment will affect the statement of profit or loss and statement of financial position.	✓

Explanation

Any irrecoverable debts should be written off at the year end – this means removing them from the sales ledger account and recording an irrecoverable debts expense.

The allowance for doubtful debts should be reviewed each year end (as a minimum) and adjusted accordingly.

The dual effect of the doubtful debt adjustment is to increase or decrease the allowance account in the SOFP and also increase or decrease the doubtful debts adjustment account in the SPL.

CHAPTER 9 Bank reconciliations

Activity 1: Bank reconciliation (recap)

(a) – (c)

Cash book

Date 20X3	Details	Bank £	Date 20X3	Cheque no.	Details	Bank £
01 April	Balance b/f	28,737	01 April	5678	ABC Ltd	8,880
18 April	QTK Ltd	20,550	05 April	5679	SRG Ltd	14,700
26 April	KT Ltd	1,770	12 April	5680	HAL Ltd	3,000
10 April	**Bank interest**	**180**	15 April	DD	Power Ltd	1,950
26 April	**R57 Ltd**	**1,350**	21 April	5681	ERT Ltd	8,100
			24 April	5682	TGN Ltd	2,280
			22 April		**Bank charges**	**150**
			22 April	**BACS**	**RDC Ltd**	**891**
			30 April		**Balance c/d**	**12,636**
		52,587				52,587
1 May	**Balance b/d**	**12,636**				

Note that there is a difference of £3,900 between the opening cash book balance of £28,737 and the opening balance on the bank statement of £32,637.

This relates to cheque number 5672 for £3,900 which would have been an uncleared cheque brought forward at 1 April. As such this would have been included in the reconciliation as at 31 March and so does not need to be included in this reconciliation.

(d)

Bank reconciliation statement	£
Balance per bank statement	13,146
Add:	
Name: KT Ltd	1,770
Total to add	1,770
Less:	
Name: TGN Ltd	2,280
Total to subtract	2,280
Balance as per cash book	12,636

Activity 2: Adjustments to the cash book (example 1)

Adjustment	Amount £	Debit ✓	Credit ✓
Adjustment (1)	90	✓	
Adjustment (3)	360	✓	
Adjustment (5)	1,100		✓

Tutorial workings (cash book):

Narrative	Amount £
Unadjusted balance per cash book	4,190
Adjustment (1)	90
Adjustment (3)	360
Adjustment (5)	(1,100)
Adjusted balance per cash book	3,540

Tutorial workings (bank statement):

Narrative	Amount £
Balance per bank statement	7,150
Cash sales (note 2)	200
Cheques received from customer (note 4)	400
Outstanding cheques to suppliers (note 6)	(4,210)
	3,540

Activity 3: Adjustments to the cash book (example 2)

Adjustment	Amount £	Debit ✓	Credit ✓
Adjustment (3)	30	✓	
Adjustment (4)	1,919		✓
Adjustment (5)	360	✓	

Tutorial workings (cash book):

Narrative	Amount £
Unadjusted balance per cash book	(7,871)
Adjustment (3)	30
Adjustment (4)	(1,919)
Adjustment (5)	360
Adjusted balance per cash book	(9,400)

Tutorial workings (bank statement):

Narrative	Amount £
Balance per bank statement	(12,056)
Unrecorded lodgements (note 1)	2,956
Automated payment to supplier (note 2)	(550)
Cash receipts (note 6)	250
	(9,400)

Activity 4: Bank statement

Adjustment	Amount £	Debit ✓	Credit ✓
Adjustment (2)	4,210	✓	
Adjustment (3)	6,543		✓
Adjustment (6)	1,000	✓	

Tutorial workings (cash book):

Narrative	Amount £
Unadjusted balance per cash book	21,434
Bank charges (Adjustment 1)	(46)
Refund of rates overpayment (Adjustment 4)	135
Dishonoured cheque (Adjustment 5)	(440)
Adjusted balance per cash book	21,083

Tutorial working (bank statement):

Narrative	Amount £
Balance per bank statement	19,750
Outstanding cheques (note 2)	(4,210)
Unrecorded lodgements (note 3)	6,543
Automated payment (note 6)	(1,000)
	21,083

Activity 5: Advanced bookkeeping – knowledge

(a)

	✓
Bank interest charged to the account in error	✓
Direct debit for £500 for insurance	
Bank charges of £70	
Cheque paid to a supplier on 29 December and included in the cash book but not yet received and cashed by the supplier	✓
Receipt from a credit customer by electronic transfer (BACS)	

Explanation

The direct debit, bank charges and BACS receipt are all potential adjustments to the balance per the cash book if these items have not been recorded in the cash book in the first place.

The bank interest needs to be removed from the balance per the bank statement as it has been charged in error. The cheque paid to the supplier is an unpresented cheque so has not yet been recorded by the bank, requiring the balance per the bank statement to be adjusted.

(b)

	True ✓	False ✓
A bank reconciliation should be performed on a regular basis (eg monthly).	✓	
The bookkeeper may have to update the cash book for items on the bank statement which are not yet included in the business's general ledger.	✓	
Outstanding lodgements are normally a cash book adjustment.		✓
Cheques sent to suppliers which have not yet cleared the bank statement are normally a cash book adjustment.		✓

Explanation

Bank reconciliations should be performed regularly to ensure that the cash book is kept fully up to date. As most banks issue statements monthly, monthly preparation is the most common.

The bookkeeper may have to update the cash book for items in the bank statement but not yet in the cash book and therefore not yet in the general ledger. This might include items such as interest or bank charges.

Outstanding lodgements are receipts that have been recorded in the cash book but not yet paid in at the bank. Therefore, they should be an adjustment to the balance per the bank statement.

Equally, unpresented cheques are payments that have been recorded in the cash book but as they have not yet cleared the bank statement; an adjustment is required to the balance per the bank statement.

CHAPTER 10 Control account reconciliations

Activity 1: Sales ledger control account reconciliation

(a)

Sales ledger control account

	£		£
Balance b/d	18,234	Bank	16,321
Sales	29,211	Discounts allowed	2,421
		Sales returns	5,311
		Purchases ledger control account	500
		Irrecoverable debts	360
		Balance c/d	22,532
	47,445		47,445
Balance b/d	22,532		

(b)

	£
Sales ledger control account balance as at 1 September 20X1	22,532
Total of sales ledger accounts as at 1 September 20X1	22,532
Difference	Nil

Workings:

Total of sales ledger accounts at 1 September 20X1:
£2,690 + £5,321 + £1,273 + £9,408 + £3,840

Activity 2: Purchases ledger control account reconciliation

(a)

Purchases ledger control account

	£		£
Bank	10,325	Balance b/d	12,325
Discounts received	3,721	Purchases	22,573
Purchases returns	2,811		
Sales ledger control account	500		
Balance c/d	17,541		
	34,898		34,898
		Balance b/d	17,541

(b)

	£
Purchases ledger control account balance as at 1 September 20X1	17,541
Total of purchases ledger accounts as at 1 September 20X1	18,041
Difference	500

As the reconciliation shows a difference of £500 this will require further investigation to identify the cause. This highlights the important role that reconciliations play in controlling the financial affairs of organisations.

Activity 3: Reconciling the sales ledger control account and the sales ledger

Adjustment	Amount £	Add ✓	Deduct ✓
Adjustment (3)	5,492		✓
Adjustment (4)	180	✓	
Adjustment (6)	364		✓

Tutorial workings (subsidiary sales ledger balances):

Narrative	Amount £
Per scenario:	16,600
Adjustment (3)	(5,492)
Adjustment (4)	180
Adjustment (6) (2 x £182)	(364)
Adjusted subsidiary sales ledger balance:	10,924

Note. Adjustment (2) does not change the sales ledger totals.

Tutorial workings (sales ledger control account):

Narrative	Amount £
Per scenario:	10,674
Adjustment (1)	450
Adjustment (5)	(200)
Adjusted sales ledger control account balance:	10,924

Activity 4: Reconciling the purchases ledger control account and the purchases ledger

Adjustment	Amount £	Debit ✓	Credit ✓
Adjustment (1)	1,520	✓	
Adjustment (3)	1,460	✓	
Adjustment (4)	900		✓

Tutorial workings (subsidiary purchases ledger balances):

Narrative	Amount £
Per scenario:	4,406
Adjustment (2)	390
Adjustment (5)	(300)
Adjustment (6)	(150)
Adjusted subsidiary purchases ledger balance:	4,346

Tutorial workings (purchases ledger control account):

Narrative	Amount £
Per scenario:	6,426
Adjustment (1) (2 × £760)	(1,520)
Adjustment (3)	(1,460)
Adjustment (4)	900
Adjusted purchases ledger control account balance:	4,346

Activity 5: Advanced bookkeeping – knowledge

(a)

	✓
Cheques received from customers omitted from the sales ledger control account.	✓
A credit note entered on the debit side of a customer's account in the subsidiary sales ledger.	
A sales invoice omitted from a customer's account in the subsidiary sales ledger.	
A purchases day book total posted to the sales ledger control account.	✓
A BACS receipt recorded on the debit side of the customer's account in the subsidiary sales ledger.	

(b)

	✓
Cheques received from customers omitted from the sales ledger control account.	
A credit note entered on the debit side of a customer's account in the subsidiary sales ledger.	✓
A sales invoice omitted from a customer's account in the subsidiary sales ledger.	✓
A purchases day book total posted to the sales ledger control account.	
A BACS receipt recorded on the debit side of the customer's account in the subsidiary sales ledger.	✓

CHAPTER 11 The trial balance, errors and the suspense account

Activity 1: Journals and the suspense account

(a)

Journal

Account name	Debit £	Credit £
Rent	350	
Sales ledger control account		350

(b)

Journal

Account name	Debit £	Credit £
Suspense	1,900	
Machinery accumulated depreciation		1,900

(c)

Journal

Account name	Debit £	Credit £
Discounts allowed	500	
Sales ledger control account		500

(d)

Journal

Account name	Debit £	Credit £
Stationery expense	1,460	
Suspense		1,460

(e)

Journal

Account name	Debit £	Credit £
Capital	18,000	
Suspense		18,000

Workings (NB: not part of the assessment answer):
Suspense account

Details	Amount £	Details	Amount £
Balance b/f	17,560	Stationery expense (d)	1,460
Machinery accumulated depreciation (b)	1,900	Capital (e)	18,000
	19,460		19,460

Activity 2: Adjustments and the extended trial balance

(a)

Extract from the extended trial balance

Ledger account	Ledger balance Debit £	Ledger balance Credit £	Adjustment Debit £	Adjustment Credit £
Accrued expenses		1,050		
Administration expenses	14,039			
Allowance for doubtful debts		1,400	**108**	
Allowance for doubtful debts – adjustment				**108**
Bank		1,970		**230**
Discounts allowed	2,100		**100**	
Insurance expenses	2,400			**950**
Irrecoverable debts	300			
Prepaid expenses			**950**	
Purchases	106,032			
Purchases ledger control account		21,324		
Sales		179,323		
Sales ledger control account	25,840			
Suspense		130	**230**	**100**
Travel expenses	8,245			

(b)

Journal entries	Debit £	Credit £
Administration expenses		14,039
Profit or loss account	14,039	
Narrative:		
Being: Transfer of administration expenses for the year ended 31 August 20X9 to the profit or loss account		

Activity 3: Extract from the trial balance

Extract from the trial balance as at 31 August 20X9:

Account	Ledger balances £	Trial balance Debit £	Trial balance Credit £
Office costs		6,321	
Purchases	30,100	30,100	
Purchases returns			775
Recycling rebates			11,550
Salaries	13,500	13,500	
Sales	58,304		58,304
Sales returns		4,367	
VAT			9,440

Activity 4: Advanced bookkeeping – knowledge

(a)

	✓
Error of commission	
Reversal of entries	✓
Error of omission	
One-sided entry	

(b)

	True ✓	False ✓
The suspense account can appear in the financial statements.		✓
All errors cause an imbalance in the trial balance.		✓
A trial balance is prepared before the financial statements.	✓	
A trial balance includes the closing balances of the subsidiary sales ledgers.		✓

CHAPTER 12 The extended trial balance

Activity 1: Adjustments and the extended trial balance

(a) (1) Plant depreciation

Account name	Debit £	Credit £
Depreciation charges	2,000	
Plant accumulated depreciation		2,000

Workings:

£20,000 × 10%

(2) Closing inventory

Account name	Debit £	Credit £
Closing inventory (SOFP)	1,500	
Closing inventory (SPL)		1,500

(3) Wages

Account name	Debit £	Credit £
Wages expense	900	
Suspense		900

(4) Rates

Account name	Debit £	Credit £
Rates	250	
Rent		250

(b)

Extended trial balance

Ledger account	Ledger balances		Adjustments		Statement of profit or loss		Statement of financial position	
	Dr £	Cr £	Dr £	Cr £	Dr £	Cr £	Dr £	Cr £
Bank		7,435						7,435
Plant at cost	20,000						20,000	
Closing inventory			1,500	1,500		1,500	1,500	
Depreciation charges			2,000		2,000			
Opening inventory	800				800			
Purchases	20,301				20,301			
Purchases ledger control		5,755						5,755
Plant accumulated depreciation				2,000				2,000
Rates	1,600		250		1,850			
Rent	2,866			250	2,616			
Sales		49,126				49,126		
Sales ledger control	8,325						8,325	
Suspense	900			900				
Wages expense	7,524		900		8,424			
Profit/loss for the year					14,635			14,635
TOTAL	62,316	62,316	4,650	4,650	50,626	50,626	29,825	29,825

Activity 2: Completing the extended trial balance

Extended trial balance

Ledger account	Ledger balances		Adjustments		Statement of profit or loss		Statement of financial position	
	Dr £	Cr £	Dr £	Cr £	Dr £	Cr £	Dr £	Cr £
Allowance for doubtful debts		4,243	400					3,843
Allowance for doubtful debts – adjustments				400		400		
Bank	80,213			2,600			77,613	
Capital		80,000						80,000
Closing inventory			36,000	36,000		36,000	36,000	
Depreciation charges			20,000		20,000			
Office expenses	50,000			1,000	49,000			
Opening inventory	31,000				31,000			
Payroll expenses	30,632			250	30,382			
Purchases	210,422		750		211,172			
Purchases ledger control account		43,221						43,221
Sales		433,764				433,764		
Sales ledger control account	50,323						50,323	
Selling expenses	5,068				5,068			
Suspense		3,100	3,850	750				
VAT		18,330						18,330
Vehicles at cost	155,000						155,000	
Vehicles accumulated depreciation		30,000		20,000				50,000
Profit/loss for the year					123,542			123,542
TOTAL	612,658	612,658	61,000	61,000	**470,164**	**470,164**	**318,936**	**318,936**

Activity 3: Advanced bookkeeping – knowledge

(a)

	✓
It ensures the accuracy of the sales and purchases ledger accounts.	
The extended trial balance can form the basis for the preparation of the financial statements.	✓
It is used in place of the financial statements.	
It ensures that all transactions are recorded in the financial statements.	

Explanation

The sales and purchases ledger accounts are memorandum accounts and are not part of the general ledger. Therefore, they are totally separate from the extended trial balance which starts with the year-end balances from the trial balance (sourced from the general ledger), processes the year-end adjustments and arrives at the figures for the final account.

The extended trial balance is often used as a step in the process of preparing final accounts rather than a replacement for the final accounts.

It does not act as a guarantee that all transactions are recorded in the financial statements as it will not take into account entries missing from the general ledger and trial balance or adjustments that have not been processed.

(b)

	True ✓	False ✓
A bank overdraft will be shown on the debit side of the extended trial balance, in the statement of financial position column.		✓
The irrecoverable debt expense will be shown in one of the statement of profit or loss columns in the extended trial balance.	✓	
Drawings will be shown in one of the statement of financial position columns in the extended trial balance.	✓	
VAT will be excluded from the extended trial balance.		✓

BPP
LEARNING MEDIA

Explanation

A bank overdraft is a liability and therefore a credit balance in the statement of financial position.

The irrecoverable debt expense is a profit and loss account and will appear as a debit balance in the extended trial balance.

Drawings (when an owner withdraws money from the business for personal use) reduce capital in the statement of financial position. As capital is a credit balance (what the business owes the owner), drawings are recorded as a debit balance in the extended trial balance and statement of financial position.

VAT should be included in the extended trail balance. It will either be a debit balance (if amounts are owed by HMRC to the business) or a credit balance (if the business owes amounts to HMRC) in the statement of financial position.

Chapter 1: Bookkeeping transactions

1 (a) **Receipt of capital into the business bank account of £40,000.**

Account name	Debit £	Credit £
Bank	40,000	
Capital		40,000

(b) **Purchase of goods for resale on credit of £12,000 inclusive of VAT.**

Account name	Debit £	Credit £
Purchases	10,000	
VAT control account	2,000	
Purchases ledger control account		12,000

Workings:

VAT is calculated as: £12,000 × 20/120 = £2,000

The amount posted to purchases is the net amount of £10,000 (£12,000 – £2,000) as the VAT element is recoverable from HMRC so is not an expense to the company. Instead the VAT element of £2,000 is debited to the VAT control account. However, the business has to pay the gross amount £12,000 to the supplier so this is the amount that must be credited to the purchases ledger control account.

(c) **Payment for goods purchased on credit for £8,000 to a credit supplier.**

Account name	Debit £	Credit £
Purchases ledger control account	8,000	
Bank		8,000

2   **(a)** **Payment of electricity from the bank account of £5,500.**

Account name	Debit £	Credit £
Electricity	5,500	
Bank		5,500

  (b) **Sale of goods to a credit customer for £15,000. Ignore VAT.**

Account name	Debit £	Credit £
Sales ledger control account	15,000	
Sales		15,000

  (c) **Receipt from a credit customer for goods sold on credit for £12,000.**

Account name	Debit £	Credit £
Bank	12,000	
Sales ledger control account		12,000

3

	Debit	Credit
Money withdrawn from the bank account by the owner	Drawings	Bank
Cash purchase (ignore VAT)	Purchases	Bank
Cash sale (ignore VAT)	Bank	Sales

4   **Bank**

	£		£
Balance b/d	15,000	Purchases ledger control account	10,000
Sales ledger control account	18,000	Rent	1,000
		Electricity	600
		Balance c/d	21,400
	33,000		33,000
Balance b/d	21,400		

5 **Sales**

	£		£
Sales returns	2,000	Sales ledger control account	42,000
Profit or loss account	40,000		
	42,000		42,000

6 **Select the correct day book from the picklist to match each description.**

Description	Day book
Where sales invoices issued to credit customers are recorded	Sales day book
Where non-standard transactions are recorded	Journal
Where cash payments and cash receipts are recorded	Cash book
Where prompt payment discounts taken up by customers are recorded	Discounts allowed day book
Where credit notes issued to customers for items returned are recorded	Sales returns day book
Where credit notes issued by suppliers for items returned are recorded	Purchases returns day book
Where prompt payment discounts offered by suppliers and taken up by the business are recorded	Discounts received day book
Where invoices received from suppliers for credit purchases are recorded	Purchases day book

7 **VAT control account**

	£		£
Sales returns	1,000	Balance b/d	6,000
Purchases	8,000	Credit sales	10,000
Discounts allowed	400	Cash sales	600
Bank	2,800	Purchases returns	1,200
Balance c/d	5,800	Discounts received	200
	18,000		18,000
		Balance b/d	5,800

Chapter 2: Accounting principles

1

	Asset, liability, capital, income or expense	SOFP or SPL
Trade payables (purchases ledger control account)	Liability	SOFP
Sundry income	Income	SPL
Purchases	Expense	SPL
Bank (debit column of TB)	Asset	SOFP
Wages expense	Expense	SPL
Property, plant and equipment	Asset	SOFP
Discounts allowed	Expense	SPL

2

Assets £	Liabilities £	Capital £
30,000	10,000	20,000

Workings:

Assets consists of the Motor vehicle (£20,000) plus Inventories (£6,400) plus Bank (£3,600).

3

	✓
Integrity	
Objectivity	
Professional competence and due care	✓
Confidentiality	
Professional behaviour	

The trainee lacks the experience and skills required to prepare the accounts.

4

	✓
Physical controls	
Written record of procedures	
Authorisation of transactions	✓
Reviews	

Explanation

This is a small organisation. The most appropriate procedure is for the business owner to authorise transactions.

Chapter 3: Purchase of non-current assets

1 **(a)**

£	11,050

Workings:

Cost of machine £10,000 + delivery costs £150 + installation costs £600 + professional fees £300

(b)

£	1,500

Workings:

Maintenance contract £1,000 + costs of advertising new product £500

2

	Capital expenditure ✓	Revenue expenditure ✓
Kitchen equipment for use in the business	✓	
Administrative costs		✓
Installation costs	✓	
Professional surveyors' fees	✓	
Repairs		✓

3

Description	Method
An old motor vehicle is given in part exchange for a new asset.	Part exchange
A photocopier is financed by the business paying an initial deposit to the finance company followed by a fixed number of instalments. After all instalments have been paid, the photocopier will be owned by the business.	Hire purchase
Office furniture is acquired. The supplier invoice states 'Payment must be made within 45 days from the date of purchase'.	Cash purchase

4

Account name	Debit £	Credit £
Machine at cost	16,000	
VAT control account	3,200	
Bank		19,200

Explanation

The business is VAT registered and can reclaim the VAT from the tax authorities. Therefore, it is not capitalised as part of the cost of the asset.

5

Journal to record the bank loan

Account name	Debit £	Credit £
Bank	16,800	
Loan		16,800

Journal to record the purchase of the machine

Account name	Debit £	Credit £
Machine at cost	16,800	
Bank		16,800

Workings:

£14,000 × 20% = £2,800 VAT

Total cost is £14,000 + £2,800 = £16,800

The VAT cannot be reclaimed from the tax authorities as the business is not VAT registered. Therefore, it must be added to the cost of the asset.

Chapter 4: Depreciation of non-current assets

1   The main accounting concept underlying the depreciation of non-current assets is the | accruals | concept.

2

£	9,000

Workings:

$(12,000 / 48,000) \times 36,000$

3   **(a)**

£	3,731

     (b)

£	6,929

Workings:

	£
Original cost	16,400
Depreciation to 31 December 20X7 $(16,400 \times 35\%)$	(5,740)
Carrying amount at 31 December 20X7	10,660
Depreciation to 31 December 20X8 $(10,660 \times 35\%)$	(3,731)
Carrying amount at 31 December 20X8	6,929

4

£	31,500

Workings:

Depreciation charge = $(£240,000 - £135,000) \times 30\% = £12,500$

5

£	2,800

Workings:

Depreciation charge = $£24,000 \times 20\% \times {}^{7}/_{12} = £2,800$

6 **(a)**

	Office equipment		Machinery
£	5,200	£	17,500

Workings:

Office equipment: £5,200 (£26,000 ÷ 5 years)

Machinery: £17,500 (£85,000 – £15,000) × 25%

(b)

	Office equipment		Machinery
£	13,200	£	32,500

Workings:

Office equipment: £13,200 (£8,000 + £5,200)

Machinery: £32,500 (£15,000 + £17,500)

7

	✓
The difference between the non-current asset's carrying amount and the estimated scrap proceeds	
The anticipated resale value of the non-current asset at the end of its useful life to the business	✓
The cost of the non-current asset minus the accumulated depreciation	
The amount paid for the non-current asset at the date of purchase	

Explanation

The estimated scrap proceeds (or resale value) at the end of the asset's useful life is the residual value (rather than the difference between the carrying amount and its estimated scrap proceeds). The cost of the asset less the accumulated depreciation is the definition of the 'carrying amount'. The amount paid for the asset at the date of its purchase is known as its 'purchase price' or 'cost'.

Chapter 5: Disposal of non-current assets

1

Statement	True ✓	False ✓
A non-current assets register is not part of the general ledger.	✓	

2

	Gain	Loss
£ 720		✓

Workings:

	£
Proceeds	600
Less carrying amount*	(1,320)
Loss on disposal	(720)
Carrying amount at disposal date:	
Original cost	2,200
20X5 depreciation 2,200 × 40%	(880)
Carrying amount at date of disposal	1,320*

3

	Gain	Loss
£ 100	✓	

Workings:

	£
Proceeds	5,800
Less carrying amount*	(5,700)
Gain on disposal	100
Carrying amount at disposal date:	
Original cost	7,200
20X6 depreciation 7,200 × 25% × 2/12	(300)
20X7 depreciation 7,200 × 25% × 8/12	(1,200)
Carrying amount at date of disposal	5,700*

4   **(a)**

A loss on disposal can also be described as	under-depreciation

(b)

A gain on disposal can also be described as	over-depreciation

5

£	25,000

Workings:

£3,200 + £21,800 = £25,000

Chapter 6: Accruals and prepayments

1   **(a)** Rent paid in advance for the following accounting period would appear

as | prepaid expenses | in the statement of financial position.

   (b) Motor expenses owing to the local garage at the year end would appear

as | accrued expenses | in the statement of financial position.

2   **(a)** In the statement of profit or loss the heat and light expense would be:

£	870

In the statement of financial position there would be | accrued expenses | of:

£	200

   (b) In the statement of profit or loss the rental income would be:

£	340

In the statement of financial position there would be | prepaid income | of:

£	40

   (c) In the statement of profit or loss the insurance expense would be:

£	1,100

In the statement of financial position there would be | prepaid expenses | of:

£	300

(d) In the statement of profit or loss the commissions income would be:

£ | 200

In the statement of financial position there would be accrued income of:

£ | 20

3 Motor expenses

	£		£
Bank	845	Prepaid expenses (150 × 6/12)	75
		Profit or loss account	770
	845		845

4 Electricity expenses

	£		£
Bank	8,950	Accrued expenses (reversal)	470
Accrued expenses	180	Profit or loss account	8,660
	9,130		9,130

Chapter 7: Inventories

1

Statements	£
The cost of each item is	27
The net realisable value of each item is	40
In the statement of financial position the 120 units will be shown at a value of	3,240

Workings:

Cost = £25 + £2 = £27

Net realisable value = £43 – £3 = £40

Statement of financial position value = 120 units × £27 = £3,240

2

Account name	Debit £	Credit £
Closing inventory (SOFP)	1,140	
Closing inventory (SPL)		1,140
Being: the year-end adjustment to record closing inventory		

Workings:

250 – 60 = 190 units

190 units × £6 = £1,140

3

£	2,500

Workings:

£4,000 – £1,100 – £400 = £2,500

Net realisable value is calculated as the selling price (£4,000) less the estimated costs to completion (£1,100) and the selling costs (£400). The costs of conversion of £1,400 are ignored here as they are included in the calculation of cost since they have already been incurred.

4

	✓
First in, first out	✓
Lower of cost and net realisable value	
Average cost	
Last in, first out	

5

£	34,000

Workings:

£60,000 – £26,000 = £34,000

Chapter 8: Irrecoverable and doubtful debts

1

Account name	Debit £	Credit £
Irrecoverable debts	3,000	
Sales ledger control account		3,000

2

Trial balance (extract)

Ledger account	Ledger balance	
	Dr £	Cr £
Sales ledger control account (60,000 – 4,000)	56,000	
Irrecoverable debts	4,000	
Allowance for doubtful debts		1,000
Allowance for doubtful debts - adjustments	1,000	

3

Account name	Debit £	Credit £
Bank	2,500	
Irrecoverable debts		2,500

4

Trial balance (extract)

Ledger account	Ledger balance	
	Dr £	Cr £
Sales ledger control account	30,000	
Allowance for doubtful debts		1,188
Allowance for doubtful debts – adjustments		12

Workings:

	£
Opening balance per sales ledger control account	30,000
Less specific allowance	(600)
	29,400
General allowance (£29,400 × 2%)	(588)
∴Total allowance:	
Specific	600
General	588
Total closing allowance	1,188
Calculating the allowance for doubtful debts – adjustments	
Opening allowance (per scenario)	1,200
Adjustment (to TB – SPL)	(12)
Closing allowance (to TB – SOFP)	1,188

5

Trial balance (extract)

Ledger account	Ledger balance	
	Dr £	Cr £
Sales ledger control account	45,000	
Allowance for doubtful debts		1,341
Allowance for doubtful debts – adjustments	141	

Workings:

	£
Opening balance per sales ledger control account	45,000
Less specific allowance	(900)
	44,100
General allowance (£44,100 × 1%)	(441)
∴**Total allowance:**	
Specific	900
General	441
Total closing allowance	1,341
Calculating the allowance for doubtful debts – adjustments	
Opening allowance (per scenario)	1,200
Adjustment (to TB – SPL)	141
Closing allowance (to TB – SOFP)	1,341

Chapter 9: Bank reconciliations

1

Questions	Answer
When the electricity payment is entered into the cash book, will it be a debit or credit item?	Credit
Will the electricity payment be included on the debit or credit side of the bank statement?	Debit

2

Questions	Answer
When the receipt is entered into the cash book, will it be a debit or credit item?	Debit
Is the receipt included on the debit or credit side of the bank statement?	Credit

3

Description	Term
Cheques paid out by the business which have not yet appeared on the bank statement.	Unpresented cheques
Money paid into the bank by the business but which has not yet appeared as a receipt on the bank statement.	Unrecorded lodgements

4

Questions	Answer
If the bank statement shows a credit balance, does the business have a positive or negative cash balance?	Positive
If the bank statement shows a debit balance, does the business have a positive or negative cash balance?	Negative

5

Adjustment	Amount £	Debit ✓	Credit ✓
BACS payment	900		✓

Chapter 10: Control account reconciliations

1

WT & Sons – Sales ledger account

	£		£
Balance b/d	2,600	Sales returns	798
Sales	5,400	Discounts allowed	120
		Purchases ledger control account	200
		Bank	3,042
		Balance c/d	3,840
	8,000		8,000
Balance b/d	3,840		

2

Adjustment	Amount £	Debit ✓	Credit ✓
Adjustment (1)	100	✓	
Adjustment (2)	450		✓
Adjustment (5)	210		✓

Workings (subsidiary sales ledger balances):

Narrative	Amount £
Per scenario:	41,586
Adjustment (3) (£769 – £679)	(90)
Adjustment (4) (2 × £16)	(32)
Adjustment (6) (2 × £125)	(250)
Adjusted subsidiary sales ledger balance:	41,214

Workings (sales ledger control account):

Narrative	Amount £
Per scenario:	41,774
Adjustment (1)	100
Adjustment (2)	(450)
Adjustment (5)	(210)
Adjusted sales ledger control account balance:	41,214

3

Adjustment	Amount £	Debit ✓	Credit ✓
Adjustment (1)	300		✓
Adjustment (2)	270		✓
Adjustment (3)	267	✓	

Workings (subsidiary purchases ledger balances):

Narrative	Amount £
Per scenario:	39,741
Adjustment (3)	(267)
Adjustment (4)	(90)
Adjustment (5)	(187)
Adjustment (6)	(200)
Adjusted subsidiary purchases ledger balance:	38,997

Workings (purchases ledger control account):

Narrative	Amount £
Per scenario:	38,694
Adjustment (1)	300
Adjustment (2)	270
Adjustment (3)	(267)
Adjusted purchases ledger control account balance:	38,997

4

Questions	£
What is the total wages expense for August?	70,000
What is the total amount to be paid to HMRC in respect of the August payroll?	25,700

Workings:

Total wages expense: Gross wages of £62,500 plus employer's NIC of £7,500 = £70,000

HMRC = £7,500 + £8,300 + £9,900 = £25,700

5

Statements	True ✓	False ✓
It is a record of how much is paid to each individual employee each month.		✓
It should have a balance of zero at the end of the period once all payroll entries have been made.	✓	
It is debited with gross pay.		✓
It is credited when net pay is paid to employees.		✓
It is where all payroll liabilities are initially recorded with a credit entry.	✓	

Chapter 11: The trial balance, errors and the suspense account

1

Statements	True ✓	False ✓
An error of principle will be detected by an imbalance in the trial balance.		✓
A one-sided entry will be detected by an imbalance in the trial balance.	✓	

2

This is an error of	original entry

3

Journal

Account name	Debit £	Credit £
Purchases ledger control account	1,100	
Purchases returns		1,100

4

Journal

Account name	Debit £	Credit £
Depreciation charges	8,000	
Accumulated depreciation		8,000

5

Journal

Account name	Debit £	Credit £
Sales ledger control account	12,000	
Suspense		12,000

6

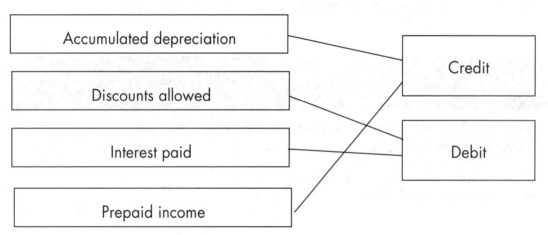

Account balance	Trial balance
Accumulated depreciation	Credit
Discounts allowed	
Interest paid	Debit
Prepaid income	

Chapter 12: The extended trial balance

1

Questions	Solution
In the statement of profit or loss columns, if the total of the debit column is higher than the total of the credit column, has a profit or a loss arisen during the period?	Loss
In the statement of profit or loss columns, if the total of the credit column is higher than the total of the debit column, has a profit or loss arisen during the period?	Profit

2

Ledger account	Statement of financial position – Debit or Credit column
Bank overdraft	Credit
Allowance for doubtful debts	Credit
VAT – due from HMRC	Debit
Loan to employee	Debit
Accumulated depreciation	Credit
VAT – owed to HMRC	Credit

3

	✓
Both a debit and a credit	✓
A debit	
A credit	
No entry	

4   The closing inventory figure is a ⟦ credit ⟧ entry in the statement of profit or loss columns and a ⟦ debit ⟧ entry in the statement of financial position columns of the extended trial balance.

5

Ledger account	Statement of profit or loss – Debit or Credit column
Allowance for doubtful debts – adjustment: increase in the allowance	Debit
Sales returns	Debit
Purchases returns	Credit
Depreciation charges	Debit
Allowance for doubtful debts – adjustment: decrease in the allowance	Credit

Synoptic assessment preparation

The *Advanced Bookkeeping* assessment learning objectives will be tested in the *AAT Advanced Diploma in Accounting* synoptic assessment. Therefore, at this stage in your studies, it is useful to consider the style of tasks you may see in the synoptic assessment.

However, it is recommended that the *AAT Advanced Diploma in Accounting* synoptic assessment is only taken when all other units have been completed.

Questions

1   This task is about ledger accounting for non-current assets.

You are working on the accounting records of a business for the year ended 31 March 20X7.

- VAT can be ignored.
- An item of computer equipment was part-exchanged on 1 October 20X6.
- The original item was bought for £3,690 on 14 August 20X4.
- Depreciation is provided at one-third of original cost per year on a straight-line basis.
- A full year's depreciation is applied in the year of acquisition and none in the year of disposal.
- A part exchange allowance of £1,350 was given.
- £3,480 was paid from the bank to complete the purchase of the new equipment.

Required

(a) Complete the disposals account. Show clearly the balance to be carried down or transferred to the statement of profit or loss, as appropriate.

Disposals

	£		£
▼		▼	
▼		▼	
▼		▼	

Picklist:

Balance b/d
Balance c/d
Bank
Computer consumables
Computer equipment accumulated depreciation
Computer equipment at cost
Depreciation charges
Disposals
Profit or loss account
Sales
Sales ledger control account

(b) Calculate the purchase cost of the new computer equipment from the information above.

£	

2   This task is about preparing a trial balance and reconciliations.

You are working on the accounting records of a business with a year end of 31 March.

You have five extracts from the ledger accounts as at 31 March 20X7:

Bank

		£			£
31.03.X7	Balance b/d	8,103			

Internet and telephone costs

		£			£
31.03.X7	Balance b/d	1,480			

Irrecoverable debts

		£			£
			31.03.X7	Balance b/d	230

VAT

		£			£
			31.03.X7	Balance b/d	4,296

Vending machine income

				£			£
				31.03.X7	Balance b/d		2,010

You need to start preparing the initial trial balance as at 31 March 20X7.

Required

(a) Using all the information given above and the figures given in the table below, enter amounts into the appropriate trial balance columns for the accounts shown.

Do NOT enter zeros into unused column cells. Do NOT enter any figures as negatives.

Extract from the trial balance as at 31 March 20X7:

Account	Ledger balance £	Trial balance	
		Debit £	Credit £
Bank			
Drawings	26,000		
Internet and telephone costs			
Irrecoverable debts			
Loan interest received	50		
Loan receivable	2,000		
VAT			
Vending machine income			

You are now ready to prepare the bank reconciliation.

The balance showing on the bank statement is a credit of £7,162 and the balance in the cash book is a debit of £8,103.

The bank statement has been compared with the cash book and the following differences identified:

(1) Bank interest received of £68 has not been entered into the cash book.

(2) Cash sales receipts totalling £260 have been entered into the cash book but are not yet banked.

(3) A direct debit payment of £427 has been recorded in the accounting records as £400.

(4) An automated payment to a supplier of £710 has been recorded correctly in the cash book but delayed by the bank due to an error in the account number given.

(5) A BACS receipt of £1,090 from a customer has been entered into the cash book but is not yet showing on the bank statement.

(6) A cheque from a customer for £3,850 has been dishonoured by the bank. When adjusting the accounting records, an incorrect amount of £3,508 was entered.

Required

(b) Use the following table to show the THREE adjustments you need to make to the cashbook.

Adjustment		Amount £	Debit ✓	Credit ✓
	▼			
	▼			
	▼			

Picklist:

Adjustment (1)
Adjustment (2)
Adjustment (3)
Adjustment (4)
Adjustment (5)
Adjustment (6)

3 This task is about accounting adjustments and journals.

You are working on the accounting records of a business with a year end of 31 March. A trial balance has been drawn up and a suspense account opened. You now need to make some corrections and adjustments for the year ended 31 March 20X7.

You may ignore VAT in this task.

Required

Record the journal entries needed in the general ledger to correct the errors noted below.

You do not need to give narratives.

Do NOT enter zeros into unused column cells.

Select the account names from the picklist at the end of the question.

(a) Travel expenses of £620 have been posted to the vehicle at cost account in error. The other side of the entry is correct.

Journal

Account name	Debit £	Credit £
▼		
▼		

(b) A repairs and maintenance expense of £84 was paid for using cash. Only the credit side of the double entry was made.

Journal

Account name	Debit £	Credit £
▼		
▼		

(c) No entries have been made for closing inventory as at 31 March 20X7. The cost of closing inventory at 31 March 20X7 is £17,820. Included in this amount are goods that cost £3,540 and have a net realisable value of £3,100.

Journal

Account name	Debit £	Credit £
▼		
▼		

(d) Discounts allowed of £2,290 have been posted on both sides of the double entry as £2,920.

Journal

Account name	Debit £	Credit £
▼		
▼		

Picklist:

Bank

Closing inventory – statement of financial position

Closing inventory – statement of profit or loss

Depreciation charges

Discounts allowed

Office furniture accumulated depreciation

Office furniture at cost

Repairs and maintenance

Sales

Sales ledger control account

Suspense

Travel expenses

Vehicles accumulated depreciation

Vehicles at cost

Solutions

1

(a)

Disposals

	£		£
Computer equipment at cost	3,690	Computer equipment accumulated depreciation	2,460
Profit or loss account	120	Computer equipment at cost	1,350
	3,810		3,810

Workings:

Computer equipment accumulated depreciation: £3,690 × ⅔ = £2,460

(b) **Calculate the purchase cost of the new computer equipment from the information above.**

£	4,830

Workings:

£1,350 + £3,480

2   (a)

Account	Ledger balance £	Trial balance Debit £	Credit £
Bank		8,103	
Drawings	26,000	26,000	
Internet and telephone costs		1,480	
Irrecoverable debts			230
Loan interest received	50		50
Loan receivable	2,000	2,000	
VAT			4,296
Vending machine income			2,010

(b)

Adjustment	Amount £	Debit ✓	Credit ✓
Adjustment (1)	68	✓	
Adjustment (3)	27		✓
Adjustment (6)	342		✓

3 **(a)**

Journal

Account name	Debit £	Credit £
Travel expenses	620	
Vehicles at cost		620

(b)

Journal

Account name	Debit £	Credit £
Repairs and maintenance	84	
Suspense		84

(c)

Journal

Account name	Debit £	Credit £
Closing inventory – statement of financial position	17,380	
Closing inventory – statement of profit or loss		17,380

Workings:

The goods which cost £3,540 need to be written down to their net realisable value of £3,100, resulting in a reduction to closing inventory of £440 (£3,540 – £3,100), because accounting standards (IAS 2 *Inventories*) requires inventory to be valued at the lower of cost and NRV. This brings closing inventory down to £17,380 (£17,820 – £440).

(d)

Journal

Account name	Debit £	Credit £
Sales ledger control account (2,920 – 2,290)	630	
Discounts allowed (2,920 – 2,290)		630

Glossary of terms

It is useful to be familiar with interchangeable terminology including between IFRS and UK GAAP (generally accepted accounting principles).

Below is a short list of the most important terms you are likely to use or come across, together with their international and UK equivalents.

UK term	International term
Profit and loss account	**Statement of profit or loss (or statement of profit or loss and other comprehensive income)**
Turnover or Sales	Revenue or Sales revenue
Operating profit	Profit from operations
Reducing balance depreciation	Diminishing balance depreciation
Depreciation or depreciation expense(s)	Depreciation charge(s)
Balance sheet	**Statement of financial position**
Fixed assets	Non-current assets
Net book value	Carrying amount
Tangible assets	Property, plant and equipment
Stocks	Inventories
Trade debtors or Debtors	Trade receivables
Prepayments	Other receivables
Debtors and prepayments	Trade and other receivables
Cash at bank and in hand	Cash and cash equivalents
Long-term liabilities	Non-current liabilities
Trade creditors or Creditors	Trade payables
Accruals	Other payables
Creditors and accruals	Trade and other payables
Capital and reserves	Equity (limited companies)
Profit and loss balance	Retained earnings
Cash flow statement	**Statement of cash flows**

Accountants often have a tendency to use several phrases to describe the same thing! Some of these are listed below:

Different terms for the same thing
Nominal ledger, main ledger or general ledger
Subsidiary ledgers, memorandum ledgers
Subsidiary (sales) ledger, sales ledger, receivables ledger
Subsidiary (purchases) ledger, purchases ledger, payables ledger

Bibliography

Association of Accounting Technicians (2014) AAT *Code of Professional Ethics.* [Online]. Available from: https://www.aat.org.uk/sites/default/files/assets/AAT_Code_of_Professional_Ethics.pdf [Accessed 28 April 2016]

International Accounting Standards Board (2003) IAS 2 Inventories. In *International Financial Reporting Standards.* Available from: http://eifrs.ifrs.org [Accessed 28 April 2016]

International Accounting Standards Board (2003) IAS 16 Property, Plant and Equipment. In *International Financial Reporting Standards.* Available from: http://eifrs.ifrs.org [Accessed 28 April 2016]

Index

REVIEW FORM

How have you used this Course Book?
(Tick one box only)

☐ Self study

☐ On a course_____

☐ Other _____

Why did you decide to purchase this Course Book? *(Tick one box only)*

☐ Have used BPP materials in the past

☐ Recommendation by friend or colleague

☐ Recommendation by a college lecturer

☐ Saw advertising

☐ Other _____

During the past six months do you recall seeing/receiving either of the following?
(Tick as many boxes as are relevant)

☐ Our advertisement in Accounting Technician

☐ Our Publishing Catalogue

Which (if any) aspects of our advertising do you think are useful?
(Tick as many boxes as are relevant)

☐ Prices and publication dates of new editions

☐ Information on Course Book content

☐ Details of our free online offering

☐ None of the above

Your ratings, comments and suggestions would be appreciated on the following areas of this Course Book.

	Very useful	Useful	Not useful
Chapter overviews	☐	☐	☐
Introductory section	☐	☐	☐
Quality of explanations	☐	☐	☐
Illustrations	☐	☐	☐
Chapter activities	☐	☐	☐
Test your learning	☐	☐	☐
Keywords	☐	☐	☐

	Excellent	Good	Adequate	Poor
Overall opinion of this Course Book	☐	☐	☐	☐

Do you intend to continue using BPP Products? ☐ Yes ☐ No

Please note any further comments and suggestions/errors on the reverse of this page. The BPP author of this edition can be emailed at: lmfeedback@bpp.com.

Alternatively, the Head of Programme of this edition can be emailed at: nisarahmed@bpp.com

REVIEW FORM (continued)

TELL US WHAT YOU THINK

Please note any further comments and suggestions/errors below